Feminine Spirituality in America

Feminine Spirituality in America

From Sarah Edwards to Martha Graham

A M A N D A   P O R T E R F I E L D

Temple University Press

Philadelphia

Fred. 22.50/20.25/9/14/82

Library of Congress Cataloging in Publication Data

Porterfield, Amanda, 1947–
   Feminine spirituality in America.

   Includes bibliographical references and index.
   1. Women—United States—Attitudes.
   2. Feminism—United States.   3. Sex role in
literature.   4. Spirituality. I. Title.
HQ1426.P67   305.4′2′0973   80-12116
ISBN 0-87722-175-8

Temple University Press, Philadelphia 19122
Published 1980
Printed in the United States of America

To my mentor,
William A. Clebsch

Contents

Acknowledgments

Chapter One	Introduction	3
Chapter Two	Bridal Passion and New England Puritanism	19
Chapter Three	The Domestication of Theology	51
Chapter Four	Witchcraft and Sexuality in Literature	83
Chapter Five	Women Under the World	99
Chapter Six	Women Transform the World	109
Chapter Seven	Emily Dickinson	129
Chapter Eight	Science, Social Work, and Sociology	155
Chapter Nine	Changing the Space Inside a Room	177
Chapter Ten	Modern Grace	189

| Notes | 203 |
| Index | 231 |

Acknowledgments

The ideas developed in this book are deeply influenced by the ideas of others. Of all the acknowledgments that are due, the first and foremost belong to William A. Clebsch. Although I could not hold him responsible for all of the particular ideas developed in this book, the assumptions that undergird it are shaped by an approach to the historical study of religion that I learned from him. This book is part of my ongoing conversation with him about the spiritual lives of American characters.

The ideas presented here would be different and smaller were it not for the ideas of good teachers, colleagues, students, and friends. Among the people whose thinking has expanded my own I single out special thanks to Jerry Irish, David Kennedy, Albert Gelpi, George Dekker, Rosemary Rader, David Langston, Jay Fliegelman, Huston and Kendra Smith, David Miller, and Lynda and Michael Sexson.

I extend my appreciation to Giles Gunn and Martin Marty for their good wishes for this project in its various stages. The encouragement of these two scholars has helped me write this book.

I am grateful to Ronald Cavanagh for his sustained support of my work on this project. Through his good offices and those of Donald Kibbey, I enjoyed a Syracuse University faculty development grant during the summer of 1976.

Louis Nordstrom worked carefully with a manuscript draft during the summer of 1978. With his talents as poet and philosopher, and with the affection of a brother, he urged my prose to greater clarity.

I thank all the members of the Religion Department of Syracuse University. The supportive and creative environment I enjoy in my department has been invaluable in my work.

To the good people at Temple University Press, I extend thanks for their fine and careful work. I am especially grateful to Michael Ames for his commitment to this book.

My mother, my father, and my brother John have loved me through all the transformations I have experienced during the writing of this book. And last I acknowledge my dear and loving husband, Mark Kline.

Amanda Porterfield
Syracuse, New York
October 1979

Feminine Spirituality in America

One

Introduction

She sweeps with many-colored Brooms—
And leaves the Shreds behind—
Oh Housewife in the Evening West—
Come back, and dust the Pond!

You dropped a Purple Ravelling in—
You dropped an Amber thread—
And now you've littered all the East
With Duds of Emerald!

And still, she plies her spotted Brooms,
And still the Aprons fly,
Till Brooms fade softly into stars—
And then I come away—

Emily Dickinson, 1861

In her poem about many-colored brooms, Emily Dickinson compared the work of a sunset with the sweepings of a housewife. The performance of the evening sky is associated with a familiar domestic task, and by implication, the ordinary task of sweeping up a house resembles nature's transformation of herself from day to night. In this poem, Dickinson pursues the esthetic dimension of her metaphor: it is beauty that characterizes the habits of the cosmos. The domestic economy of nature is spelled out in colorful extravagance, not in bleak efficiency. In putting away the sun, nature litters as she goes, loosing her threads and coloring up her sky. In this celestial cleansing, nature spills herself lavishly to become dark and starry.

If this poem about nature works by its associations with feminine cycles and sweepings, it is rendered all the more humanly profound by its spiritual associations. In the meaning of Dickinson's poem, as in the lives of a number of exemplary American women, domestic beauty is a metaphor for spiritual transformation. The last two lines of Dickinson's poem indicate that a beautiful sunset, home, or soul is only a preparation for heaven. And yet Dickinson's demure relation to the kingdom of the stars is an indirect claim to spiritual power. The relation between feminine spirituality and God is a complementary relation as common and as mysterious as the relation between day and night.

Dickinson's poem illustrates a spiritual tradition that has persisted through enormous changes in social and intellectual consciousness and has embraced and encouraged both self-expression and the self's capacity for transformation. The receptivity to change and the capacities to see one's environment as a home and oneself as a maker of a home characterize a tradition of spirituality that has played a powerful role in the history of American culture.

There have been men as well as women who have experienced the world as a home and found religious challenge and satisfaction in that experience. Three of America's most eminent religious thinkers—Jonathan Edwards, Ralph Waldo Emerson, and William James—grounded their theoretical work in experiences of being at home in the universe.[1] The experience of the universe's hospitality to the human spirit has persisted as a mode of spirituality important to America's most well-respected thinkers and illustrative of a noble aspect of American culture. The feminine spirituality that is the subject of this book differs from the manly spirit of being at home in the universe only, but significantly, in how concretely and commonly the metaphor has been experienced. Because they have often acted and imagined themselves as homemakers, women have found access to the universe's hospitality through the expansion of their own feminine desires, responsibilities, and powers. Whether by social, biological, or divine cause, American women have cultivated a domestic consciousness, and in its finest hours domestic consciousness has been agent and avenue to beauty.

As in Dickinson's poem about brooms, the process of maintaining and transforming environments, whether by domestic or ecological activism, is primarily and fundamentally an esthetic process. Nature seems to spill her images and display her colors not by any law of efficient order but by accidents of splendor.[2] The gratuitous impact of beauty is the attractive heart of domesticity as it is of nature. The ultimate satisfactions of domesticity are more akin to the pleasures of surprise and beauty than to the steady rewards of efficient productivity. Meals and rooms, gardens and clothes, children and husbands, brothers and fathers, are loved and sponsored not because they are efficient, interchangeable productions but because they may be played with pleasure.

A pleasure principle, which works deeper than morality, motivates this esthetic consciousness and characterizes feminine spirituality. By the logic of this psychology, power is to be played with rather than seized. If American women have received pleasure by submitting to authority, they have also often received authority by submitting to pleasure. The spiritual authority of American women has often involved the ability to make obedience a pleasure.

Because of their capacities to see domestic space with an esthetic eye and to extend domestic consciousness toward being at home in the universe, American women have often commanded social esteem and spiritual authority. More than a few American women have compelled admiration, even adoration and obedience—a phenomenon that testifies more to the attractive powers of femininity and domesticity than to the political authority of women.

This positive view of the spiritually persistent, politically latent powers of femininity is not to be confused with the point of view of Catharine Beecher, who celebrated woman's moral superiority. If it is true, as the Puritans believed, that people who experience beauty act beautifully, it is also true that beauty is not apprehended by moral self-righteousness. It is the access to beauty, not the claim to superior moral judgment, that American women may claim as their gift by right of their own history.

This is a book about spirituality in America. Spirituality refers to personal attitudes toward life, attitudes that engage an individual's deepest feelings and most fundamental beliefs. It encompasses the religious attitudes and experiences of individuals and may often be used as a synonym for religiousness. But spirituality covers a larger domain than that staked out by religion because it does not require belief in God or commitment to institutional forms of worship. It is what William James described as an individual's "total reaction upon life . . . that curious sense of the whole residual cosmos as an everlasting presence, intimate or alien, terrible or amusing, lovable or odious, which in some degree everyone possesses."[3]

This is not a book about everyone's spirituality in America. It is a study of a spiritual tradition identified by feminine attitudes and expressions. The first thesis of this book is that femininity characterizes a powerful and lasting tradition of spirituality in America. From the Puritan era to the present, many Americans of Christian heritage have perceived the nature of spirituality to be intimately related to feminine responses to life.

As for what "femininity" means, the reader will find no *a priori* definition. I begin with the most minimal assertion, namely, that femininity refers to attitudes and experiences that are perceived to characterize women. However one understands femininity, that understanding grows out of one's observation and study of women. Correspondingly, this book seeks to understand feminine spirituality by studying the spiritualities of women. We are not concerned here with all American women or with all aspects of femininity, but with the overlap of feminine attitudes toward life and spiritual attitudes of Christian origin.

While an understanding of femininity depends on perceptions

about women, insofar as it is an attitude of the soul, femininity
has not been restricted to women. In their spiritual responses to
a masculine God men have found it possible to imagine themselves as womanly beings. For example, the religious self-
understandings expressed by Edward Taylor, Francis Asbury,
and Henry Ward Beecher exemplify distinctly feminine attitudes
of the soul. Within their different historical eras and theological
frameworks, as the reader will see, these three men joined the
tradition of feminine spirituality and enlarged its domain.

Femininity and spirituality are not monolithic concepts, nor
are they points of view unaffected by historical change.
Throughout the course of American history both femininity and
spirituality have adapted to enormous social and intellectual
change and have found expression in a rich variety of activities
and beliefs. Adaptability is, in fact, an essential characteristic
common to both femininity and spirituality. Their persistent
association with one another by Americans of Christian heritage
helps give these adaptable terms some definition.

Feminine spirituality can be characterized by its illustrations
but not captured by conceptual definition. A conceptual definition is different from the thing itself, just as a definition of
melody is not itself a melody. To become familiar with melody it
is important to hear melodies. And we hear—and remember—
a melody by recognizing its particularity. As with melody, feminine spirituality is particular and various by nature. This book
approaches its subject through illustrations, presenting a variety
of feminine Americans whose spiritual lives are as singular as
memorable melodies. To reach a general understanding of feminine spirituality in America, I have explored relations among
these exemplary spiritual lives within the context of the history
of American culture.

The women whose lives have attracted my study have reminded me, by some personal characteristic, vocational dilemma,
or image held sacred, of one another. The women discussed in
this book belong together, as if their dilemmas and achievements
were of the same family, as if they were kin to one another across

great distances of time, space, and historical change. The women discussed here represent a family of spiritual characteristics and attitudes.

Insofar as I have looked to remarkable persons for the clearest illustrations of types of spiritual consciousness, I have followed the methodology of William James' *Varieties of Religious Experience.*[4] The reader will encounter here a selective array of women, most of them economically and educationally privileged and all of them articulate about spiritual life. The women included for discussion have been selected not because they represent "typical" spiritual consciousness as in a demographic survey, but because they illustrate spiritual consciousness in vivid and distinctive ways. In exemplary, and in some cases, extreme fashion, these women display personality characteristics and devotional attitudes that represent a gallery of spiritual types.

As a study of stages and states of spirituality, James' *Varieties* follows Jonathan Edwards' *Treatise on the Religious Affections* in its examination of vivid case histories and also in its presentation of the psychological structures characteristic of Christianity. In the spirit of that tradition in American religious thought, the conceptual structure of this book is based in a Puritan understanding of spirituality and the historical developments traced here have Puritanism as their point of origin. As for what is distinctly feminine about Puritan spirituality, this book shows how New England Puritans compared the life of a saint to the preparations of a bride and to the sustained bride-consciousness of a devoted wife. By this comparison, Puritans explained the nature of Christian spirituality as a feminine attitude toward God. Aspirants to sainthood were encouraged to imagine God as Bridegroom and Husband, a point of view that associated religiousness with femininity and that made religious life an adventure of paradox and self-conflict for men. This book traces the future history of the feminine dimension of Puritan spirituality.

In recent scholarship, significant insights have been offered about the influence of Puritan religious consciousness on the history of American culture. To take one important example, in

The Puritan Origins of the American Self, Sacvan Bercovitch shows how significant the relation between the Puritan God and the Puritan self has been for the history of American culture and self-consciousness. Bercovitch shows how the Puritan ideas and images of God were dynamically opposed to Puritan ideas and images of the human self. As Bercovitch tells it, in the process of becoming a Christian, the Puritan was a warrior against himself, striving to annihilate his own self and to imitate Christ. Bercovitch's psychological scrutiny of Puritan theology has influenced my own general perspective, but my argument differs from his when it considers the relation between feminine Puritan selves and an omnipotently masculine God. There I have found weddings rather than wars.[5]

In my interpretation of American spirituality, the husband-wife relation so precisely defined by the Puritans effected a lasting distinction between masculinity and femininity. This distinction may be described in terms of a set of relationships between gender on the one hand and power and authority on the other. As a legacy of Puritan conceptions of God, man, and woman, American men have had to vie with authority while American women have had to receive it.

Having to receive authority has been a paradoxical business. On the one hand, taboos against women warring for authority have functioned to deny women certain experiences of power. On the other hand, the capacity to receive authority is its own kind of power, a power that has enabled women to exercise authority, when it is received, with a security and righteousness not granted to those who fight for it. Another way to view this matter is to acknowledge that for a number of memorable American women, disqualification from political authority enabled the pursuit of an interior life that brought its own kind of power and lent these women spiritual authority in the eyes of their communities. One could say that although American women have often renounced or been refused direct political and economic power, they have often made up for this in power they experienced in realms of religious experience and esthetic expression. A Marxist or Freudian might interpret this feminine recourse as escapism or sublimation; a humanist would study the nature and meaning of its compensations.

The feminine notion of sainthood, as practiced by the Puritans, has perpetuated itself in the democratic privacy of American family life. To be sure, some Americans in later generations came to view the gratifications of sainthood and femininity with skepticism, but this skepticism notwithstanding, the association of femininity with spirituality has been forcefully and continually acknowledged by both women and men. Feminine spirituality has been a common experience and has ordinarily been practiced at home. In fact, feminine spirituality has involved the creation and maintenance of "home life" as much as it has involved the capacity to receive authority. Feminine spirituality involves the capacity to sacralize space or, in other words, an intuitive, esthetic sensitivity to environmental spaces, a sensitivity I call "domestic consciousness." Restricted to a single family and home, domestic life has often functioned to imprison women. But for some women, domestic consciousness has been an expansive spirituality, extending beyond the four walls of the home to a commitment to a larger human family, to an attention to social and environmental spaces, and to an artistic appreciation of the human soul as itself a household.

In presenting the spiritual lives of a collection of remarkable American women, I have tried to make visible thematic connections among them so that each of the lives illumines the others. At the same time, I have tried to show the historical integrity of each life, establishing relations among them in a way that demonstrates the uniquenesses of each. In the genre of biography, the realistic portrayal of a historical person depends, to some degree at least, on analysis of that person's relations with other persons, such as mother, father, spouse, friend, or deity. By a similar logic, I have found that comparative analysis of the lives of women from different eras of American culture actually enhances rather than blurs the historical individuality of the subjects under study.

The connections a historian draws across time or among people depend on the original writings of the people being studied and on primary documents about them. *How* the historian draws connections depends, of course, on the historian but also on the genre that suits the connections. Insofar as this history of feminine spirituality concerns the lives of individuals, and much of it does, I have written as a biographer. The reader will find here a design of biographical portraits woven together in the context of a cultural history of perceptions about women.

In regard to the biographical approach to cultural history, the book most significant for my own work has been Kathryn Kish Sklar's *Catharine Beecher: A Study in American Domesticity*.[6] Sklar's masterful biography of Catharine Beecher is two things at once: a penetrating analysis of the inner life of an influential woman and the cultural history of an era. Sklar dramatizes nearly a century of cultural history through the inner history, or character, of an individual whose life influenced as well as measured her culture. But though my approach to the relation between personal and cultural history has followed that of Sklar's, the subject of my study is not the whole history of one woman, but an inner history of femininity itself, as it has been made manifest in the lives of American women whose spiritualities have measured and influenced their culture.

In order to present the kind of history that focuses on the spiritual perceptions *of* historical women, it is necessary to offer a second kind of history as well, a history of American perceptions *about* women. To understand any particular woman's personal aspirations and dilemmas it is important to understand her cultural context and that context inevitably involves perceptions about women. General, cultural perceptions about women are ingredients in the perceptions of any single woman.

For material that documents perceptions about women, one naturally turns to personal documents, such as journals and letters, and to didactic literature, such as essays on morals and manners. One might also turn, for perceptions about femininity and about the relation between femininity and spirituality, to fiction—to novels, short stories, and poetry. But because a novel represents a different order of reality than the reality documented in journals, letters, and moral essays, it may seem a questionable business for a historian to draw forth cultural perceptions about femininity from fiction. A novelist creates characters and situations while a letter-writer, journalist, or essayist describes, interprets, and evaluates people and events. To be sure, there are no sharp lines between creation, interpretation, and description, but, on the other hand, most people would agree to a difference in emphasis.

The differences between fiction and theology were crucially important to New England Puritans, for whom theology was the measure of truth and fiction was vanity. This attitude altered substantially under the influence of romanticism, but even then the theologian's self-consciousness about his art differed from the novelist's. Harriet Beecher Stowe could say, with perfect religious sincerity, that God wrote *Uncle Tom's Cabin*. She was claiming that God *wrote* through her as a novelist. No Protestant theologian in America has ever claimed, to my knowledge, that God wrote his sermons. A relationship with a divine creator may be present in fiction as in theology, but the nature of the relationship is different. But despite these differences, and their impact on audiences, both theology and fiction qualify as valuable resources for historians of American culture.

It is precisely because of the imaginative freedom of fiction that fiction should count, on its own terms, as historical data. The power and influence of a novel depends on how imaginatively the author portrays his characters and constructs his plot. No novelist can avoid representing the life of his culture. Novelists succeed or fail in terms of how vividly and compellingly they develop their culture's ideas and images. Fiction is not outside the bailiwick of a historian, and for cultural studies of novel-writing eras, novels are crucial resources.

It is one of the contentions of this study that novels functioned for Christians in the nineteenth century in ways that are similar to how sermons functioned for New England Puritans. It is a further and related contention that the novel came to be so influential as a genre of religious expression that it actually transformed the nature and form of theology. Theology and fiction function similarly in important respects. Neither theology nor fiction is a documentary report about life as it is literally lived. Both portray invisible realms of human experience, realms that are defined by personalities and their desires and situations. Both inform their audiences how to live by persuasively presenting the personalities and situations of unseen realities.

In the heyday of the classic American novel, in the mid- and late nineteenth century, many popular and influential novels were written by women. These novels are characteristically constructed in terms of perceptions about femininity. To a significant extent, then, in the nineteenth century it is women who were responsible for popular cultural perceptions about women. Hence the notion that one could distinguish between perceptions of and about women by separating the writings of men from the writings of women is a distinction inappropriate to the materials at hand. It is of crucial importance to my study of feminine spirituality that, in the nineteenth century at least, perceptions *about* women were to a large extent constructed in the minds of women, that is, in terms of perceptions *of* women.

The question then becomes, for the historian, how to discriminate the spiritual perceptions of women from spiritual perceptions about them. Or, to put the question another way, in what ways would biographical accounts of historical women differ from a discussion of literary heroines? It has seemed to me that, as far as the historian can tell, the individual lives of most women and perceptions about them have merged to become a collective, cultural history accessible to the historian through the novels these women read and the sermons they heard. For the historian, the distinction between *of* and *about* can only be made in the cases of those women who registered their dissent from cultural perceptions about women or who actually influenced, by the example of their own lives or by the literature they wrote, cultural perceptions about women. It has been my intention to explore cultural perceptions about women in order to understand the lives and contributions of the women who rebelled from, altered, or dramatically confirmed those conventions. I have mined the histories of American theology and literature and presented those histories in relation to changing social structures. But my aim has always been to return to individuals—to a selected group of women who made a mark that historians can read. I have understood the more visible cultural history as the material of the internal dilemmas and desires of particular women. I have used cultural history as the grist for a history of individuals.

The relation of my work to Ann Douglas' *The Feminization of American Culture* may be best understood in terms of this issue of the difference between biography and cultural history. Douglas has presented a compelling and beautifully researched study of cultural perceptions about femininity in nineteenth-century America. She has claimed about the Victorian era, as Betty Friedan claimed about the "feminine mystique" of the 1950's, that femininity functioned as a religious ideal that exerted enormous power over nearly all dimensions of culture.[7] Douglas agrees with Friedan that the idolization of femininity has served to weaken the moral fiber and intellectual energy of American culture and to imprison women in stereotypes about themselves. I have agreed with Douglas and Friedan that idealized perceptions about femininity have played a powerful role in the cultural history of America, that the values and aspirations of American women have been shaped by cultural assumptions about femininity, and that countless women have been enslaved by idealized perceptions about femininity. My study differs from theirs in that it is focused on spiritual biography and, hence, its discussions of perceptions about femininity are set in relation to the spiritual experiences of a constellation of great women. This biographical direction of my work has, it must be stated, shaped my understanding of the feminine mystique and my evaluation of the feminization of American culture. I agree that idealized perceptions about femininity can function negatively and repressively for women but that recognition has not led me to an ideological treatment of cultural perceptions about femininity.

I have learned to appreciate how idealized perceptions about femininity have been experienced as elements of profound spiritual visions.

Douglas contends that theology and fiction merged during the nineteenth century and that theology was trivialized in the process. It is certainly true that the development of the novel influenced the form and content of theology, and I agree with Douglas that theology suffered as a result. One need only think of the difference between the minds of Hooker, Shepard, and Edwards and those of Bushnell, Henry Ward Beecher, and Moody to appreciate how great a loss American theology suffered in intellectual energy and structure during the time from the Puritan era to the Victorian. I would add, however, that the decline of theology is not necessarily to be equated with the decline of religious experience or spiritual awareness. The creative freedom of fiction may, for many women, actually have stimulated rather than repressed individuation. What I argue for is an understanding of the relation between art, theology, or ideology on the one hand and subjective life on the other in which subjective life is the vessel without bottom or lid in which images and ideas are established, disestablished, rebelled against, altered, or reanimated. This is contrary to a substantialist or ideological view of the human self; it is rather a notion of countless selves as countless spaces in process. The stuff present in the invisible space of these selves include ideas, images, values, and desires. In the case of the few women whose lives I have selected for particularly close study, the religious images about femininity available to them from their culture were stirred and recomposed in exciting ways. In a culture replete with religious ideas and images about femininity, some women were able to internalize those "fictions" in ways that brought them close enough to God to be his lover, his mother—or even himself.

Ann Douglas has paid special attention to Margaret Fuller because Fuller objected, more radically and self-consciously than any other nineteenth-century American woman, to the fictionalizing mania of her culture. I, on the other hand, have paid special attention to Emily Dickinson because Dickinson internalized, more radically and self-consciously than any other nineteenth-century American woman, the images of fiction and the ideas of theology as the material of her own spiritual adventures. Dickinson internalized life to an extraordinary degree and to magnificent proportions. She internalized civil war, the collapse of theology, flowers in her garden, God, Jesus, the Devil, and Prince Charming—all became personalized as the images, ideas, fictions, theologies, and histories of her own polytheistic self. Since, in her poetry, she left a long, detailed, and intelligent account of her inner life, she made it possible, perhaps more than any other American woman, for others to write about her spirituality.

The lives selected here for discussion all exemplify a process of transformation. Since the type of spiritual transformation most celebrated throughout American history has been religious conversion, I have used the nature and process of religious conversion as an important model for understanding a variety of types of spiritual transformation among American women. The spiritual transformation of Catharine Beecher, for example, involved a conversion-like process during which she lost her desire to be converted to evangelical Christianity.[8] In the case of Emily Dickinson, transformation is the most persistent subject of her poetry. Even in her meter she communicates the discontinuity and power of transformation.

For converted Christians, for Catharine Beecher and for Emily Dickinson, spiritual transformation has seemed to involve moments when the bottom falls out or the lid flies off, moments in which some sudden infusion of energy enables ideas and images to be radically rearranged. In the paradigm of conversion, in which old ideas and images are rearranged in pious harmony, the infusion of volatile energy is identified as grace. Grace has been reported by American Christians and understood by their theologians as an experience of beauty and, often, as an ecstatic experience. Ecstatic experiences of spiritual transformation can involve—for women at least as commonly as for men—such dramatic physical and emotional expression as weeping, singing, and dancing.[9]

Given the association between the dramatic expression of spirituality and the transformational energy Christians call grace, I have seen choreographer and dancer Martha Graham as an outstanding exemplar of feminine spirituality in twentieth-century America. Although she did not experience grace as a *Christian* experience, grace for Graham was admittedly a religious experience involving divinity, spiritual transformation, and the beauty of balance. Graham chose explicitly religious themes as the subjects for most of her choreographic works. Almost every dance she created focused on the religious dilemmas and sexual desires of a female character—the Virgin Mary, Emily Dickinson, and Medea, to name three—and I have understood the corpus of her work as an exploration of relations among vividly feminine religious personalities. As has been said about Dickinson, Graham's work is her life. In the history of her dances Graham sought spiritual transformation and cultivated grace. The feminine personalities she created in dance bear family resemblances to the spiritual lives portrayed in this study.

Two

Bridal Passion and New England Puritanism

A Wife—at Daybreak I shall be—
Sunrise—Hast thou a Flag for me?
At Midnight, I am but a Maid,
How short it takes to make a Bride—
Then—Midnight, I have passed from thee
Unto the East, and Victory—

Midnight—Good Night! I hear them call,
The Angels bustle in the Hall—
Softly my Future climbs the Stair,
I fumble at my Childhood's prayer
So soon to be a Child no more—
Eternity, I'm coming—Sir,
Savior—I've seen the face—before!

Emily Dickinson, 1862

❧ The religious attitudes of the small band of men and women who settled Massachusetts Bay Colony have deeply influenced American culture. We remember the Puritans as stern, judgmental, and self-consciously serious people whose disciplined stubbornness tamed a wilderness and established a civilization. We have inherited their determined practicality and their self-consciousness, and we blame them, on occasion, for our intolerances and neuroses.

19

Although we are aware of the influence of the Puritans on
American culture, we give too little scrutiny, in our reflections
about them, to the religious vision that they claimed as their
identity and motivation. Puritans experienced the world and
understood history as a complex reality established by and for
the glory of God. The Puritans' experience of the overwhelming
power and infinite knowledge of God shaped their understanding of themselves and lay at the root of their experiments in
church and state.

The Puritans not only worked under—and with—the wrath of
God, they also experienced—and loved—the beauty of God. The
sermons, journals, letters, and poems written by men and
women of Massachusetts Bay reveal the exuberance with which
they lived in the world. They experienced not only the agonies of
failure before God but also the pleasures of living with glory.
The writings that record the pleasures of religious experience
reveal a joyfulness in the hearts of some Puritans at least, a
joyfulness that softens our stereotyped image of their long, dour
faces.

For New England Puritans, religious life was more than a
conceptual enterprise; it was the personal experience of spiritual
events that composed the glory of God. In this kind of religious
life, moments of ecstasy were actually and acutely sensational, as
were moments of despair. God could enjoy as well as criticize his
fleshly creation and, correspondingly, human responsiveness
could find expression in physical joy as well as in worldly denial.
Although many Puritan devotions were as gloomy and tortured
as hell, experiences of ecstasy characterize an essential, vitaliz-
ing element in the tradition of American Puritanism.

Ecstasy announced itself in no less virtuous and respected a
person than Sarah Pierrepont Edwards, third-generation resi-
dent of Massachusetts, wife of New England's greatest divine,
and matriarch of the celebrated Pierrepont-Edwards lineage.
The religious experiences of Sarah Edwards, as interpreted
through the psychology of her husband Jonathan, may be seen as
illustrating the vitality of Puritan spirituality at the moment of

its culmination and transformation in the religious enthusiasms of the Great Awakening.

Early in 1742, amidst the excitement of the Great Awakening, Sarah Edwards intensely experienced the grace of God, and in *Some Thoughts Concerning the Present Revival* (1742), Jonathan Edwards quoted from his wife's written account of her dramatic experience.[1] Engulfed in the beauty of Christ, Sarah Edwards felt "swallowed up with light and love." In this "heavenly Elysium" she "swam in the rays of Christ's love, like a little mote swimming in the beams of the sun." A "constant stream of sweet light" flowed between her heart and the heart of Christ. Her experience of swimming in the sun as it swallowed her was prolonged and recurrent; "More than once" she felt this grace "for five or six hours together, without any interruption."[2] Her own narrative records a moment "so intense . . . I could not forbear rising up and leaping with joy and exaltation." Sarah Edwards did not swim metaphorically in the trope of divine light—she danced before her Lord. And as she was renowned for her "peculiar loveliness of expression," one suspects that she showed off beautifully the grace she received.[3]

In Sarah Edwards' experience, as in her husband's theology, the nature of grace was the exercise of it or, in other words, grace, like God himself, was a "Divine and Supernatural Light." The "constant stream of sweet light" running between Christ and Sarah Edwards illustrated her husband's theories of religious experience. As he described the activity of grace, the spirit of God communicated itself as a "vital principle" within the saint's soul, a communication that moved the saint to reemanate that holy vitality. This divine light did not shine on the saint's soul as on a dark body, but "exerts and communicates himself in his own proper nature"[4]—as if the principle of light were planted in the soul, so that the soul itself became a source of light. Sarah Edwards participated in the nature of God himself and, conversely, his nature shone in her beauty.

The movement of grace enjoyed itself in the display of the universe. To explain how the universe was in such harmonious

motion, Jonathan Edwards argued that color was an expression
of the simple moving principle of "mere light." Mere light divides
and recombines itself in "rays" of varying patterns. Edwards
took the beautiful harmony of nature's colors—"the suitable-
ness of green for the grass and plants, the blue of the skie, the
white of the clouds, the colours of flowers"—to be light reveal-
ing and displaying itself in kaleidoscopic form. To paraphrase
Edwards, those who experienced the movement of light itself
could see God moving colorfully in nature. They could also see,
and see themselves swimming in and swallowed by, the nature
of God. Just as the fullness of white light contains and harmon-
izes all colors, so sheer light or "brightness" itself, "mankind
have agreed," represents "glory and extraordinary beauty."[5]

The bright glory and extraordinary beauty of divine light
"swallowed up" Sarah Edwards, instilling in her body and soul
the very principle that sanctified her, enabling not only the
streaming light of her intercourse with Christ, but also her
powers of social expression. If we interpret the remarks of
her admirers within the context of her husband's theology, her
beauty was a display of color that revealed the movement of light
itself. The supernatural simplicity of divine light infused her
being and dwelt there as a vital principle of new nature. As an
exemplar not only of faith but of God, Sarah Edwards could
figure for others as a sacred text. "The works of God are but a
kind of voice or language of God," wrote Jonathan Edwards,[6] and
Sarah, like Scripture, communicated the Word itself. The beauty
of her virtue embodied God.

By the canons of Puritan epistemology the words of a religious
text or the "lovely tinctures of the morning and evening"[7] do not
themselves possess the spirit that determines them. Like the
whole beauty of nature itself, Sarah Edwards' virtuosity lay in
her capacity to point to divine authority. A model of God's love
for others, the beauty of her comportment was nothing in and of
itself. To be full of God for others required emptiness of self, and
we shall return to the pains and dilemmas of this religious
dynamic. But first it is important to set the experiences and

beauty of Sarah Edwards within the context of a certain dimension of Puritan spirituality. Behind her experiences of grace and her power to represent the nature of God stood a century of New England experiences of Christ. The experiences and powers of Sarah Edwards illumine a theological tradition that encouraged sensational religious experiences and associated Christian virtue with the beauty of femininity.

In their public and private literature the first generation of New England Puritans compared the joys and responsibilities of saints to the preparations of a bride and the privileges of a wife. Of course, the characterization of Christian spirituality as a bridal relation to Christ did not originate with the New England Puritans. Ancient allegory made Christ the husband of the church and the believer's soul the bride of the Lord. Insofar as they relied on the image of marriage to describe the Christian's relation to deity, the Puritans depended on tradition. But they departed from tradition in their evaluation of human marriage. Marriage between man and woman was not a sacrament for the Puritans. From our modern, secular perspective it might seem that transfering the celebration of marriage from a sacramental to a civil office, as the Puritans did, diminished the religious significance of marriage. In fact the Puritans intended the opposite, namely, to highlight the religious significance of marriage. They also intended, in their desacralization of marriage, to emphasize the religious responsibilities and privileges of Christian women who were wives in this world.

To see this point of view it is necessary to understand how the Puritans placed the sacraments in relation to the rest of Christian life. As participants in the reformation of Christianity, Puritans limited the sacraments to baptism and communion. They purified the definition of a sacrament, insisting that it refer exclusively to the celebration of an individual's relation with God. The sacraments of baptism and communion were ritual acknowledgments of the Christian's private relation with God and, consequently, marriage between man and woman simply did not qualify as a sacrament.[8] To disqualify marriage as a sacrament did not imply that marriage, or any other human relation or activity, was secular. Every experience was, for Puritan Christians, laden with religious significance. The religious plantation of New England should be understood in terms of this emotional and theological commitment. The separation of civil and ecclesiastical functions did not imply that civil life was areligious. In the religious experiment of Massachusetts Bay, Puritans established church and state as separate but complementary institutions. They distinguished the religious responsibilities of the two institutions to purify the functions of the church and to enforce religious responsibilities on the officers and members of the state. The marriage of man and woman was, like all Puritan institutions, of religious significance. Beyond this, marriage had special meaning: the loving union of man and woman was an analogy for the relation between God and the Christian.

A favorite text for drawing the analogy between feminine devotion and Christian spirituality was the parable in Matthew in which "the kingdom of heaven" is "likened unto ten virgins." In that parable "five of them were wise" and "took oil in their vessels with their lamps." The five "foolish" virgins "took no oil with them" and were found unprepared when "at midnight there was a cry made, Behold the bridegroom cometh, go ye out to meet him." The unprepared virgins hurried to purchase the oil needed to greet the light of their Lord, but in their absence "the bridegroom came" and the "ready" virgins "went in with him to the marriage, and the door was shut." When the foolish ones returned they begged their Lord, "open to us. But he answered . . . I know you not."[9]

With this parable as his text, Thomas Shepard, eminent among the first generation of Massachusetts Bay theologians, delivered a long and rich series of lectures to his Cambridge parish from June, 1636, to May, 1640. In these lectures, Shepard interpreted the ten virgins as the visible church, stating clearly that "all church members are and must be visible saints . . . virgins espoused to Christ." From the initial analogy, Shepard went on to compare church membership to the joys and responsibilities of betrothal. In warm tones, he described how the true church member actively awaits the coming of Christ as an espoused virgin prepares to join her bridegroom. Loving, hoping, church members longed for the hour when Christ would arrive, resplendent in his bridal array, to carry his faithful lovers into the heavenly chamber of eternal marriage. Shepard warned that at Christ's coming, some who profess Christianity would be found unprepared, just as "a woman may be espoused to another, and yet her foul apparel is on." Only those church members dressed for Christ would consummate the midnight marriage.

During his four years of sermons on the parable, Shepard constantly stressed the attractiveness of Christ: "He is worthy of love, there is beauty in him why thou shouldest desire him." Shepard also took care to emphasize that believers possess no virtue of their own that deserves Christ's love. Thus while the espoused saint loves the bridegroom for his compelling beauty, she has no beauty—except in his eyes. Nor do good works effect salvation, for Christ "does not suspend his love on our grace or holiness." The source of Christ's love for believers is his *own* graciousness, and in the profusion of his divine beauty, God fills those who love him with his own loveliness. "He will rejoice in thee . . . as a bridegroom does over the bride: Not because of any beauty in thee, for there is none, but . . . for his own sake."[10]

In 1707, seventy years after Shepard's lectures, the young Boston minister Benjamin Colman published his sermons on the same parable. The urbane Colman delighted in the theatrical splendor of the second coming, foreseeing Christ's arrival "on a burning refulgent Cloud" to inaugurate "the most pompous Show the World can ever see or Heaven afford." In Colman's sumptuous interpretation, Christ will take his pleasure in the virgins who greet him. To describe that pleasure Colman put poetry from the Song of Solomon in the mouth of Christ, who says to his brides as they are ravished by his purity, "Behold thou art fair my Love—Thou art all fair, there is no Spot in thee."

Beatification is a process of beautification in which Christ "cleanses" his virgins until they are spotless mirrors "and then takes Pleasure in his own Image." With joy in his own abundant beauty Christ adorns his lovers with his own "graces." To illustrate the nature of saintliness Colman chose the sensual imagery of washed bodies arrayed in luxurious garments and, again quoting from Canticles, exclaimed at the wonderful generosity of Christ: "That he should be at the Cost to *cloath us with Broider'd Work, and deck us with Ornaments* that we may appear worthy of being His!" Like Shepard, Colman placed his descriptions of the sensual privileges of election within the context of the ultimate attractiveness of Christ: the saint is inflamed with love for her bridegroom for "in her Eyes he is altogether lovely and his Presence and Graces are the infinite Bliss she craves."[11]

In his sermons Colman extended the parable of espousal to an analogy between sanctification and marriage. "The Relation wherein Christ proposes and offers himself unto us agrees in many respects to the Conjugal or Marriage Relation." Colman defined the mystical union of sanctification as the marriage of God and man: "A Marriage makes *Two* to become One, so that he is joined to the Lord in one Spirit." The conjugal analogy served Colman doubly well, for marriage involved a hierarchy of authority as well as a union of love. In grace as in marriage the sovereignty of one commanded the subservience of the other. The "Duties" of a Christian "are like those which a *Wife* engages in her Marriage: for instance: Intire, unfeigned, fervent, and perpetual *Love* to Christ." With greater explicitness and more assurance about heaven than Shepard, Colman enumerated the "Privileges" of the marriage covenant with Christ and specified "the Fruits of this tender Affection" as "*Provision, Protection, and Conduct* from Christ." Christians could anticipate eternal pleasure as well as reward. Colman assured his readers that in heaven wives of Christ will "partake in his Honours and Inheritance" and live in "everlasting *enjoyment* of Christ."[12]

Although Colman's ornate pieties contrast with Shepard's steadier and humbler devotions, in their sermons on the parable of the ten virgins the ministers drew forth similar theories of religious experience. Both used the motif of bride-consciousness to connote the purity of religious love. And both showed how the loveliness of the bride-saint depended on the beauty of Christ. In the sermons of Colman and Shepard, religious experience was finally an esthetic experience. God ruled all reality— Puritans assumed that sinners and even pagans were aware of that. But Christians were distinguished by their perception and reflection of God's beauty.

When Shepard and Colman used betrothal as an analogy for religious life, they encouraged their parishioners and readers to conceive of themselves as brides. Betrothal was a common experience or expectation among New England Puritans, and a woman could participate in the analogy by imaginatively extending her own experience as preparing bride and obedient wife. Because of the congruence between her social and religious roles the life of any virtuous woman could be a parable of sainthood. But for a male parishioner to identify with the analogy between marital and religious love, a metaphoric change of gender was required. As rulers and husbands on earth, and thus in some sense as imitators of divine sovereignty, men were precariously balanced between social authority and religious humility. In his religious life as a bride of Christ a man might come to regard his earthly authority as an obstacle to the humility that accompanied holiness.

The personal poetry of Edward Taylor represents a particularly intense love relation between believer and Christ and a case in point of a male Puritan who appropriated a feminine persona to confess his spirituality. Minister of the frontier parish of Westfield, Massachusetts, from 1671 until his death in 1729, Taylor forbade his heirs to publish his poetry,[13] perhaps because the effusiveness of his style did not correspond to the "plain style" encouraged in Puritan writing, perhaps because he regarded the emotional ardor of his verse as a wholly private expression of his relation with God, or perhaps because he became a different person through his poetry, a maiden rather

than a minister, and his maidenhood depended on the lack of its
publicity. The amorous language of the Song of Solomon inspired many of his meditations, especially those in which he
anticipated union with Christ. His "Meditation One" begins
with wonder at Christ's promise of marriage:

> What Love is this of thine, that Cannot bee
>   In thine Infinity, O Lord, Confinde,
> Unless it in thy very Person see,
>   Infinity, and finity Conjoyn'd?
>   What hath thy Godhead, as not satisfide
> Marri'de our Manhood, making it its Bride?

His meditation on "The Spouse" also expresses astonishment at
the news that God will marry man:

> I know not how to speak't, it is so good:
>   Shall Mortall, and Immortall marry? nay,
> Man marry God? God be a Match for Mud?
>   The King of Glory Wed a Worm? mere Clay?
>   Thy Maker is thy Husband. Hearst thou this?[14]

In both verses Taylor contrasts the power of God with the
weakness of humanity. God unites himself with human beings
not because they deserve it but in a gratuitous celebration of his
own power. The creator relishes his handiwork despite the fact
that his mortals are no finer than mud or worms. In the power of
his ardor God satisfies himself by rejoining to himself his defiled
creation. The creation—and the Christian—do not initiate, they
respond. Marriage—man taking the weakness of woman for his
bride—symbolizes God's way of union. Just as Benjamin Colman
used marriage to illustrate the theological coincidence of union
and hierarchy, so Taylor found the paradox of matrimony an apt
representation of the miracle of sanctification.

Furthermore Taylor, like Shepard and Colman, stressed the
beauty of holiness, the essentially esthetic quality of religious
experience. Illustrating Christian beauty through sensual imagery, he portrayed Christ's power to make men holy as a spiritual

experience akin to the sexual. One stanza from "The Reflexion" represents Taylor's way of describing Christ's beauty and his beatification of believers:

> *Shall not thy Rose my Garden fresh perfume?*
> *Shall not thy Beauty my dull Heart assaile?*
> *Shall not thy golden gleams run through this gloom?*
> *Shall my black Velvet Mask thy fair Face Vaile?*
> *Pass o're my Faults: shine forth, bright sun: arise*
> *Enthrone thy Rosy-selfe within mine Eyes.*[15]

In this poem, Taylor imagines himself as soil in which God plants his Rose, a typological symbol of Christ. Longing for the smell of the Rose, the poet begs God to "assaile" his heart with Beauty and "run through" his dark sinfulness with divine light. The light of God pierces into the dark body of man to his heart, generating there a rose that grows from the heart through the eyes of the poet. The Rose that blossoms forth in the poet's vision is an image of the sun as Christ is an image of God, living through this dark world as an embodiment of the beauty of God.

As did Jonathan Edwards, Edward Taylor understood the influence of God as a divine and supernatural light. But despite the fecund naturalism of Taylor's conceits, the earth, soiled in sin, is a mask veiling true reality rather than the shadow-realm of divine life.[16] For Edwards, darkness was part of the divine economy. In his attitude toward the nature of nature, and toward the evil nature of human nature, Edwards understood the whole creation to be the harmonious expression of divine being. His wife illustrated, and perhaps elicited, the point. In contrast, Taylor wrote poetry like a sensualist addicted to his guilt. Perhaps the public majesty of the ministry was a mask of authority that hid the impassioned privacy of the poetry through which he experienced and expressed his soiledness, his weakness, and his longing for the piercings of divine light and the perfumes of Christ.

Taylor's poetry testifies that yearning after God could take its pattern and imagery from dynamics of sexuality. God was dominatingly male in the literature and consciousness of Puritans, and in his intimate spirituality, Taylor assumed a complementary feminine stance toward God. But apart from the question—or problem—of gender, the yearning for and enjoyment of love was a quality of feeling common to both men and women. The experience or anticipation of a love that unified oneself with another offered an analogy for sanctification that transcended the inexchangeable determinations of gender. The union of sanctification—or of marriage—was effected by the surrender of feminine to masculine power; the potential for mystic union existed inside the partnership of unequals. Since theological symbols are shaped by social experience, the unification of married selves must have been a deeply felt and not uncommon experience.

Indeed, extant journals, letters, and poems written by both men and women document how personal experiences of wedlock could be earthly illustrations of religious union. The love between John and Margaret Winthrop exemplifies this interplay of sexual passion within and beyond this world. Their absences from one another became opportunities for each to discover and express by letter the presence of their love. Since Margaret Winthrop's second pregnancy prevented her from accompanying her husband to New England on the *Arbella* in 1630, during their separation each set aside the hour between five and six on Monday and Friday evenings for thoughts of the other. During this absence the governor of Massachusetts Bay wrote: "Oh how it refresheth my heart to thinke that I shall yet againe see thy sweet face in the lande of the livinge, that lovely countenance that I have so much delighted in, and beheld with so great contente." Margaret Winthrop's love for her husband matched his for her. She wrote to her absent spouse: "It is now late and bed time and I must bid thee good night before I am wilinge for I could finde in my hart to sit and talke with thee all night."[17]

Because spouse and God compelled analogous responses, Puritan Christians were forced to guard against transfering devotion away from God. In the spirit of this constraint, as he looked forward to his marriage to Margaret Tyndal, John Winthrop addressed her as "the happye and hopeful supplie (next Christ Jesus) of my greatest losses." Another of Winthrop's absences— this time to settle with Anne Hutchinson in Boston—prompted him to remind his wife that it was proper for God to have "detayned" him: God "hath a greater interest in me than thy self." Margaret Winthrop matched her husband's religious obedience. In 1628, on learning of his illness in London, she found in his ill health and her anxiety a gracious warning from God: "Thus it pleaseth the Lord to exercise us with one affliction after another in love; lest we should forget our selves and love this world too much, and not set our affections on heaven where all true happyness is for ever."[18]

For the Winthrops, as for several other notable couples, marriage was a career of earthly passion rivaled and checked by passion for God. Edward Taylor wrote with conviction to his espoused, Elizabeth Fitch, "that Conjugall love ought to exceed all other." And he showed her how heated that love could be: his love for her was "a golden ball of pure fire." But he cautioned that this earthly love "must be kept within bounds too. For it must be subordinate to God's Glory." Taylor notified his beloved that he could not deliver his whole heart to her—"for that I trust is sent to Heaven long since"—but assured her that whatever heart-portion God permitted him to distribute in the world would "safely and singly fall to your share."[19] God granted passion among men and women as a hint and analogy of divine graciousness. Once having been granted passionate love, it was tempting but idolatrous to fall wholly in love with the signs and shadows of God's grace.

Thomas Shepard, whose *Parable of the Ten Virgins* we have already encountered, wrote in his autobiography about a bittersweet instance of God's use of human love to display the nature of his own suit. To show his "goodness and sweetness," God "fitted" Thomas Shepard with a holy wife. In her husband's words, Joanna was "a most sweet humble woman, full of Christ, and a very discerning Christian, a wife who was most incomparable loving to me and every way amiable and holy and endued with a very sweet spirit of prayer." God permitted Thomas Shepard to live with a true helpmeet, a wife whose Christian virtues were shaped for her husband's needs. As far as Thomas' religious interests were concerned, the Shepard marriage was made in heaven. And he acknowledged the plain truth of his good situation: "I did marry the best and fittest woman in the world unto me."[20]

But lest he love Joanna too much for herself and too little for her capacity to point him to divine love, Thomas understood that God used Joanna's affliction in childbirth to expose the frailty of earthly love. He appropriated his wife's pain, as well as her virtues, as God's useful lessons to him. After Joanna had labored four days, Thomas wrote that "the Lord did teach me much." He confessed that he "had need" of Joanna's sickness, "for I began to grow secretly proud and full of sensuality, delighting my soul in my dear wife more than in my God." Thomas needed Joanna's ill health because he loved her more than he thought a mortal deserved or God allowed. Whether in jealousy or in the spirit of a relentless pedagogy, "the Lord by this affliction of my wife learnt me to desire to fear him more and to keep his dread in my heart."[21]

Finally, during another difficult childbirth, God "took away" Joanna Shepard. Her husband's grief was deep—perhaps inconsolable. In the voice of a heartbroken man, he recorded that God's chastisement left him with a loneliness that deprived him not only of Joanna but of God himself. God "refused to hear prayer when I did think He would have hearkened and let me see His beauty in the land of the living." Thomas had found shining in Joanna—who "was fit to die long before she did"—the beauty of God. God had "manifested" his "tender care" through her life, and at her death he felt God "withdraw." Thomas Shepard concluded his autobiography with remorse over his inability to learn from his anguish: "Thus God hath visited and scorged me for my sins, and sought to wean me from this world; but I have ever found it a difficult thing to profit ever but a little by the sorest and sharpest afflictions."[22]

Thomas Shepard, like Edward Taylor and John and Margaret Winthrop, believed that marital love was sacred, but only when it was experienced as a gift that reflected the graciousness of God. A good marriage signified God's blessing and man's prevision of sanctification, but the more a marriage reflected God's beauty, the more vulnerable was that union to God's disruption with a reminder of his greater love. The ill health, absences, or death of a spouse were at once torment and blessing. The greater the earthly love, the greater space for torment at the beloved's affliction; and the greater the torment, the greater space God had for working in the Puritan's heart. In view of the religious opportunity offered by such anguish, John Davenport instructed the recently widowed Lady Mary Vere that though her "relation . . . to this earthly husband . . . ceaseth in his death, . . . the relation you have to our heavenly husband remayneth inviolable." Davenport found a striking metaphor for his lesson: "it is but a conduit pipe that is broken." The "fountaine" was "still open" to Lady Mary.[23] The grace of God, like water from a fountain, was poured into the soul of Lady Mary. By this analogy, a husband mediated God's grace to his wife, for he, like the heavenly husband, was superior and required her submission, obedience, and devotion. But a husband, like a conduit pipe, was dispensable, while a wife, like a pitcher for the waters of grace, was a receptacle for the fountain of God.

As religious subjects, that is, as worshipers of God, seeking to purify, chasten, and humble their souls and to become ever more religious, women could prepare for religious dependence through matrimony, as Mary Vere had learned of God's sovereignty first through her devotion to her husband and later through his death. In contrast, a man might mediate or even represent the sovereignty of God, but to receive and radiate grace he must somehow learn what leadership and social authority tended not to teach him, namely, humility. As models of how to love and depend on God women could also teach others, especially those who needed instruction in dependence, as Joanna Shepard's sweet humility tutored her husband's spirituality. Graceful women might finally function as religious objects, as God filled Joanna Shepard with himself, disclosed his beauty through her presence, and withdrew, with her, at her death.

Thus Puritan women were religiously favored on at least three counts, as religious subjects, as religious models, and as religious objects. First, a woman's dependent status in marriage could train her for a correct relation with God. Second, a woman with expertise in humility might win the respect and attention of others and others might pattern their religiosity on the model of her presence. In her third religious posture, a beloved Puritan woman might reveal the nature of God. This posture of power was also a posture of great danger, as we shall see in the case of Anne Hutchinson. In the case of Joanna Shepard, the power her husband perceived her to have seemed reason enough for God to have ended her life.

These three religious postures, each of which permitted an analogy between wifehood and sainthood, were postures perceived to characterize women. For the woman's side of the story —that is, for some statement from a Puritan woman about her own self-perceptions as a wife and as a Christian—we turn to the poetry and occasional prose of Anne Bradstreet, New England's first published poet. A central theme in Bradstreet's writing was her own comparison of the attractions of earthly and heavenly love. In a poem addressed "To my Dear and Loving Husband" she expressed the intensity of her matrimonial union:

> If ever two were one, then surely we.
> If ever man were lov'd by wife, then thee;
> If ever wife was happy in a man,
> Compare with me ye women if you can.
> I prize thy love more than whole Mines of gold,
> Or all the riches that the East doth hold.
> My love is such that Rivers cannot quench,
> Nor ought but love from thee, give recompence.
> Thy love is such I can no way repay,
> The heavens reward thee manifold I pray.
> Then while we live, in love lets so persever
> That when we live no more, we may live ever.[24]

In this generous and passionate poem, Bradstreet describes the nature of her love for her husband Simon, and his for her, and she uses religious symbolism to portray the qualities and intensity of their love. The union of Anne and Simon Bradstreet suggests a mystical interpenetration of selves that, if it perseveres, will deserve immortality: "That when we live no more, we may live ever." As in Christ's covenant of grace, Anne does not deserve her husband's love: "Thy love is such I can no way repay." Although she cannot earn Simon's love by works, she can offer in gratitude and absolute devotion a love of her own that also transcends repayment: "My love is such that Rivers cannot quench."

Her matrimonial bliss notwithstanding, in other writings Bradstreet carefully distinguished earthly affection from eternal reality. While her soul's dilemma lay in judging which suitor commanded her ultimate devotion, her religious practice lay in repeatedly exercising her choice for God. Even though "To my Dear and Loving Husband" demonstrates that her love for Simon mirrored the ardor of a saint's love for Christ, other poems and meditations define her passion for her husband as secondary to her passion for God.

Her poem "In my Solitary houres in my dear husband his Absence" is a religious lesson to herself. One stanza reads:

> Tho: husband dear bee from me gone,
>   Whom I doe love so well;
> I have a more beloved one
>   Whose comforts far excell.

This poem goes on to say that if she does not continually see God within her husband, children, and friends, then "they are no Joy but woe." Only by affirming "In Thee Alone is more than All, / And there content I'll take" can she honestly pray for Simon's return. Anne and Simon, if God rejoins them, will rededicate their union to God's glory "and serve Thee better than before." And in another context, in a meditation after "a sore fitt of fainting, which lasted 2 or 3 dayes," Bradstreet acknowledged that sickness "was so much the sorer . . . because my dear husband was from home (which is my chiefest comforter on earth)." Though Simon failed her by his absence, "my God, who never failed me, was not absent, but helped me, and graciously manifested his love to me."[25]

Turning toward God for ultimate satisfaction was a difficult and lifelong process. In "The Flesh and the Spirit" two sisters debate about "things that are past, and things to come." The poem is one of Bradstreet's finest, and the debate a real one. Flesh offers riches, pleasure, and fame. Flesh is solid, wonderful, and various: "Sister, quoth Flesh, what liv'st thou on / Nothing but Meditation? . . . Earth hath more silver, pearls and gold, / Then eyes can see, or hands can hold." But Spirit finishes the debate. What Spirit offers that Flesh cannot is the peace of permanence—freedom from change, affliction, and death. Heaven is an eternal security:

> The City where I hope to dwell,
> There's none on Earth can parallel;
> The stately Walls both high and Strong,
> Are made of pretious Jasper stone.[26]

Bradstreet expected life after death to be permanently beautiful and peaceful and she expected the moment of death to be a transformational experience that would exalt her body with ecstasy. In a poem of 1669, Bradstreet pictured the ecstasy she anticipated in death:

> What tho my flesh shall there consume
>   it is the bed Christ did perfume
> And when a few yeares shall be gone
>   this mortall shall be cloth'd upon
> A Corrupt Carcasse downe it lyes
>   a glorious body it shall rise.

In this poem Bradstreet describes how, in a sensual if invisible manner, her flesh will receive grace as a bed is permeated by perfume. As we have seen, Edward Taylor used a similar conceit, describing God's grace as "fresh perfume" for his garden and entreating divine beauty to "assaile" his "dull Heart" and be planted there as a Rose. By figuring her body as a bed made for Christ, Bradstreet associates sanctification with sexual intercourse. She anticipates that, as she surrenders her body, with all its faults, to death, it will be penetrated by the spirit of God and thereby transformed into a permanently beautiful body, fit to marry the king of heaven. Her poem concludes with the prayer "Lord make me ready for that day / then Come deare Bridegrome Come away."[27]

The career of a Christian wife might have its worldly satisfactions as well as its heavenly rewards, but the journey could be fraught with frustration as well. A virtuous wife was a model of saintliness for the whole community. But the characteristic that made good women into saints was the capacity for humble surrender. A woman who took her own experiences seriously enough to use them as the basis for teaching others about God at once fulfilled and endangered her role as obedient wife and humble saint.

Anne Hutchinson's career offers a dramatic illustration of this dilemma. Hutchinson attacked the ministers of Massachusetts Bay for preaching the covenant of works and suggested, to their displeasure, that they measured saintliness by conventions of ostensible virtue.[28] Believing that the covenant of grace implied immediate, personal revelation, she understood religious virtue to be a matter between God and the souls of individuals and not a matter of convention or public morality. Consistent assurance of her own dependence on God gave her confidence to preach God to others. Radically submissive to God's revelations, she became a social authority at pointing out divine authority. Hutchinson's accusers detected an antinomian threat to social order in her sharp distinction between religion and convention and perhaps in the lack of distinction between her spiritual assurance and her femininity. Along with their theological censure the ministers judged her social authority inappropriate for a woman and charged her with religious sedition against the fifth commandment—she had acted more "a Husband than a Wife, and a

Preacher than a Hearer, and a Magistrate than a Subject." Unlike other women discussed in this chapter, Anne Hutchinson was not united to a powerful husband—John Winthrop described William Hutchinson as "a man of very mild temper and weak parts, and wholly guided by his wife."[29] Perhaps because her husband did not compete with God for sovereignty over her, Anne Hutchinson depended on God with a radical assurance that disturbed and threatened her community.

It is interesting to ponder a comparison of the spiritual lives of Anne Hutchinson and Edward Taylor and to wonder whose dilemma was more debilitating and whose odyssey more fulfilling. In his private poetry Taylor exchanged his ministerial masculinity for a femininity that enabled the confessions and enjoyments of his soul. He assumed a receptive humility that invited the approach of God as his lover. If we suppose that Taylor was uncomfortable with his own virility, we must acknowledge that we remember him not for his ministry but for the sensual beauty of his poetry.

In her attentiveness to the revelations of God's will, Anne Hutchinson extended her dependence into union and absorbed the powers of her lover. One cannot assume too quickly that feminine surrender was inevitably an unenjoyable or oppressive experience. A woman mystically inclined might discover great power in a freedom from the narrow circumstances of self. Loss of ego could be a small price to pay for union with God and nonalienated participation in his power. But if we suppose that Hutchinson experienced empowerment, we must also recall the consequences she paid.

Perhaps Taylor and Hutchinson, in risking their gender identities, each found exchange of gender a circular and amplifying process. Even if few perceived or rose to the challenge, the theology that compared grace to betrothal and sanctification to marriage invited that kind of enlargement of self. As Edward Taylor wrote, the religious soul could "see," in the "very Person" of God, "Infinity, and finity Conjoyn'd."

We have seen that the theology that associated marriage with sanctification had a source in Puritan social experience: the union of a loving wedlock could be a gift full of grace and a preview of heaven. Theology in turn shaped its social source: the union of a loving wedlock became an instrument of God, its beauty regarded as dependent on God and its disruptions accepted as teachings. The union of sanctification presupposed a hierarchical relationship in which the Christian, by assuming a posture of feminine surrender before God's masculine power, was taken at midnight, penetrated by grace, and swallowed in light. Earthly marriage mirrored the hierarchy of religious experience: the powers of God were like those of a husband who exercised sternness and enjoyed the beauty of his power; the duties and joys of a saint were like those of a woman captivated by love. Religious women could extend their feminine virtues into their relation with God and, in the extension of their surrender, experience moments of unification with God, moments in which they were swallowed in God's beauty and partook of his power.

We return to the life of Sarah Edwards, and to the correspondence between her life and her husband's theology, for further discussion of the relation between Puritan spirituality and femininity. In the eyes of Jonathan Edwards, who reformulated the essentials of Puritan spirituality in the mid-eighteenth century, his wife's union with God illustrated the beauty of holiness. As a model for others of religious and domestic virtue, Sarah Edwards assumed the fortunes and dilemmas of public virtuosity. Throughout her life she stood as an authority at pointing out divine authority and in time of spiritual crisis she explored both the power and the painful contradictions of that role. Like Anne Bradstreet, her relation to her husband provided a model for her relation with God and her religious struggles focused on their competition for her dependence.

Sarah Edwards was a beautiful woman. Samuel Hopkins, a disciple of Jonathan Edwards who studied theology in the Edwards' home, described Mrs. Edwards as "more than ordinarily beautiful." Her grandson Timothy Dwight, who also became a prominent theologian, ascribed her "peculiar loveliness of expression" to her inner virtues of "cheerfulness, and benevolence." Dwight also admired her remarkable "intelligence"—in his estimation "the native powers of her mind were of a superior order."

By the age of five Sarah Pierrepont had manifested an uncommon piety, "exhibit[ing] the life and power of religion, and that in a remarkable manner."[30] By the time she was thirteen, reports of her spirituality had attracted the notice of young Jonathan Edwards. He described a "young lady" so loved by God that he often "fills her mind with exceeding sweet delight," promising her she will be "caught up into heaven." Young Edwards wrote that "God loves her too well to let her remain at a distance from him always." He noted, perhaps for his own benefit, how "conscientious" Sarah was to please God with her behavior: "you could not persuade her to do anything wrong or sinful, if you would give her all the world."[31]

In her marriage to Jonathan Edwards, Sarah Pierrepont so capably fulfilled the responsibilities of a minister's wife that she "secure[d] the high and increasing approbation of all who knew her." Hopkins praised her superior "diligence and discretion" at managing the worldly affairs of the Edwards' household; Sarah "took almost the whole direction of the temporal affairs of the family without doors and within." Her prudent and cheerful management "was particularly suited to the disposition of her husband, who chose to have no care, if possible, of any worldly businesss." In Hopkins' estimation, her studied restraint from criticizing her neighbors clearly revealed her virtue. He described how she managed gossip: when a person's "imperfections" were under consideration, she made it her practice to respond with what might "excuse" or commend them. And if she herself were negatively criticized, "she could bear injuries and reproach with great calmness." Like a fountain of holiness, Sarah Edwards "was ready to pity and forgive those who appeared to be her enemies."[32]

As wife of Northampton's imposingly tall and brilliantly learned minister, and as mother of eleven remarkably healthy children, Sarah Edwards occupied a special status in her community. Pious, intelligent, competent, and lovely to look at, she embodied the perfections of womanhood. She seems to have worked to appear virtuous before others. Jonathan Edwards' praise of her conscientiousness about pleasing God suggests how highly conscious she was of her virtues and piety. One can imagine that the young lady who stood steadfast against "anything wrong or sinful" exhibited a certain self-righteousness. Perhaps her well-rounded virtuosity was enough to provoke occasional resentment. If not, her studied efforts to divert gossip and the "great calmness" with which she bore criticism suggest that her artful equanimity may have provoked "those who appeared to be her enemies."

Although Sarah Edwards' personal pride may have motivated some of her public humility, her apparent qualities corresponded to those that identified a saint. Or to put it closer to home, her reputation exhibited the virtues that defined her husband's psychology of religiousness. Just as Timothy Dwight attributed Sarah's "peculiar loveliness of expression" to inner graciousness, so Jonathan, for whom the beauty of holiness was at once palpable and wholly spiritual, may have perceived his wife's sensual attractiveness as an agreeable expression of her piety. In his personal spirituality and in his theology, Jonathan Edwards consistently identified deity with beauty. As a young man he was "much in reading" the Song of Solomon, especially those passages that described "the loveliness and beauty of Jesus Christ." As his early religiousness developed he described his relish for holiness as a compelling sensation of *divine* beauty." "There was nothing in [holiness] but what was ravishingly lovely, . . . everything else was like mire and defilement."[33] Just as God used Joanna Shepard to "let" Thomas "see His beauty in the land of the living," so Jonathan Edwards found his wife's presence an illustration of divine comeliness.

Jonathan Edwards drew on Thomas Shepard's theology of beauty as he developed his own psychology of saintliness. Edwards used Shepard's *Parable of the Ten Virgins* as a major source in his *Treatise Concerning Religious Affections* (1746), in which he quoted from Shepard on more than seventy-five occasions.[34] As presented in the *Affections,* one sign which distinguished a saint was an apprehension of divine beauty: "a love to divine things for the beauty and sweetness of their moral excellency" defined "the first beginning and spring of all holy affections." It was God's beauty that "renders all his other attributes glorious and lovely."[35] The saint, who perceived the beauty of God, embodied the beauty of God.

In *The Nature of True Virtue* (1755; published posthumously in 1765) Edwards identified true virtue as the union of self with "being in general." To paraphrase Edwards, the beauty of being itself flowed through the truly virtuous person. By perceiving the harmony of creation, such a person saw his or her own place in the universal scheme and also saw the beauty in other lives. In this last major work Edwards described how lovers of being inevitably attract one another: "When any one under the influence of general benevolence, sees another being possessed of the like general benevolence, this attaches his heart to him, and draws forth greater love to him, than merely his having existence." When the hearts of both are united to the beauty of the universe, each "heart is extended and united to" the other. Each "looks on" the other's "interest as its own." "Pure love to others" was "a kind of enlargement of the mind, whereby it so extends itself as to take others into a man's self: and therefore it implies a disposition to feel, to desire, and to act as though others were one with ourselves."[36] Near the conclusion of his treatise, Edwards shows how the "natural affection" of sexual love is "of the same denomination" as religious affection. He describes how natural and religious affections may mingle with each other to make heterosexual union a preparation for and manifestation of true love. In "a virtuous love between the sexes . . . there may be the influence of virtue mingled with instinct; and virtue may . . . guide it to such ends as are agreeable to the great purposes of true virtue."[37]

For Jonathan Edwards, as for earlier Puritans, religious love not only drew individuals to God, it drew couples together in love affairs that partook of the beauty of the universe. In such love affairs two become one in a union that mirrored and celebrated the nature of God. Jonathan Edwards' experience of marriage may speak through his abstractions. The deep mutual love between the Edwardses and the religious context of their "uncommon union" resound in Jonathan's deathbed message to Sarah:

> It seems to me to be the will of God that I must shortly leave you; therefore give my kindest love to my dear wife, and tell her, that the uncommon union, which has so long subsisted between us, has been of such a nature, as I trust is spiritual, and therefore will continue forever: and I hope she shall be supported under so great a trial, and submit cheerfully to the will of God.[38]

The sincerity that permeates this passage combines sexuality with spirituality in a testimony to the beauty that grounded their love and made their parting bearable. By Jonathan Edwards' own principles, one could not describe experiences of pure love without having tested them. His marriage provided experience for his theories about the nature of God and the nature of religious experience.

Sarah Edwards' religious virtues served her husband's theology in public as well as in private ways. He used her narration of her ecstatic experience as the centerpiece in his argument that the Great Awakening was of divine origin. In *Some Thoughts Concerning the Present Revival,* Jonathan Edwards argued that the revivals were the work of God and neither the false products of vain imaginings nor the work of Satan. In this argument it was important to show that the enthusiasms of the Greak Awakening were—on the whole—true, joyful, and socially constructive. His wife's experience of swimming in the divine light that swallowed her illustrated how human passions[39] could be tremendously moved and still exhibit the harmony of true holiness. True religion was the sensational experience of grace and grace was the blend of flight and balance.

In his account of his wife's ecstatic experience, Jonathan Edwards carefully followed descriptions of her jubilations with evidence that her experiences were not "enthusiasm, and the fruits of a distempered brain." To illustrate the important point that religious fervor was not madness, he edited Sarah Edwards' own written account of the experience. And to show that her "enlightenment" ran counter to Satan's work, he interpreted her ecstatic experience within the context of her impressive history as a charitable Christian. He shaped his wife's story into a portrait of evangelical humility. A professing Christian for twenty-seven years, Sarah Edwards was neither "in the giddy age of youth" nor an "unexperienced Christian." Nearly all her life she had been "growing in grace, and rising, by very sensible degrees, to higher love to God . . . and mastery over sin and temptation." Her religiousness was stirred—not begun or deluded—during the Great Awakening.[40]

Edwards pointed out that his wife's humility increased after her experience of 1742. "Under smaller discoveries and feebler exercises of divine affection" she had manifested "a disposition to censure and condemn others." But in her episode of heightened awareness, she encountered "a peculiar sensible aversion to a judging of others." Criticizing others "appeared hateful, as not agreeing with that lamb-like humility, meekness, gentleness and charity, which the soul then, above other times, saw the beauty of, and felt a disposition to." Sarah Edward's experience also gave her "a new sense and conviction" concerning "the importance of moral and social duties and how great a part of religion lay in them."[41] With his wife portrayed as a model of Christian piety, her aspiration to benevolence showed Jonathan Edwards' readers that sensitivity to religious experiences led to humble and responsible behavior.

In his edited version of his wife's experience Edwards not only balanced and polished her story, he also omitted the specifics of her spiritual and physical aggravations. Although distortion is perhaps too strong a word, he did choose not to describe the despair that initiated her religious episode or the details of the ecstatic behavior that frightened the Northampton townspeople. In particular, Jonathan Edwards omitted, in his rendering of the narrative, his own role in his wife's soul-searching and her analysis of the depression that prepared her for the experiences that followed. Sarah Edwards' own written account, however, describes how "on Tuesday night, Jan. 19, 1742, . . . I felt very uneasy and unhappy, at my being so low in grace." She received "great quietness of spirit" during the night, but

> the next morning I found a degree of uneasiness in my mind, at Mr. Edwards' suggesting, that he thought I had failed in some measure in point of prudence, in some conversation I had with Mr. Williams, of Hadley, the day before. I found, that it seemed to bereave me of the quietness and calm of my mind, in any respect not to have a good opinion of my husband. This I much disliked in myself, as arguing a want of a sufficient rest in God, and felt a disposition to fight against it, and look to God for his help, that I might have a more full and entire rest in him, independent of all other things.[42]

Measuring her progress in religious purity and judging for herself its limitations, Sarah Edwards noted that more than three years earlier she "ma[d]e a new and most solemn dedication of herself to [God's] service and glory." Since that time she had become resigned to life or death according to God's will and had succeeded in weaning herself from dependence on earthly concerns in all but two points of "disturbance":

> 1st. My own good name and fair reputation among men, and especially the esteem and just treatment of the people of this town; 2ndly. And more especially, the esteem, and love, and kind treatment of my husband.[43]

Noting her imperfections in a spirit of objectivity, Sarah Edwards now hoped to overcome them and to shed her attachment to her "fair reputation among men" and to the "esteem, and love, and kind treatment" of her husband.

As Sarah Edwards told it, after bringing her imprudence to her attention, her husband left Northampton for two weeks of preaching in other parishes. Preaching in his absence was young and fiery Samuel Buell, who, in later years, admitted to "indecent heats" as a preacher during the Awakening.[44] Sarah Edwards fought with her jealousy of Buell's success as the visiting minister until, in a state of religious awakening, her resentment disappeared. Now she accepted Buell's success, even if it were to extend "to the enlivening of every saint, and to the conversion of every sinner, in the town." In this generous mood, "these feelings continued," and she wrote that she "never felt the least rising of heart to the contrary, but my submission was even and uniform, without interruption or disturbance."[45]

Immediately after this release from anxiety about Buell's competition with her husband, Sarah Edwards experienced nine days of extraordinary emotion. Periods of peace were interspersed with many public faintings and spurts of "earnest" conversation. Then came a moment "so intense . . . I could not forbear rising up and leaping with joy and exhultation." In her description of the neighbors' reactions to her behavior, Sarah disclosed that she had made a public—and alarming—spectacle of herself. Recalling the second Friday of Edwards' absence, she wrote:

> Towards night being informed that Mrs. P—— had expressed her fears lest I should die before Mr. Edwards' return, and he should think the people had killed his wife; I told those who were present, that I chose to die in the way that was most agreeable to God's will, and that I should be willing to die in darkness and horror, if it was most for the glory of God.[46]

From her elevated viewpoint Sarah may indeed have spied the

resentment and hatred that eight years later secured the Edwards' dismissal and sought their humiliation. But in her exultation, she was above it all and, one suspects, enjoying herself immensely, even enjoying her "willing[ness] to die in darkness and horror, if it was most for the glory of God." Exposing her worst fears, she maintained that, even if her community were "enemies . . . venting their malice and cruelty upon me," her strength in God would make it "impossible" to "cherish any feelings towards them but . . . love, and pity, and ardent desires for their happiness."[47]

Whether Sarah was exercising prophetic insight or indulging her paranoia, for her the importance of the event lay in her realization that she was not obliged to meet other people's standards for a virtuous wife of a minister of God. Her only responsibility was to God. And her joyful obedience to God would now put her even beyond reach of her husband's criticism. She would still fulfill "with alacrity . . . every act and duty" of a virtuous wife, but now only God, not Jonathan, would measure her virtue. From her new perspective she saw her husband as a man like any other. She even speculated that should his "tenderness" change to "extreme cruelty," her "happiness would remain undiminished and entire."[48] Sarah's imagining that "extreme cruelty" lurked on the other side of her husband's "tenderness" suggests that, in her mind at least, Jonathan Edwards shared certain personality traits with God. In anticipating her indifference should Edwards turn cruel, she acknowledged that her happiness lay elsewhere and that her husband, after all, was only a man.

There is no need to argue that Sarah Edwards was a perfect—or perfectly humble—woman to feel sure that her experience of 1742 deepened her self-awareness and offered her a freedom and independence that was new, enjoyable, and worthy of celebration. Both before and after her experience Sarah had stood for others as a model of Christian and feminine virtue. The beauty, sweetness, and competence that characterized her social presence made it easy for her to assume that those qualities also characterized her relation with God. But in the self-evaluation that preceded her experience Sarah Edwards convicted herself of the desire and effort to compel the esteem of others. The fact that she analyzed her dilemma and experienced its dissolution shows that, at the very least, she worked out the problem— and experienced herself—at a deeper level. And it is of no little importance that she received this deepened awareness through an experience of embodied ecstasy. Whatever her solar experience "did for her," however much her comportment was improved or her virtues purified, for nine days she participated in the immediate beauty of her world. To paraphrase Sarah Edwards herself, everything else should be viewed in that light.

Sarah and Jonathan Edwards were typical Puritans in their understanding of marriage as an analogy for the relation between the Christian and God. It is impossible to overstate the importance of analogy for Puritan thinking. The relation between the Christian and God was itself an analogy, an analogy of opposition. For example, Puritans testified to the power of God by opposite analogy, that is, by describing the weakness of humanity. For the analogy to hold, both parts were needed. Without power of his own, man depended for his life on the power of God. And to display his power, God created man as his servant. Similarly, spirit used flesh as God used nature: the body of the world pointed away from itself to its creator.

To take another example, Puritans catalogued their sins and blemishes by way of oppositional analogy to the beauty of God. This particular analogy was especially crucial for the Puritans because they took the experience of God's beauty to be the heart of Christian awareness. Puritans communicated the experience of God's beauty with rigorous humility. Their testimonies to God's beauty always involved confession of their own blemishes. This double message allowed for celebrating the sensual beauties of life within the confines of worshiping a transcendent God. The oppositional analogy between humanity and God involved a hidden connection: behind the relentless contrasting of humanity and God lay sensual, human experiences that pointed, along the narrow path of dogma, to divine beauty.

It was love, a love far stronger than justice, that paired the beauty of God and the disgrace of humanity. The Puritans described the relation between God and the saint as a miracle of love. God's grace was an act of love that made possible the saint's love of God. The capacity for love was the characteristic common to God and the saint and the bond that joined them together. By the power of divine love, God and the Christian became partners devoted to one another, partners in union. The Puritans' most discerning ministers discovered an analogy for this unifying love in their marriages. In the union of a loving marriage the differences between man and women were brought into complementary relation. In such a marriage two were joined together as one.[49]

One of the most striking phenomena about the New England Puritans is that their greatest ministers and governors—Thomas Shepard, John Winthrop, Simon Bradstreet, Edward Taylor, and Jonathan Edwards, for example—loved their wives beyond measure. These men found their wives to be earthly representatives of God's beauty. For these men a loving wife was not only a model Christian but also an expression of the beauty of the world that pointed beyond itself to divine beauty. And the enjoyment of God's beauty was the essence of Puritan spirituality. Although Puritans cloaked their experiences of divine beauty in the authoritarian conceptualizations of dogmatic theology, encounters with the beauty of God and creation motivated and sustained their theology. Experience of the beauty of God was the treasure the Puritans buried in a harsh theology. If it was the masculine side of humanity that was responsible for implementing God's stern truth on earth, it was the feminine side of humanity that represented God's beauty.

As man and woman were joined together in a loving marriage, so the Godhead itself was a union of truth and beauty. Marital love could reveal the very nature of God. This interpretation of the mystical implications of Puritan marriage must be carefully qualified. Although the *unification* of marriage could reveal the nature of God, the *relation* of marriage was an analogy for the covenant of grace and in the covenant of grace God dealt with believers one at a time. Given the oppositional relation between humanity and God, husbands dared not extend their customary authority to their relation with God. Wives, on the other hand, were enjoined to expand upon their submissiveness in their relation with God. A Christian wife might be a model Christian, but a Christian husband had to relinquish his authority in his relation with the heavenly husband.

The widely sown cultural and psychological legacies of Puritan bride-consciousness include esthetic as well as religious expression. The spiritual awareness of beauty has not always been defined, as it was for the Puritans, by the framework of dogmatic theology. To understand how feminine spirituality has been disseminated to esthetic realms beyond the domain of rigorous theology it is important to see how theology itself was transformed in Christian America.

Three

The Domestication of Theology

❦ During the late eighteenth and early nineteenth centuries theology relaxed its dialectical standards and softened to include expressions of artistic sentiment about God, nature, and humanity. On the one hand, this softening process weakened the conceptual fiber of theology. On the other hand, the demise of theology's rigor and authority enabled women to situate the awareness of beauty characteristic of feminine spirituality in a wide variety of cultural contexts.

To describe this transformation a bit differently, one could say that the love of a sternly transcendent God could only be sustained by a few religious intellectuals. The Puritans recognized this elitism in their requirements for church membership, including the unprecedented requirement that the candidate be able to report, and report correctly, his relation with God. As the colonial population in America grew, so did the population of religious people whose statements about God and man did not conform to the abstract theology of Puritanism. By force of cultural expansion, the white man's God became more accessible to humanity and the readiness to claim his love became a Christian command. As Christians liberalized theology, God became weaker, his love more available, his compassion melting his opposition to man. At a certain stage in this remarkable process, religious thinkers began to imagine God as a woman, a point of view that turned the heart of Puritanism inside out.

Feminine characteristics were attributed to God by such influential nineteenth-century theologians as Horace Bushnell, Henry Ward Beecher, and Dwight Lyman Moody. These theologians could envision the feminine nature of God because their imaginations were shaped by cultural conventions that idealized womanhood. This chapter offers a history of the American idealization of womanhood, showing how the threads of this history are intertwined with threads that represent changes in the nature of American theology. As we have seen, the analogies drawn by the Puritans between a saint and a betrothed virgin, bride, or devoted wife illustrated the Puritans' understanding of the nature of love toward God. As Puritan theology lost its grip on America, attention was drawn away from feminine love toward God to the beauty of feminine nature, in and of itself.

The "belle-ideal" of womanhood gained currency in America during the late eighteenth century and in the course of the nineteenth century became thoroughly Americanized as a broadly acclaimed and widely accepted life style for urban, middle-class women.[1] The American idealization of femininity was more than a polite convention; it became interwoven into the defense and promulgation of Christian religion. Obeisance to the ideal of womanhood assumed the force of religious worship. But this deification of qualities inherent in woman's "nature" did not reflect the expansive vitality of the Puritan mode of feminine spirituality nor did it encourage experiences of self-awareness or ecstasy such as those Sarah Edwards enjoyed. Women became imprisoned by the very conventions that idealized them.

As they came to expression in America, the polite conventions that, on the one hand, idealized the nature of womanhood and, on the other, confined the activities and thoughts of women had roots in Puritan theology. But if the conventions that idealized womanhood had the social power of Puritan theology, as merely social conventions, they offered less spiritual depth and elasticity than Puritan femininity, which involved one's relation to God as well as to human company. For the Puritans, femininity was, to a certain extent, accessible to men as well as to women because it implied a relationship with God. Although it required some imagination, a man could adopt, as his religious posture in his relation with God, the role of preparing virgin or obedient wife. As Edward Taylor's poetry shows, a man could even express his religious experience of femininity in bodily language. But the theology that associated femininity with spiritual responsiveness became, by the end of the eighteenth century in America, an ideology that stereotyped women as weak characters with small capacities.

The historical process reducing femininity from an attitude toward God to a set of stereotypes was accompanied by the collapse of the Puritans' religious vision to a short-sighted, secularized point of view. These two histories are interwoven with one another. A history of perceptions about femininity may be read in the context of the history of theology in America and a history of theology may be read in the context of changing American perceptions about femininity. In the spirit of these interweavings, the discussion that follows measures the dimming of the Puritan vision and the accompanying constriction of women's roles and powers, studies the expression of stereotyped perceptions about femininity in literature and the effect of those stereotypes on religion and theology, and, finally, shows how the new theology, impoverished by stereotypes about femininity, actually stimulated the imaginations of literary women who reanimated, in fiction, a spiritual vision of femininity.

During the early years in New England men and women worked together in their wilderness struggle for self-preservation and in their creation of a religious society. *Magnalia Christi Americana* (1702), Cotton Mather's history of Christ's work in America, describes how the Christian "founders" of America had been persecuted for their holiness in the Old World and driven to the vast and terrible "desarts of America" to face famine, disease, cruel winters, and Indian wars. From Mather's perspective this history of terror illumined the courage and purpose of the early New Englanders. The founders had perceived their social experiment as a holy mission and themselves as religious utopians. Mather described how God had singled out the New World as the home of his chosen people, delaying the discovery of America until the "resurrection of literature" and the "Reformation of religion." With the Renaissance and the Reformation as the scenery behind them, the men and women who established New England saw themselves as players in the last act of a cosmic drama and took the Bible as the script of their particular history. Massachusetts Bay governor John Winthrop envisioned New England as "a city on a hill" where a novel government of goodness, justice, and honesty would provide a model for Europe and actualize God's final redirection of the history of the world.[2]

The presumptuousness of this vision was inflated by megalomania and sustained by an intolerance that approached fanaticism. But in theory, and in the practice of the most saintly Puritans, the deification of self and community was mirrored by a self-criticism that loved to find the devil and confess his powers. For the Puritan saints, the self, or ego, was the devil and the devil could play the role of God. The courage of humility could unmask the devil, but in the vigilant willfulness to surrender, the self knew that the game of unmasking was never won.[3]

But the saints grew fainter, at least in proportion to the rest of the population, and the Puritans' cosmic social vision succumbed to myopia. Within a few decades it became clear that the Old World regarded the New not as a utopian model but as a provincial outpost. And the founders' vision of a social order structured by religious commitment narrowed and flattened as New Englanders became increasingly preoccupied with the isolation of their own situation. As Perry Miller described the plight of New Englanders: "Having failed to rivet the eyes of the world upon their city on the hill, they were left alone with America."[4] And so, having lost the eyes of the larger world, the New England Puritans riveted their eyes on themselves. Surrounded by mirrors of self-flattery that managed the optical illusion, they carried on and acted out the old vision in a meaner perspective.

Left alone with America, some took advantage of the economic opportunities of the New World in a way that demonstrated little adherence to the idea that the new land and its people existed to glorify a critical God. As the population expanded and the vision dimmed, nostalgic, "conservative" clergy took to berating parishioners for worshiping land and trade above God. In 1730, Thomas Prince summarized a century of altered priorities: the New World had been settled as a "plantation religious," not as a "plantation of trade"; God had responded to the piety of the founding fathers with the gift of material prosperity; and now, in heinous ingratitude to God, Americans were cultivating prosperity for its own sake. The "daughter"—material reward—was "killing" its spiritual "mother."[5]

Women, and perceptions about them, were affected by these changing perceptions of American destiny and by the provincial materialism and short-sighted spirituality that increasingly characterized their culture. As long as spiritual receptivity was not circumscribed and as long as religious surrender remained a social priority, then saintly women, whose capacities for receptivity and surrender were tutored by their socialization as wives, enjoyed a certain social esteem.

To the religious power potentially available to Puritan women had been coupled a real economic power. The demands of New England life recruited the energies of able-bodied women as well as men. The home was an economic center and many Puritan women were competent managers of household industries, industries upon which the community and each family depended for survival. In a society without separate institutions to shelter and rehabilitate the poor and disabled, the home was itself a "welfare institution" and the wife its supervisor. Colonial women stepped with relative ease into the larger business community as tavern keepers, merchants, artisans, and midwives, and they enjoyed proprietary and contractual rights under colonial laws far exceeding their rights under English or later American law. For almost a hundred years women in Massachusetts voted for elective offices. New England's Puritan women participated more fully in economic and political life than did women in the contemporary European world or in the later world of national culture.[6]

Seventeenth-century European social theorists denounced female learning and advocated limiting the middle- and upper-class woman's sphere to socially marginal functions. But in the New World of America there was relatively little opportunity for the cultivation of a life style of feminine frailty and leisure.[7] New England settlers regarded learning as an accompaniment to piety and already, by 1649, Rhode Island was the only New England colony without compulsory education for children of both sexes. In all colonies some town schools educated older girls as well as boys. The reign of Queen Elizabeth, which was a lively and positive memory in the New World, reminded colonists that women could wield intelligence and deserved education. As Anne Bradstreet put it, lamenting social theories that sought to curtail women's spheres of activity, "Let such as say our Sex is void of Reason, / Know tis a Slander now, but once was Treason."[8] The remoteness and special situation of New England retarded the assimilation of European social thought denouncing sexual equality. European ideas restricting woman's sphere were appropriated and imitated in urban areas only as the exigencies of frontier life gave way to a diversified economy and the cultivation of leisure.

The earliest European work on women widely read by Americans was *The Ladies Library*, published in London in 1714 and offered for sale in Philadelphia in 1738. The *Library* gave many Americans their first opportunity to read works such as Lord Halifax's moral essay on the nature of womanliness, *The Lady's New Year Gift* (1688), in which Halifax emphasized woman's emotional sensitivity and physical softness. Womanhood and learning were contradictory and incompatible, and Halifax did not encourage women to read or study, even as a means to piety. He stressed the innate differences between the sexes and argued that men's superior powers of reason justified their authority.

> Your *Sex* wanteth our *Reason* for your *Conduct*, and
> our *Strength* for your *Protection*: *Ours* wanteth your
> *Gentleness* to soften, and to entertain us . . . You
> have more strength in your *Looks*, then we have in
> our *Laws*; and more power by your *Tears*, than we
> have by our *Arguments*.[9]

With a back-handed compliment that was to become a successful and hackneyed moral argument, Halifax showed how the
superiority of women lay in their inferiority. He did not appeal to
a balanced or vital dynamic of sexual interchange but to a lopsided arrangement in which women offer men the entertain-
ment they want in exchange for the security they need. And by
juxtaposing tears with arguments and looks with laws Halifax
showed that the strength and power of women were matters of
appearance. While the Puritan association of femininity and
spirituality was revealed by embodied beauty, in Halifax's paean
beauty lay more on the surface than in spiritual depth. Womanhood was set apart from the world through the agency of sentiments that made beauty a cartoon, security a necessity, and
honor an imprisonment.

Flattering woman for her physical softness, emotional sensitivity, and charming incapacity to reason, protect, or provide for
herself represented an attitude that complemented the ideology
of rationalism. As they developed in the eighteenth century, the
American versions of Enlightenment rationalism generally assumed that the world was constructed for the acquisition of
property and happiness by individuals, generally characterized
the nature of man by his capacity for work, and associated work
with reason, will, and emotional detachment. The perception of
women as gentle rather than willful, pretty rather than productive, and emotional rather than rational not only disqualified
them from direct participation in the world of workmanship but
also separated the nature of man from the nature of woman by a
set of radically opposed categories of feeling, acting and think-

ing. The Puritan vision had not only succumbed to myopia; American self-consciousness developed an astigmatism as well, a fractured point of view that dissociated reason from emotion and correspondingly and persistently divided men from women.

Rationalist assumptions about the nature of man and his place in the cosmos influenced theology during the eighteenth century as religious leaders of "liberal" persuasion worked to defend Protestantism in an increasingly secular culture. With growing explicitness, the determinism of Calvinism and the omnipotence of God were replaced by man's capacity to will his own virtue. Liberals argued that it was more meaningful to understand religion as gradual progress toward moral virtue than in terms of mysterious acts of regeneration.[10]

Rationalist assumptions may even be detected in the work of "conservative" theologians who spoke against new-fashioned theology and its spirit of compromise. While Jonathan Edwards' psychology stressed the integration of the will, emotions, and reason and defined religious virtue as the whole person's self-conscious participation in the coherence of universal beauty, Edwards' own interpreters—Samuel Hopkins, Nathaniel Emmons, Jonathan Edwards, Jr.—defended the necessity of redemption, original sin, and the sovereignty of God's will in a way that qualified God's sovereignty by defining human nature in terms of self-willed reason and qualified God's transcendence by measuring his morality by human standards of justice. This point of view assumed, in a rather perverse manner, something of the humanism that characterized the liberal opposition.[11] Both conservatives and liberals located God's power not in his beauty but by the measure of his rational morality—or irrational immorality. By the end of the century New England theology had become a shadow of its former self, its religious vision shortened, sundered, and defensive.

As theology grew rigid and decayed, Americans became increasingly interested in reading fiction. By the end of the eighteenth century America boasted a handful of her own novelists. Two of these authors, Susanna Rowson and Charles Brockden

Brown, used their experiments in "fiction" to depict the inferior
social situation of women and to urgently criticize the assumptions that cast women out from the world of men. In much of
their writing, Rowson and Brown showed that the genre they
helped to create in America served a double purpose—to portray
and to criticize. Like theology, the early American novel described the way the world was and judged how the world ought
to be.

Susanna Rowson's *Charlotte Temple* (1791),[12] the first American
novel written by a woman, portrays and criticizes the reigning
idealization of feminine spirituality. This "Tale of Truth" describes the fall of a virtuous maiden into the real world of
deception, passion, and avarice. The innocent English school girl,
Charlotte Temple, agrees to accompany her French teacher La
Rue to enjoy "fruit and pastry" with gentlemen of the world.
This first small step to satisfy a curiosity about the world beyond
her school walls seals Charlotte's fate. From fruit and pastry she
descends through seduction, elopement, exile in America, aban-
donment, and poverty to death in childbirth. Rowson explicitly
makes her heroine's plight a moral lesson for young women
readers. The real world—of business, war, pleasures, and passion—is a world legislated by and for men. A woman cannot
survive independently in that world and retain her goodness.
Her fate depends on whether she is protected or victimized by
men. Angry at the wardens of woman's fate, Rowson intrudes
her own voice into the story: "My bosom glows with honest
indignation, and I wish for power to extirpate those monsters
from the earth."[13]

Since the world is as it is, not as it should be, Rowson begs her
young readers to "kneel down each morning and request kind
heaven to keep you free from temptation." Should temptation
appear and virtue be tested, "pray for fortitude to resist the
impulses of inclination when it runs counter to the precepts of
religion and virtue." It is a woman's lot that her inclination and
virtue often do run counter to one another—"be assured," Rowson warns, "it is now past the days of romance." Feminine virtue

must be protected to survive; a woman who acts on her desires is bound for evil. The worldly La Rue, who indulges her pleasures and passions at the expense of Charlotte's virtue, spends seven years "in riot, dissipation, and vice, till overtaken by poverty and sickness," she repents and dies.[14] The message of *Charlotte Temple* is that to survive virtuously, women must be kept in the Temple of their innocence and never allowed out on the Avenue.

Through her male protagonist, Charlotte's "gentleman" Montraville, Rowson portrays the independence men have to determine their own morality. Montraville's father warns him against the folly of forsaking his independence as a soldier of fortune to marry a country maid. Though the reader is led to hope that if Montraville had married poor, virtuous Charlotte, the two might have lived happily together in America, he retains his independence and abandons Charlotte to her fate as a victimized woman in the New World. Although he suffers for the demonic role he plays in Charlotte's fate—"to the end of his life [he] was subject to severe fits of melancholy"—nevertheless his "strong constitution," his military career, and his later and legal wife's "tender assiduities" and substantial fortune reform him honorably.[15] Charlotte's sin was fatal; Montraville is scarred but redeemed.

Rowson attributes freedom of will to the masculine half of humanity and portrays women as dependent for their virtue on the sovereignty of husbands and fathers. Her novel offers an index to how changing notions of the nature of virtue affected perceptions about women. For Thomas Shepard, Benjamin Colman, and Jonathan Edwards, a virtuous person radiated God's beauty. Sarah Edwards' religious experience illustrated both the ecstasy and the struggle for social independence that characterized the beauty of virtue for American Puritans; in tune with herself and the universe, Sarah's dependence on God effected her independence from husband and community. Charlotte's fortune contrasts sadly with Sarah's fulfillment. In Rowson's novel, beauty and virtue are interdependent, as they were for the Puritans, but virtue has become wholly determined by

social convention and Charlotte's beauty fades in direct proportion to her social dis-grace.[16] In Charlotte's twice-fallen world,
women are as susceptible to disgrace as they are dependent on
maintaining their attractiveness in the eyes of others.

Literalisms govern the world of *Charlotte Temple*. Sovereignty
and dependence, once symbols of the heights and depths of
religious experience, have collapsed into two-dimensional, inex-
changeably gender-specific rules for human intercourse. While
Montraville is free for self-reliance and free to choose virtue or
vice, Charlotte is not. She is at the mercy of men, and incapable
of virtue without masculine protection. For the Puritans, sovereignty and dependence were imitated on earth but had final
referent and critical check in the trans-social relation of the
heavenly husband to his preparing virgins. In Rowson's novel
Charlotte is the victim of a literalist definition of the maidenhood typology. God's power has also been severely limited: the
best he can do is sweeten her deathbed with the hope of forgiveness in the remote world of afterlife.

In *Alcuin: A Dialogue* (1798), Charles Brockden Brown derides
the views about women that Susanna Rowson dramatized in
Charlotte Temple. Brown's social philosophy was influenced by
such radicals and free-thinkers as William Godwin, Mary Astell,
and Mary Wollstonecraft. Many of Brown's female characters—
Constantina Dudley in *Ormond* and the heroine of *Jane Talbot*—
are well-educated and open-minded philosophers of marriage
who are quick to point out perversions, but retain a respect for
marriage when that relation is one of love and respect. Although
contemporary readers regarded Brown's writings with moral
suspicion, they serve our purposes well. The vivid descriptions
of contemporary perceptions about women offered in his writing stem, in part, from his detachment from popular values.[17]

In Brown's *Dialogue*, the impoverished writer Alcuin visits an
intellectual gathering place where Mrs. Carter, "who was always
at home," presides over the teapot. The naive fellow opens a
conversation by inquiring whether Mrs. Carter is a Federalist.
With polite circuity she suggests that since women have no

political power it may be irrelevant for them to form political opinions. When Alcuin confesses surprise she warms to a rhetorical question: "What have I, as a woman, to do with politics?" She points out, with some irony, that America had recently declared itself a nation of independence with political justice declared for all. But the American "government . . . , which is said to be the freest in the world, . . . excluded [women] from all political rights without the least ceremony. Lawmakers thought as little of comprehending us in their code of liberty, as if we were pigs or sheep." If American women are political animals, they existed as such only to be fed and slaughtered, combed and sacrificed, or so Mrs. Carter discretely implies. Since she is quite "conscious of being an intelligent and moral being" Mrs. Carter will not "smile . . . at tyranny" or acquiesce to the "gospel" of male superiority. She answers Alcuin flatly, "No, I am no federalist."[18]

Mrs. Carter would expand the rationalism of the nation's founding fathers and correct their errors in logic: "Men and women are partakers of the same nature. They are rational beings; and as such, the same principles of truth and equity must be applicable to both." She argues that if women were educated to use their reason they would no longer be characterized by the incapacity to reason that disqualified them from serious education. Displaying her own powers of logic, she reasons that assumptions of masculine authority are irrational prejudices. Marriage itself is shaped by the "law and force" of "spurious obligations" rather than by the principle of thought. The institution of marriage functions to imprison women in "servitude" and to celebrate the "tyranny of men."[19]

To say the very least, Mrs. Carter does not enjoy being "subject . . . to the will of another."[20] Like later spokeswomen for American feminism, she espouses a humanistic ideology that, in the exercise of its rationalism, would discount rather than indulge the peculiarities of gender. As "an intelligent and moral being," Mrs. Carter has been forced into a corner. Qualities that had once distinguished femininity now discount the intelligence and strength of women. Mrs. Carter's alternative is to argue that there are no real differences between men and women. She responds to the lopsided philosophy of rationalism with an argument that would include women in its domain. But the assumption that reason transcends and minimalizes all differences among people has sorry implications for the valuation of human relationships. As a far-sighted character, Mrs. Carter may expect the acceptance of women as rational creatures to enlarge perceptions of reason and transform the philosophy of rationalism.

Charles Brockden Brown and Susanna Rowson exposed popular distinctions between male rationality and female emotionalism as elements of a debilitating ideology that functioned to curtail the social responsibilities of women and to diminish the lives of both men and women. Earlier in the century, the categorization of human activity as either reasonable or emotional made its appearance in quite a different context. During debates over the nature of the Great Awakening and the religious enthusiasm it spawned, religion itself was categorized by either of two assumptions, one that true religion was rational and the other that it was a matter of feeling and emotional warmth. These divisive definitions of religion, each of which involved perceptions about femininity, had a dramatic effect on the history of religion and theology in America.

During the Great Awakening (1740-1742), even as Jonathan Edwards was endeavoring to preserve the integration of reason and emotion, ministers who opposed the revival did so on the grounds that emotional enthusiasm was anathema not only to particular canons of theology but to the very enterprise of theology. Reason, theology, morality, and masculinity stood as one against emotional enthusiasm. And, as a related development, religious enthusiasm came to be associated with feminine emotionalism, an indication that as early as the Awakening women had begun to be associated with an incapacity for rational restraint and propriety. The Boston liberal Charles Chauncy, who defended a reasonable Protestantism and was scandalized by the "Errors and Disorder" of the Awakening, noted that women were likely victims of the indiscriminate emotionalism of the revivals: "Enthusiasm has made a strong attempt to destroy all property, to make all things common, *wives* as well as goods."[21] Charleston's Commissary Alexander Garden, who identified religious enthusiasm as a weapon of Catholicism, characterized Rome as an evil and adulterous mother who employed her emotional skills to attract her victims:

> We know *Rome* has her *Seed* and *Harvest* Missionaries. Her *Seedsmen* sow INFIDELITY AND ENTHUSIASM, to distress and unsettle weak Minds, often to *Distraction;* and then appear the *Harvest Men;* to *heal* their wounds, and *gather* them home into the *Bosom* of their *Mother,* from whom they had gone astray.[22]

"Pietistical enthusiasm" is a term that characterizes those eighteenth-century Christians who "felt" their relation to God and who subordinated or even disregarded the rational defense of doctrine in the name of a personalized, emotional sensitivity.[23] Pietistical enthusiasts located religiousness in emotional sensitivity while rationalists stressed the moral order of Christianity. Jonathan Edwards stood nearly alone in the eighteenth century in his belief that emotion and reason were both structured by desire. Edwards defended the emotionalism of the Great Awakening as predominantly religious, while at the same time he argued that high emotions were not always purely religious: "There is nothing that belongs to Christian experience that is more liable to a corrupt mixture than zeal." But because Edwards believed that affections and understanding always acted together he found it his "duty to raise the affections of my hearers and high as I possibly can, provided that they are affected by nothing but truth."[24]

Pietistical enthusiasm exercised a wide and lasting influence on religious expression in America. The *Bethlehem Diary,* the journal of the Pennsylvania Moravians, provides vivid illustrations of religious emotionalism as it flourished in America among members of an enclave of pietistical enthusiasts. In 1743, during one of the "love feasts" that characterized their worship, the Moravians in Bethlehem, Pennsylvania, concentrated on personal receptivity to God's love, encouraging worshipers to "feel" God's love in themselves and each other as they became "vividly aware of the Savior's death and blood." Like their German brethren, the Pennsylvania Moravians elicited religious emotion by elaborating and concretizing the agonies of Christ's death: "tender and hardened sinners render / Tribute of teardrops burning, with sighs and wistful yearning, / For our dear Savior's blood, that hot and gushing flood.[25]

This concentration on the physical and emotional graphics of Christian suffering distinguishes pietistical enthusiasm from the piety of Puritan spirituality. While Edward Taylor had figured himself as a worm before Christ's infinite majesty in a poetic conceit that displayed his humility, the Moravians exceeded Taylor's sensual indulgence in their description of believers as "maggots . . . attach[ed]. . . to His gaping wounds." Like the New England Puritans, the Pennsylvania Moravians found marriage an apt characterization of the relation between Christ and saint and encouraged a feminine posture toward God, but whereas Puritans like Thomas Shepard had celebrated the joys of bethrothal to Christ, Moravians emphasized the suffering and blood-letting Christ endured to purchase his wife, the church. As a "watchword" in the *Diary* put it, / "May ev'ry one of you be found / In Him, by Virtue of each Wound, / Till all may to his Marriage come, / When he his Blood-bought Wife leads Home."[26]

Moravian theology, love feasts, and song rituals influenced John and Charles Wesley, their followers, and the theology and practice of American Methodism. The love feasts that characterized Moravian ritual were important in "cementing Methodist fellowship" during the early nineteenth century, and the hymn-singing central to Methodist worship had a source in Moravian ritual. Many Moravian hymns were translated by Methodists and incorporated in popular psalmodies. John Wesley translated "My Soul before thee prostrate lies," a hymn in which the Christian soul is figured as a woman's body surrendered to "her Source." The soul's femininity underscored the humility as well as the sensuality of religious love: "No more her praise let nature boast, / but in thy will may mine be lost."[27]

The American Methodist organizer Francis Asbury, who characterized religiosity as a melting of the heart, discovered "a degree of effeminacy cleaving to me, but abhor it from my very heart." In 1772, alert to dangers and perversions lurking in pietistical sensationalism, Asbury stressed his "particular Desire" that his students "be kept at the utmost Distance . . . from softness and effeminacy of Manners."[28] Asbury detected, in himself and in his disciples, such symptoms of "effeminacy" as "nervous complaints." A diagnosis of effeminacy was inevitable: the religion Asbury preached associated Christian spirituality with traits perceived as characterizing women, such as weakness, empathetic suffering, and high-strung sensitivities.

Observers of enthusiastic religion in America have noted that woman appeared to be particularly susceptible. This apparent vulnerability to religious enthusiasm has been associated with the emotionally volatile nature of feminity. And further, something about religious excitement has been perceived to resemble and spark the sexual excitement of women. Reports of frontier revivals in the early nineteenth century suggested that women were more liable to participate in the "fallings" that occurred during camp meetings than were men. One of the most serious problems that early frontier revivalists faced was how to handle the sexual exercise that occasionally followed the religious. In reports of these incidents it was often women who were mentioned for their promiscuity.[29]

The association between feminine sexuality and feminine spirituality was a troublesome one; Chapter Four considers the fears of witchcraft that accompanied that association. But there were women who managed to explore the connection between sexuality and spirituality in a context of such holiness that they avoided being perceived as demonic. Phoebe Palmer, Methodist perfectionist and spokeswoman for the Holiness movement, was one such pious sensualist.

Mrs. Palmer's book, *The Way to Holiness,* and her monthly magazine, *The Beauty of Holiness,* offered techniques for the achievement of perfect sanctification. In 1843, she articulated an "altar
phraseology" that identified the altar as the symbol of "Christ
the Sanctified" and the yearning Christian as the "living sacrifice" upon the altar. If the Christian were conscious that he was
"on the altar" he might know that he was sanctified.[30] In Mrs.
Palmer's perfect way, the Christian yearned to be ravished by
the holiness of Christ. Preparation for such holiness involved
laying oneself down, in imagination, on the symbolic body of
Christ and waiting for the experience of a mystical moment.

The perception that emotional sensitivity characterized both
pietistical enthusiasm and femininity led some Christians to
believe that women were naturally pious and that the maintenance of religion depended on women. In 1791, Sarah Edwards'
grandson, Timothy Dwight, reported that "were the church of
Christ stripped of her female communicants, she would lose
many of her brightest ornaments, and I fear, two thirds of her
whole family."[31] The interdependence between women and
Christianity was extended during the nineteenth century to
claims that the nature of woman was inherently Christlike. In
1869, in *Women's Suffrage: The Reform against Nature,* Hartford theologian Horace Bushnell wrote that man is to woman as *law* is to
gospel and that woman-nature was the "more effective . . . side
of the divine power; that which is the power of God unto salvation." Bushnell argued that women were particularly adept at
religious virtuosity because the identifying "quality" of the female brain was the capacity for "delicate feeling and bright
insight, . . . dramatic fancy-play, and a facility and grace of
movement . . . closely related to beauty." Woman was gifted
with special powers for apprehending beauty and an organism
that illustrated beauty. Her "upper octave voice" and "her small
hands" portrayed the subtlety essential to beauty and her pale,
soft skin luminated the "principle of beauty lying under it."[32]

Extending the correspondence between woman and Christ,
Bushnell argued that Christian virtue entailed a lifetime of self-
sacrifice. Compassion, suffering, and beauty joined together to

make woman the representative of Christ. The self-sacrifice natural to women could exert real power over those who found themselves objects of maternal martyrdom. While a father, who governs by reason, might earn the "respect of his children," a mother's love was compelling enough to win the "ineradicable, inexpungable possession of the life of her sons and daughters." In her self-denying compassion a mother "fastens a feeling so deep in the child" and elicits reverential obedience.[33]

This fascination with the innately religious dimensions of femininity not only celebrated women as imitators of Christ, but offered a new image of God and helped reconstruct Protestant theology. For example, in 1858 the Brooklyn preacher Henry Ward Beecher compared God's role in human existence to a mother rocking her child. Beecher stressed the maternal compassion of God, who "pardons like a mother, who kisses . . . offence into everlasting forgetfulness." The laws that once expressed God's nature have been replaced by kisses. The nature of woman has risen to heaven and the flattery of femininity applied to God himself has become religious veneration. As Beecher went on, "God Almighty is the mother, and the soul is the tired child; and he folds it in his arms, and dispels its fears, and lulls it to repose, saying, 'Sleep, my darling; sleep. It is I who watch thee.'" God has become the eternal maternal and believers cling like hungry infants to the Christian equation between divinity and femininity: "God clasps every yearning soul to his bosom."[34]

While Beecher's sermons and books were directed toward middle- and upper-class Americans, in later decades the theology of mother-love reached those of lesser affluence through the sermons of revivalist Dwight Lyman Moody. Moody, who drew crowds immense enough to fill—or require construction of—the largest halls in America's major cities during the 1880's and 1890's, equated mother-love with the love of God. Grace for Moody was "unlimited mercy, undeserved favor, and unmerited love" and was precisely like the love a mother offered her children. While children, like sinners, unceasingly try a mother's love, mothers, like God, forgive and forgive and forgive: "There is no woman that loves on this earth like a mother. There is no love on earth so strong as a mother's love. . . . Nothing will separate a true mother from her child. She will love him through all his sin and inequity. . . . God takes that for an illustration." Taking another tale of mother-love as a vivid "illustration" of God's nature, Moody brought his religious point home: "The mother would take from a child its loathsome disease, right out of its body, and put it into her own—such is a mother's love." If the population of the world were extrapolated from Moody's sermons, it would be peopled mostly by dying mothers and prodigal sons. The death of a pious mother often provoked such love and sorrow in a son that he returned Home to God. In other illustrations, the remembrance of a dead mother's love was a catalyst for conversion. The heart-melting words of one returning son suggest the psychological omnipotence of his mother: "I have not had a kiss for years. The last kiss I had was from my mother, and she was dying."[35]

Whether one reads the gushings of Henry Ward Beecher or the poignant "illustrations" of Dwight Lyman Moody, one cannot help but sense how theology had changed since the Puritan era. Theology, as the Puritans understood that rigorously conceptual structure, simply did not exist in the sermons of Beecher and Moody. In its place were stories, illustrations, anecdotes, and sentiments. Pietistical religion, with its emphasis on emotion, and romantic idealism, with its air of bittersweet beauty, had replaced a severe and philosophical theology with stories about compassionate mothers and dying sons. Perhaps this kind of religion had its old, symbolic roots in the Mary-Jesus stories of medieval Christianity or even in the mother-goddess stories of pagan Europe. But if femininity was deified in Victorian America, something of the power of deity was compromised in the process, as if sweetness and sentimentality had replaced truth and objectivity. The sermons of Beecher and Moody do not celebrate a majestic Queen of Heaven or a tremendous Mother Earth.

Since the era of Puritan theology, the power of God had

suffered and been sacrificed. Correspondingly, the feminine passion of Christian believers shifted in emphasis from sexual passion to sacrificial passion. One might argue that the nineteenth-century preachers who emphasized sacrifice and suffering approached the heart of Christianity and, indeed, touched on powerful symbols common to many of the world's religions, including religions involving fertility rites that celebrate natural cycles of dying and rising. But Victorian Christians detested primitive power. Their suffering, sacrificed deity had only a sentimental power in the hearts of civilized Christians and little of the objective authority he exercised over the Puritans. God had taken on the personality of a surrendered believer.

A critical turning point in this journey from God's sovereignty to his martyrdom may be marked by the inroads made by literary criticism into the once narrow path of biblical exegesis. Romantic ideas about language were appropriated by such eminent nineteenth-century theologians as Bushnell, Edwards Amasa Park, and Austin Phelps, who intended to expand popular appreciation of Scripture by inviting Americans to consider the poetic qualities of its inspirations. But this literary defense worked to relieve the Bible of its special status as the final word. If Scripture could be as inspirational as fiction, fiction could teach as effectively as theology.

Indeed, fiction did function as theology for many nineteenth-century Americans as a pietism of domesticity was propagated through a rapidly expanding publishing industry. Dollars for book sales quintupled in America between 1820 and 1850, and magazines increased their output six times between 1825 and 1860. *Godey's Lady's Book,* which offered guides to and fictional illustrations of domestic harmony, was the most widely read American periodical during the 1840's and reached a circulation of 150,000 by 1860. Manuals of child-rearing and domestic economy flourished and the sentimental fiction of domestic psychology fed a seemingly insatiable reading public. Sentimental novels fictionalized the loves and troubles of home life and centered on the circuitous emotional careers of family members.

In plot, character, and moral, the sentimental story was always religious—domestic hardships were religious trials, happy home-life was heaven or just a step away, and characters often displayed typologically religious personalities.[36]

Harriet Beecher Stowe's *Oldtown Folks* (1869) illustrates both the theology of sentimental fiction and the history of that theology. In that novel, Harry and Eglantine Percival are orphans who live under the antiquated gloom of late eighteenth-century Calvinism and its equally unnatural counterpart, authoritarian foster parents. Their own mother's dying prayer— "Never doubt that God loves you, whatever happens; and, if you have any trouble, pray to him"—provides their religious inheritance, their support through travail (Tina's first husband, patterned after Jonathan Edwards' grandson Aaron Burr, is lascivious and insane), and the seed of their growing piety. When asked whether "prayer is a clew strong enough to hold amid the rugged realities of life," Harry responds: "that is my life-experiment. My mother left me that as her only legacy." Harry had inherited a feminine religiousness: his "conclusions were all intuitions" and his piety was not "the tyranny of mere logical methods as applied to the understanding of moral truth," but rather "an emanation from the heart."[37] He finds vocation in the liberal ministry and his life-experiment proves that New England theology could be humanized by the pietism of domesticity.

Harry's character illustrates how love as well as ministry could be sentimentally religious. During a revival season Harry's romantic attentions facilitate a young woman's salvation: "Esther's deliverance came through that greatest and holiest of all the natural sacraments and means of grace,—LOVE." Coincident with her conversion, Esther realizes that she is "beloved by a poet soul,—one of that rare order to whom the love of woman is a religion! a baptism!—a consecration!" In Stowe's exclamatory equation of the enthusiasms of romance and piety, love between man and woman was a "natural sacrament" and a "means of grace."[38]

Domestic felicity required a husband with the moral and

religious sensibilities of a woman, and through Harry, Stowe portrayed a man perfect in piety and in wedlock. Having stepped entirely within the circle of domestic psychology, Harry will make an ideal minister, preaching the religion of Christian nurture and romantic love, just as he will make a thoroughly domesticated husband and father. The rarefied love of sentimental romanticism functioned to moralize, chasten, and platonize sexuality, and Stowe's display of the relation between religious and marital love contrasts with the Puritan understanding of that relation. For Shepherd, Taylor, or Bradstreet, marital and religious love resembled each other as powerful passions; for Harry and Eglantine Percival romantic domesticity and Christian love were by far more sweet than strong.

The extent to which *Oldtown Folks* is a theological statement as well as a novel is suggested by comparing it to Bushnell's *Christian Nurture* (1847 and, in an extended and more widely read version, 1861). Bushnell's theological treatise, which also doubled as a child-rearing manual, questioned the Calvinist assumption of innate depravity that, to Bushnell, entailed the perverse assumption that a child's early life was an education in sin. Like Stowe, Bushnell understood emotional sensitivity as a means to piety and was critical of the doctrinal dryness and sternness that characterized old-fashioned Protestantism. *Christian Nurture* argued that religious responsibility should not be postponed until conversion but that a child's goodness should be elicited in his life at home: "the child is to grow up a Christian, and never know himself otherwise." By stressing parental responsibility for the religiousness of children, Bushnell gave the family religious justification as the ultimate authority. *Christian Nurture* supplanted the authority of the church with the authority of the home. Prayer, scripture lessons, and Sabbath pastimes could be supervised by parents at home. Critical of the tendency of the Protestant Church to foster "no element of genial warmth and love about the child" and to attribute "to religion rather a forbidding aspect," Bushnell warned parents that the church might impede rather than assist Christian nurture. Bushnell encouraged parents to assume responsibility for judging the doctrines and atmosphere of denominational churches.[39]

In Bushnell's psychology of religious growth, "the Christian scheme is really wrapped up in the life of any Christian parent, and beams out from him as a living epistle." Long before a child were able to use language or understand doctrine, he might absorb "the operative truth necessary to a new life" through the "looks, manners, and the ways of life" of his parents. Just as a child inherited physical characteristics from his parents, so he assumed their "moral characters." A Christian child required sound stock as well as training. The family was an "organic unity" and faith was an organic principle communicated primarily by the religious virtues of mothers. Just as Harry and Eglantine were sustained by the "flavor" of their mother's piety, so Bushnell interpreted Paul's assurance to Timothy that religious virtue "was a seed somehow planted in him by the believing motherhoods of the past." In Bushnell's biology of religiousness, a mother's womb is invested with moral and spiritual qualities and the home continued the nurture of prenatal existence.[40] While Harry and Eglantine were deprived of the extended womb of religious domesticity, they inherited the "clew" that helped them survive and usher in an era of familial piety.

Stowe's *Oldtown Folks* offered a history of the transformation of New England theology and in the best seller that had established her reputation as America's most influential writer, she outlined a theology of domestic politics. Slavery is evil in *Uncle Tom's Cabin* (1851–1852) because it impedes the Christian nurture of family life. The novel is full of tales, based on actual accounts, of black families destroyed and white families debilitated by the economic greed that buys and sells regardless of family ties. The Christian cabin parented by Aunt Chloe and Uncle Tom, where food and laughter, children and religion are plenty until Tom is sold down river, is a model for all other cabins, high and low, white and black. Home is heaven in *Uncle Tom's Cabin* and Stowe damns slavery not because it is a system of political and economic dependency but for nearly the opposite reason—slavery separates Americans from the organic harmony of Christian domesticity.

Little Eva, whose short career illustrates the domestic qualities of a heavenly life-style, is the Christ-like child who mends the rents and re-establishes the dependencies between this world and the next. As the feminine incarnation of the purity and obedience of the first Christ child, Eva "always dressed in white, [and] seemed to move like a shadow through all sorts of places, without contracting spot or stain." To Uncle Tom, Eva "seemed something almost divine; and whenever her golden head and deep blue eyes peered out upon him . . . he half believed that he saw one of the angels stepped out of his New Testament." Although it is not until Eva is obviously near death that she manages the conversion, she saves the black-willed Topsy for heaven and obedience when everyone else had given her up as intractable. Placing "her little thin, white hand on Topsy's shoulder," and admitting that "I shan't live a great while," Eva tells Topsy: "I love you, because you haven't had any father, or mother, or friends;—because you've been a poor, abused child!" Topsy cannot resist, and "a ray of heavenly love . . . penetrated the darkness of her heathen soul." As "the black child" wept, "the beautiful child, bending over her, looked like the picture of some bright angel stooping to reclaim a sinner."[41]

The conversion of Eva's father, St. Clare, is her most difficult. He is embittered by the cruelties of reality and cheated out of a happy home by a neurotic, whining wife. But even in this seemingly hopeless situation, Eva works her heavenly magic. She is her father's "little gospel": "Oh! Evangeline! rightly named, . . . hath not God made thee an evangel to me?" After her death, "he read his little Eva's Bible seriously and honestly," and planned to manumit his slaves. On his deathbed shortly thereafter, St. Clare murmurs Latin words entreating the Infinite Pity of Jesus. The doctor thinks "his mind is wandering," but "'No! it is coming HOME, at last!' said St. Clare, energetically; 'at last, at last!'"[42] Heaven is home in *Uncle Tom's Cabin*.

Eva's personal cross is a mother, selfish and spoiled, whose beauty wanes as her whining intensifies. Marie St. Clare, like a petulant child, spends increasingly more time in the crib of invalidism as Eva, sinking rapidly under consumption but rising steadily toward heaven, assumes the emotional responsibilities of a mother. Eva inherits the purity and piety of her grandmother, St. Claire's mother, who in his eyes "was divine!" and although she no longer lives on earth, represents "all that has stood between me and utter disbelief for years. She was a direct embodiment and personification of the New Testament." Like Eva, St. Clare's mother was an allegorical innocent dressed in white, and like Eva, she had an esthetic "genius" that worked on others not through argument or doctrine but through emotional power: "she used to sit at her organ, playing fine majestic music of the Catholic Church, and singing with a voice more like an angel than a mortal woman." Through his mother's music, St. Clare experienced the ecstasy of inarticulate religious emotion: "I would lay my head down on her lap, and cry, and dream, and feel,—oh immeasurably!—things that I had no language to say!"[43]

Eva's character documents the Christ-like similarities between motherhood and childhood. Uncle Tom completes the holy picture. In his patient suffering of a tortured martyrdom, Tom lays down his life in imitation of Christ and in so doing saves others from rebellion and for the same good fortune. Eva, the holy child, and Tom, the suffering servant, embody the two aspects of Christ most significant for Victorian Americans— purity and self-sacrifice. Throughout Stowe's novel enslaved black people, loving mothers, and sensitive children recognize Jesus in each other. Domestic religiosity welcomed qualities of docility and mutual dependency and was threatened by the willfulness and independence characteristic of the world of white men. In the guise of an anti-slavery novel, Stowe championed the authority and celebrated the power of domestic politics.

The deaths of Little Eva and Uncle Tom, hers as the final rung reached on the ladder of purity, his as a joyful release from the impurities and ladders of this world, are the most emotional moments in Stowe's novel. Death could be the best part of life and, indeed, death scenes climaxed many nineteenth-century novels, poems, and sermons. In all the happy endings, the theology of domestic space was extended to heaven. The kinship between home and heaven implied that the clues to afterlife could be secured within domestic walls. Those who failed to value their lives in domestic terms were excluded from heaven, while those who justified themselves within the values of home life lived in anticipation of death. The composite picture of domestic pietism suggests a peaceful still-life, a concentric series of sacred spaces, from womb to home to tomb and heaven, that amplify the religious point that femininity is holy.

Elizabeth Stuart Phelps, granddaughter of theologian Moses Stuart, daughter of Austin Phelps, and student of Edwards Amasa Park, takes the laurels as the great American authoress of afterlife. Her celebrated trilogy—*The Gates Ajar* (1868), *Beyond the Gates* (1883), and *The Gates Between* (1887)—not only told the way to heaven but neatly outlined heaven's domestic sociology. Transported to a permanent home, Phelps' happy Christians enjoy personal immortality in the company of their families. *Gates Ajar* enjoyed an immense popularity, selling 180,000 copies in thirty years and stimulating production of "a 'gates ajar' collar and tippet, cigar, funeral wreath, and patent medicine, the last dispensed with a free copy of the book."[44]

Gates Ajar is an allegory of a pilgrim's progress toward assurance of personal immortality. Mary's brother Roy, who "was all there was," is "shot dead" in the Civil War, and Mary's loss provokes her to question God's goodness. In the course of an opportune visit, benevolent Aunt Winifred and her cherubic daughter Faith lead Mary toward knowledge of Christ's brotherliness and Roy's continued existence. Winifred, who communicates with her deceased husband John and anticipates the recovery of her "pretty brown hair" in heaven, dies near the end of the novel with her "face at last towards the window" and a greeting on her lips: "John . . . why, John!"[45]

Winifred's metaphysical style is analogical: scripture tells that "in the Father's house are many mansions," a passage Winifred interprets to mean that "Christ is truly 'preparing' my home for me. He must be there, too, you see,—I mean John." Like all "organized society," heaven will include "homes, not unlike the homes of this world." Winifred's analogies have several distinctive qualities. First, whatever is truly pleasant must be ordained by God. For example, the "CLEAN—white—guinea pig," which pleases Faith immensely, will certainly join her in heaven. And since "a happy home is the happiest thing in the world," Winifred cannot "see why it should not be in any world." The "little tendernesses of family ties" have a religious dimension that deserves infinite continuation.[46]

Winifred describes her theology as "spiritual materialism." Her character depends, far more than do Stowe's characters, on what Ann Douglas, in *The Feminization of American Culture*, has analyzed as a piety of eternal consumerism. [47] As a storyteller, Phelps rather baldly and reductively illustrates the sentiments Stowe crafted with such ingenuity. As a literalist in her theories of self-perpetuation, Phelps' sanctification of domesticity takes the home's most trival measure. It comes as no surprise that Mark Twain found Phelps' geography of the hereafter "a mean little ten-cent heaven about the size of Rhode Island."[48]

Phelps elevated family life to an abstraction that insisted on happiness and denied pain. But if her theology was self-aggrandizing and self-indulgent, it may have been because her imagination was imprisoned by the sentimental conventions she celebrated. Harriet Beecher Stowe, on the other hand, seems to have held the beliefs and practices of domestic pietism under her mind's eye. The capacity to contain domestic pietism within her larger imagination granted Stowe an inner objectivity that she used to cement, through her enormously powerful "fiction," the values she analyzed so shrewdly. It is important to acknowledge that the theology of domestic happiness was grounded in the real values of peace and love and in the significant truth of feminine spirituality. The flaw in the domestic fantasy was that it set

women in competition with the rest of the world and denied that
the theology of home was a claim to social power.

It might well be said that changing perceptions about women
enabled theologians to discover the feminine nature of God. The
home, and thereby women, lost economic status during the late
eighteenth and early nineteenth centuries, but gained in religious
authority, a development reflecting the secularization of American
public life and the isolation of religion as a personal, family affair.[49]
As religion became a matter of family persuasion, women became
arbiters of religious life, persuasive religious authorities as well as
exemplars of religious devotion. As religion came to be invested in
every Christian family, and as America's Christian homes became
sacred enclaves, womanhood became an object of religious devotion.
In the Christian literature of the nineteenth century there are many
texts in which maternal characteristics are attributed to God. According to these texts, God's nature included capacities for nurture,
shelter, forgiveness, and sacrifice, capacities that were illustrated on
earth by virtuous mothers.

The feminization of God and the deification of femininity involved
a reinterpretation of the relation between beauty and truth. Truth
bowed to beauty in nineteenth-century American Christianity, a
posture evident in the enormous religious appeal of sentimental
fiction and in the influence of that genre on theology. Preachers and
novelists illustrated the beauty of God by demonstrating the superiority of esthetic sensitivity over rational understanding for religious
life. If theology was compromised by this situation, women often
chose not to see it that way, taking advantage of both their beauty
and their sensitivity to beauty to lay a double claim on the truth. In an
era of soft religion, many religious women found great personal
strength and wielded authority accordingly, compelling the allegiance of nearly all sectors of their culture to the religious values they
preserved in family life. With this religious strength in hand, as we
shall see in later chapters, a few women broke down the walls
between politics and religion, stepping beyond the home to play
heroic roles in social history. Others asserted the pragmatic effectiveness of religion and claimed, in the case of Christian Science, that
the beauty of religion was scientifically true.

The influence of feminine spirituality on politics, science, and institutional religion has been significant. In the nineteenth and twentieth centuries, nearly all social reform movements in America have been influenced by the maternal perspectives and domestic agendas of women who have urged that social and natural environments be cleaned up to offer their inhabitants shelter, nurture, and beauty. Though American women have made relatively few contributions to the theoretical sciences, the practical science of health care, ranging from nursing to faith healing, has depended on women with effective techniques and recipes for health—indicating the pragmatism as well as the compassion of feminine spirituality. The piety and benevolent energy of women have been sustaining forces in America's institutions of religion as well, and in church activities the feminine mode of spirituality has probably been more influential and more exercised than any other. In the realms of politics, health, and church, agents of feminine spirituality have practiced the truth according to the esthetic of domestic consciousness. The practicality inherent in domestic consciousness has yielded a pragmatic definition of truth that has made cultural activism a natural expression of feminine spirituality.

The principle of beauty central to feminine spirituality has yielded other definitions of truth as well, truths born on flights of the imagination. In the domain of artistic expression, the truths proposed by artists of feminine spirituality have often gone unrecognized or been dismissed as florid, enigmatic, and sentimental. But viewed from within the history of feminine spirituality, the awareness of truth in beauty may be of comparable significance to the Puritan awareness of beauty in truth. American Christians influenced by romanticism understood truth to be determined by beauty. Under this influence, artists of feminine spirituality presented the familial theology of Puritanism in fictional stories about human personalities and relationships. They transformed the analogical theology of Puritanism into religious stories about family life.

In the nineteenth century, through a publishing industry that expanded rapidly to meet the demands of authors and readers of poetry, novels, and short stories, hundreds of women contributed to a literary reconstruction of Christianity. This massive literary effort by lady Christians—Nathaniel Hawthorne's "damned mob of scribbling women"—exercised a dramatic effect on the history of both religion and literature in America. In terms of their place in the history of American religion, one of the most significant assertions of these authors is their testimony to personal immortality. Their postulation of the eternal afterlife of personailty has been judged as the gratuitous effort of angry women who, to compensate for being denied political authority on earth, imagined heaven as an environment governed by their own domestic values. But in fact the point of view that motivated the heavenly fiction of the nineteenth century had far more integrity and profundity than simple compensation and expressed an emotional range that was far wider than that described by frustration and anger.

Like the Puritans, these literary writers believed personality to be the fundamental element of human experience and the medium of divine expression. In their recasting of Puritan spirituality in the context of belief in the maternal dimensions of God's personality, these women relied on their own experiences as mothers—as personalities who gave birth to and nurtured other personalities—to illustrate Christian spirituality. Their sentimental optimism encouraged them to believe that religious life was clean and beautiful and that spiritual beauty involved a moral goodness that dissolved evil in acts of forgiveness. It was the creation and virtuous development of personality that God loved, and it was the purpose of religion—and literature—to remind people that their personalities ought to develop after the image of God.

The literary ladies of nineteenth-century America believed that their stories and poems were true as sincerely as they believed in personal immortality, spiritualism, animism, and prayer. And their belief in the truth of their literature was grounded in the recognition that personality was imaginatively wrought. The medium of imaginative literature was the appropriate form for this theology, corresponding to the notion that

the creation of personality—by God or by literary characterization—was more an esthetic than a dogmatic process. Although their consideration of the relation between language and
truth departed from Puritan theory, the sentimental authors of
the nineteenth century preserved a Puritan devotion to words.
They reconceived the authority of *logos* sacred to Protestantism
by inventing homely, happy stories designed to warm and stir
human hearts.

Four

Witchcraft and Sexuality
in Literature

W Sentimental novels and sermons were designed to quicken human hearts, but not to the point of passionate heat or desire. Ministers influenced by sentimental romanticism drew a connection between God's love and mother-love. Novelists expanded the connection to show the resemblances between love toward God, on the one hand, and love toward mother, toward child or daughter, and toward bride or wife on the other. In the correspondences drawn between loving God and loving girls and women, novelists tended either to avoid the subject of sexual desire entirely or, when passion was involved in the plot, punished or repressed it in the name of a purer love.

In the context of nineteenth-century popular romanticism, sexual desire and Christian love were perceived as antithetical. Indeed, from the point of view of sentimental Christianity, sexual passion was religious evil. This chapter approaches the topic of religious evil through literary perceptions about femininity in which the correlation between religious evil and sexual passion was made explicit. Chapter Five will look at the histories of two notorious women who argued publicly that sexual passion was a natural expression of femininity, and were thereupon caricatured as witches.

The religious problem of sexual passion involved perceptions about women and also, and quite dramatically, the fears of men.

Henry Ward Beecher's *Lectures to Young Men* (1844) illustrates how the celebration of feminine virtue could invert itself in a fear of feminine sexuality. Beecher believed that sexual passion threatened religious virtue and social stability. In "The Strange Woman," the most outstanding of his *Lectures,* he recounted the quick and gruesome fate of a young man who succumbs to sexual indulgence. "Who cries out?" Beecher asks his reader; "It is the voice of the son of midnight; it is the shriek of the STRANGE WOMAN'S victim!" he answers. Beecher invites his readers to "enter with me, in imagination, the strange woman's HOUSE— where, God grant you may never enter in any other way." In his tour through this hell-house, which antithetically corresponds to a Christian home, Beecher described a chambered pentagon of mounting horrors: "There are five wards—Pleasure, Satiety, Discovery, Disease, and Death." Purity is the only alternative to hell, and by purity Beecher meant not chastity but domestic haven and Christian marriage.[1]

Witchcraft offers a motif for focusing discussion of perceptions about the nature and dangers of feminine sexuality. For nineteenth-century Americans, as for New England Puritans, witchcraft represented the demonic limits of personal corruption and excited fears of social disaster. But the theology of witchcraft elaborated by nineteenth-century Americans departed drastically from its Puritan heritage even as it depended for its imagery on New England history.

John Greenleaf Whittier's "The Witch of Wenham" (1877) offers a fine example of how Victorian Americans at once borrowed and departed from their Puritan ancestors' experiences with evil. In that poem, a mother warns her son that the woman of Wenham Lake threatens his virtue and his reason. The issue between mother and son is whether the seductiveness of the Wenham woman's beauty accompanies or denies her piety. Andrew protests that she is pious and pure; in his mother's eyes "the wickedest witch in Salem jail/Is to that girl a saint." Her warning unheeded, the mother "clasped her hands, she wept aloud,/but Andrew rode away" in haste and lust to Wenham

Lake. In desperation the mother begs a minister to help her:

> "O reverend sir, my Andrew's soul
>   The Wenham witch has caught,
> She holds him with the curled gold
>   Whereof her snare is wrought.
>
> "She charms him with her great blue eyes,
>   She binds him with her hair;
> Oh, break the spell with holy words,
>   Unbind him with a prayer!"

Sexual attraction is the charm of this witchcraft, and the mother's last recourse against it is the counter-charm of a minister's prayer. But for the moment, the warmth of Christian prayer is no match for the urgent heat of Andrew's passion, and the sexual attractiveness of the siren who lives in lakeside solitude is more inviting than the protectiveness of maternal virtue. The blue-eyed "witch" is accused of using her beauty to transform buttercups into yellow birds, entice fish to eat out of her hand, command swarms of bees, and compel the eyes of young men. A Salem marshal arrests her for witchcraft and imprisons her in the attic of an old farmhouse. Andrew finds and rescues her and, as they flee across the Merrimac, the "ancient ferryman"

> Forgot, at times, his idle oars,
>   So fair a freight to scan.
>
> And when from off his grounded boat
>   He saw them mount and ride,
> "God keep her from the evil eye,
>   And harm of witch!" he cried.
>
> The maiden laughed, as youth will laugh
>   At all its fears gone by;
> "He does not know," she whispered low,
>   "A little witch am I."[2]

Stories of witchcraft were available to Americans from their New England past, and authors eager to craft a national literature that would compete with European art regarded seventeenth-century episodes of witchcraft as memorable moments in American history and as worthy subjects for literary interpretation. John Neal wrote *Rachel Dyer* (1828), one of the earliest historical novels about the Salem trials of 1692, in response to the "insolent question of a Scotch Reviewer, repeated on every side of me by native Americans—'Who reads an American book?'"[3]

Writers who took New England witchcraft as subject for historical fiction consistently associated bewitchment with the sexual power of women and in so doing reinterpreted the history and theology of witchcraft in a way that illumines our understanding of their perceptions about women. No romantic maidens were involved in the trials of 1692: those judged to be witches were older, mostly eccentric women, and a few men, and most of the accusations were made by a group of eleven-to-thirteen-year-old girls.[4] The appearance of beautiful heroines in historical fiction about witchcraft suggests that nineteenth-century Americans joined to their interest in history a fascination with a particular kind of feminine sexuality.

As we have seen, the popular novels of the nineteenth century took the beauty of woman to represent religious virtue. But the sexual seductiveness of feminine beauty, when mentioned at all, was regarded as a temptation to evil. Contemporary novels about witchcraft, which took their place within the genre of sentimental literature, pointedly illustrated how feminine beauty could arouse lust in the imaginations of men. Three novelists who took the history of Salem witchcraft as a subject for literary romance—William Henry Herbert, James Kirke Paulding, and John W. De Forest—reinterpreted history to link witchcraft with the evil excited by feminine beauty. In the witch novels of all three writers, an innocent but beautiful heroine is accused of witchcraft by a man whose already weakened virtue permits him to be drawn to a woman for her sexuality rather than her virtue.

In these three novels there are no genuine witches, no persons who wittingly practice witchcraft and none who are justly accused of it. In an earlier era the practice of witchcraft involved a complex system of beliefs and rituals that some followed and others acknowledged as powerfully real. Half a million Europeans, mostly women, were put to death for witchcraft from the fourteenth through the seventeenth centuries. The episode at Salem Village in 1692 was a late and relatively tiny outburst of persecution: from June to September nineteen Salem villagers were hanged, and one man pressed to death, for witchcraft.[5] In its pre-modern history, witchcraft and its persecution focused on the power of feminine sexuality.[6] Many of the women who were persecuted for witchcraft practiced their craft self-consciously and confessed to making agreements with the devil. By contrast, in the sentimental fiction of the nineteenth century, women accused of witchcraft were only perceived as witches, and witchcraft was always a descriptive and never a self-ascriptive term.

Witchcraft was part of the geography of Puritan consciousness. Cotton Mather pointed out that skepticism of witchcraft led to skepticism about the Devil's existence. Should religion come to such a pass, "we shall," as Mather put it, "have no *Christ* but a *Light within,* and no *Heaven* but a *Frame of Mind.*"[7] The Puritan animosity toward witches, like their fear of the devil, granted the reality and took the measure of the supernatural power of evil. Their belief in the omnipotence of God in no way qualified their recognition of the pervasiveness of evil. Evil was part of the divine economy, and Puritans were not squeamish about acknowledging it as an instrument of God. Even though evil—and the devil and his witches—hated God, God finally controlled them all. To see and spurn the devil, and to engage in combat against him was to acknowledge God's objective reality and express allegiance to him.

In contrast, romantic writers regarded witchcraft as superstition, and they criticized the Puritan persecution of witchcraft as an injustice grounded in delusion. Romantic writers were aware that witchcraft fit within the economy of Puritan consciousness, and their criticism of it carried with it a more general theological argument against Puritanism. In the theology of sentimental romanticism, God was not only good but exclusively so. Evil existed—without it a novel could hardly be written—as a misinterpretation, and a misuse, of the natural order of God's universe. Evil was an imaginative delusion, an effect of a corrupt imagination, and nineteenth-century authors of historical fiction associated the whole religious vision of the Puritans with this category of delusion. Sentimentalists regarded their Puritan ancestors as misanthropic legalists who cultivated a consciousness of evil and then attempted to ferret it out with a rigorous and literalist discipline that was callous to the goodness of this world and hostile to its beauty. From the sentimental point of view witchcraft was a superstition and as such a useful metaphor for the delusions and corruptions of the human imagination. The metaphor of witchcraft was finally directed not to those who were accused of witchcraft by Puritans, but to the Puritans themselves.

Because the imagination was celebrated as the faculty that apprehended truth, the theology of sentimental romanticism was in an important sense itself a frame of mind. It was appropriate, then, for this theology to be illustrated, explained, and defended in poems and novels as well as in sermons and didactic literature. In fact, precisely because fiction expressed and inspired the imagination, it was even more suited to romantic theology than the expository prose of doctrinal exegesis. And sentimental fiction explained history as well as theology. Novelists wrote history from the point of view of their theology. Herbert, Paulding, and De Forest, whose novels represent the historical fiction about witchcraft popular among nineteenth-century Americans, interpreted Puritan history in the terms of their own theology of the imagination.

In Herbert's *Fair Puritan* (1875) Ruth Whalley engages in a religious communion with nature that antagonizes her Puritan father. Ruth is a "Forest Maiden" whose "exquisite physical form" mirrors nature just as nature "kindle[s] into rapture" her "refined taste and poetical imagination." But nothing can soften the heart of Ruth's father Merciful, whose name is a gross travesty of his character. "This stern, fierce, proud, sneering fanatic" would turn "the fair world, with all its beauty and its joy, into a very hell."[8] Hostile toward beauty, Merciful cultivates a callousness to the forest world and to his daughter's loveliness.

Ruth has two lovers, one virtuous and one not. Sir Henry Cecil, who "cast but a passing glance upon mere charms of the person," understands that "the beauteous body was but the casket of a soul, and to be loved and treasured, or despised and cast aside, according as that soul was beautiful or not." In absolute contrast, Ruth's second suitor, Sir Edmund Andross, "casts the eyes of passion" on her "voluptuous" form and hungers for sexual enjoyment.[9] Herbert's rigid distinction between lust and love illustrates the difference between sentimental theology and the sexual attitudes that in fact characterized Puritanism. As we have seen, the theological affirmation and practical cultivation of a state of undistracted religious awareness was essential to Puritan spirituality. When consciousness and behavior were fully surrendered to God, Puritans lost the dissociation of soul and flesh in experiences of embodied consciousness.

Ruth's beauty casts a spell on Andross—though she does not intend to captivate men in this way, for she has no control, and barely an inkling, of the power that others perceive as hers. Because the enchantment offers no consummation, Andross is consumed with frustration. In "The Temptation" chapter Ruth is imprisoned in Andross' house in a luxuriously appointed room where she is offered rich foods and fine wines. "That vile panderer of his foul will" visits his captive and asks what she would do to obtain her freedom and a pardon for her father. (Merciful has been arrested for sequestering the patriarch Edward Whalley, one of the regicide judges of Charles I.) " 'I would do anything,' she answers, clasping her hands together, 'anything that I may do unreproved of Heaven.' " Andross is ready with his proposition: "Be mine . . . by the gentle bonds of love, not by the iron shackles of this world's hypocritic custom—." Ruth, "interrupting him with an air of perfect majesty," insists she and her family would "rather die all" and, when Andross approaches her in force, holds him off with a carving knife. Andross' "brow grew black as night, and his scowling eye shot forth a ray of hellish spite and fury." He rushes from the room to charge Ruth with witchcraft before the Boston magistrates.[10]

In the last moments of the novel, as she awaits death in her prison cell, Ruth is "resigned and calm," and, like Christ, she suffers in innocence. Her eyes were "fixed and straining, through the small, iron-grated loop-hole, on that far heaven, wherein she hoped ere long to live in bliss for ever." When news of the transference of power from Andross to Bradstreet's Puritan government reaches Boston, Sir Henry Cecil, who has fortuitously transfered his allegiance from crown to colony, intercepts Ruth's death procession and cuts "the bonds which fastened her fair wrists." Thus saved from meeting her death as a victim of Puritan superstition and sexual materialism, Ruth swoons "in the excess of surprise and joy."[11]

In Paulding's *Puritan and His Daughter* (1849), another father, "crop-eared" Harold Habingdon, reproaches another daughter, Miriam, for the imaginative delight she takes in nature: "knowest thou not that the indulgence of the imagination is dangerous to youth! It lures us astray from the path we are destined to tread in this weary pilgrimage." Miriam is more at home with her romantic dream world of nature than "within the narrow limits of reality."[12]

Like Ruth, Miriam is accused of witchcraft by a community whose religious misanthropy represses beauty and imagination, hates happiness, and condemns the purest of its women as evil. Tobias Harpsfield is enchanted by Miriam's inheritance. When she repulses his overtures, he at once takes his revenge and schemes for her submission by elaborate fabrications convicting her of witchcraft. Her conviction accomplished, Tobias visits Miriam in prison, promising her freedom in return for marriage, calculating that by "procuring her release in the last extremity . . . he might so work on her gratitude, if not her affections, that she would be ultimately wrought upon to give him her hand,

which being well filled, he coveted most egregiously." But like
Ruth Whalley, the unsullied Miriam would rather die than
marry an avaricious man. As she puts it with a definitiveness
characteristic of her virtue, "I had rather, ten times rather, meet
the doom prepared for those accused of witchcraft, than pledge
my faith to a man mean enough to take advantage of my
wretched condition for his own selfish purposes." Like Ruth,
Miriam faces death submissively, does not revile her accusers,
and welcomes the sacrifice that maintains and proves her virtue.
With the inward peace of innocence, she appears in her death
procession in a "snowy gown" as if she were a bride of Christ
proceeding to her betrothal. At the very last moment Tobias
confesses his evil machinations and Miriam is free to marry her
fair suitor, cavalier Langley Tyringham. The lovers retire to the
Tyringham family estate in Virginia and are married in the
Episcopal church. Although she is born a Congregationalist,
Miriam has "no scruple in worshipping with Christians in any
Christian church," and thus represents a type of American
woman whose softness cloaks her moralism: "Her most common
and natural mood was a quiet gentleness" but "dormant under
the yielding softness, the mild benignity, the smiling acquies-
cence, of the Puritan's daughter" was "latent enthusiasm, . . .
energetic purpose," and an "obstinate unyielding sense of the
right."[13] The Puritan's daughter improves upon her paternity;
her receptivity to beauty sweetens her religious fiber and her
passive demeanor preserves her virtue without fanaticism or
pride.

De Forest's *Witching Times* (1854–1857) tells a similar story
with intellectual elegance. In this novel the father is as sensitive
as his daughter: Henry Moore and his daughter Rachel have
romantic sensibilities that make them kindred spirits in a hostile
community. The humanitarian Henry has a "native tendency to
free thinking" that sets him apart from the Salem community in
his "extreme unbelief and scorn of the doctrine of witchcraft."
And yet Henry is not an irreligious man. He "believed in God
most reverently" but interpreted the Bible "after a mild and

humane fashion." De Forest conjectures that "were he living in the present day, he would be, at the worst, a Unitarian or a Transcendentalist." Henry's gentle rationalism provides an ideal masculine counterpart to his daughter's sensitivity to nature. Rachel is serenely at home in nature and, in her "leafy hermitages," she tries to "domesticate . . . the wild creatures around her" including Harry the squirrel, who habitually scurries up onto her lap to nibble the food she brings for him[14] and whose name suggests that his training is related to Henry's romantic schooling.

Rachel, like Ruth and Miriam, is the victim of the diabolical revenge of a spurned suitor. When she accepts the hand of upright Mark Stanton, Elder Nicholas Noyes maneuvers Henry's death and Rachel's ordeal in prison. Noyes has always worshiped the darker side of God. As his enchantment with Rachel's beauty develops into jealousy and then revenge, his introspections increasingly revolve around evil itself. His anxiety over whom he should accuse of witchcraft—the Moores or himself—possesses him with "horrible thoughts" and a "vague consciousness of pleasure." His preoccupying sensitivity to sin "could not restrain him from rushing blindly on in the path of his sinful imaginations—could not bend him to any lowliness of submission nor elevate him to any sublimity of pious aspiration."[15] This suitor who lusts to possess the beauty that enchants him is satanic; his actions to destroy what he cannot possess prove he is demonic. Of the three novels, De Forest's *Witching Times* offers the most subtle account of the romantic psychology of evil. The imagination of Nicholas Noyes is sensitive but corrupt: he cannot purify the possessive desires of his imagination by sacrificing them to the discipline of goodness nor can he sublimate his fantasies in any project that transcends his own lust.

The relation, suggested by Herbert and Paulding and made more explicit by De Forest, between the fanaticism of Puritanism and the sexual corruption of the imagination was pursued further by Nathaniel Hawthorne. Hawthorne's stories and novels explore the idea that religious sensitivity and feminine beauty may combine in the masculine imagination for evil as well as for good.

In "Young Goodman Brown" (1835) religious virtue and feminine purity are twin fantasies in the protagonist's imagination. When Brown is lured from his pink-ribboned bride Faith into the forest where he sees—or imagines he sees—the whole Salem community reveling as they worship the devil, no more than Noyes could he keep from rushing blindly on in the path of his sinful imaginations. When he perceives that even Faith is present, he is driven to join the unholy communion. A last-minute appeal to her wakes him as if from a dream. Real or not, Brown's night of imaginative terror has transformed a good man into a dour misanthrope forever anxious about the evil around and within him. He becomes "darkly meditative" and "on the Sabbath day, when the congregation were singing a holy psalm, he could not listen, because an anthem of sin rushed loudly upon his ear and drowned all the blessed strain."[16]

In Hawthorne's story a good man is driven to evil because he deserts his faith and Faith depends for her existence on her husband. A heroine derives her identity from her suitors: in the eyes of a Christian lover she offers a mirror for his faith; in the eyes of an unholy lover she is a sexual enchantress. A heroine's beauty is as dependent on her suitor's virtue as her demeanor is passive. Even her moral character develops inside the perceptions of her suitors, not within herself or on her own terms. Ruth, Miriam, and Rachel are of such fixed virtue that they can only shrink in abhorrence from their fiendish suitors or reflect the chaste devotion of their good young men.

Hawthorne's writing bears a peculiar relation to the historical romances of his time. Herbert, Paulding, and De Forest perceived nature as benign and characterized their heroines as emotional innocents happily at home in nature. Men who lusted after women epitomized evil by desecrating the holiness that natural beauty represents. For Hawthorne the relation between nature, women, and evil was more complicated. As a romantic, he granted the imagination religious status and portrayed the artistic and the religious visionary as similar types. But unlike his more sentimental contemporaries, Hawthorne understood that nature, women, art, and religion could threaten as well as enforce social order. As did sentimental authors, Hawthorne often chose sexual passion to represent the evil of anarchy, but unlike sentimentalists, he opened his own imagination to the anarchy of nature and the evil dimension of sexuality.

In Hawthorne's "Rappuccini's Daughter" (1844), Beatrice Rappuccini's luxuriant beauty quite literally enchants Giovanni Guasconti as, from his window, he first discovers her tending her vegetable sisters in her father's magical flower garden. Beatrice's father, whose single-minded passion for knowledge has pushed his scientific intelligence to a demonic creativity, has nourished his daughter on poisons. Just as his flowers are supernaturally beautiful because they are all poisonous hybrids of natural plants, so Beatrice's beauty—like her father's other blossoms—is deadly as well as seductive. Even before Giovanni is convinced that Beatrice has infected him physically, he recognizes that her "rich beauty was a madness to him," and he "fancied her spirit to be imbued with the same baneful essence" that was communicated by her physical touch. Her poison was "a wild offspring of both love and horror that had each parent in it, and burned like one and shivered like the other." This lurid hybrid of love and terror is Hawthorne's representation of the power of woman's beauty to enchant men and destroy their sanity. Beatrice, like other heroines accused of witchcraft, is helpless to control her own power. Her father, who thinks his daughter should have appreciated the unique power he has given her, finds that she would have preferred the weakness common among women and the love and protection of a husband.[17]

While Faith is only an allegorical reflection of Young Goodman Brown's fevered imagination, and Beatrice is the innocent victim of her father's demonic imagination, in other stories and novels Hawthorne grants his female characters powers of their own. The mother of Illbrahim, in "The Gentle Boy" (1837), is a Quaker of "mighty passions," banished from the Bay Colony as a threat to social order. Her reappearance there provokes "terrified astonishment," for her raven hair was "defiled by pale streaks of ashes" and her once beautiful face was now "wild with enthusiasm." This hellion figures as an opposite to the Madonna-like Dorothy, who has adopted Illbrahim for her son: Dorothy's "mild but saddened features, and neat matronly attire, harmonized together, and were like a verse of fireside poetry." Dorothy and the Quaker, "as they each held a hand of Illbrahim's, formed a practical allegory; it was rational piety and unbridled fanaticism contending for the empire of a young heart."[18]

While in "The Gentle Boy" Hawthorne chose easily between domestic and deviant femininity, in *The Scarlet Letter* (1851) he displayed more sympathy toward a woman who participates in passion and is conscious of her own powers. The reader first meets Hester Prynne as she stands at the prison door beside a wild rose bush that "by a strange chance, has been kept alive in history; . . . it had sprung up under the footsteps of the sainted Anne Hutchinson." Hester aroused the same fears of anarchy that, in Hawthorne's interpretation, prompted the Puritans to punish Hutchinson, Quakers, and witches: she is punished for indulging in passion unrestrained by social convention. The images of the prison and the rose, of Anne Hutchinson as heretic and saint, of Hester as adulteress and Madonna, all symbolize the ambiguity of her character. In Hawthorne's view there is a magnificence in visionary defiance and wilderness freedom, but the sins of religious heterodoxy and sexual passion disrupt community and compel punishment. Hester is Hawthorne's portrait of a lady, his paradigm of a woman whose heroism lies in the self-conscious relinquishment of passion for compassion. When she repents for her sexual passion and meets the demands of community and motherhood, her creativity becomes socially valuable in the beauty of her sewing and her benevolent life. Through his dark-haired beauties Hawthorne explored his own fascination with feminine sexuality, portraying the imagination and beauty of these women as supernatural qualities. But Hawthorne never allowed his dark women to fully satisfy their hunger for freedom.[19]

In this regard, the difference between heroes and heroines in

American literature is most striking. Cooper, Twain, and Hemingway, to name three great American adventure writers, represent their heroes forever riding through the woods, across the seas, up canyon walls, or down rivers in search of adventure, or in escape from it. In the case of Hester Prynne, who is a fine candidate for the archetypal American heroine, her story turns on how she learns to avoid travel, at least travel of the chasing, fleeing, space-devouring kind. Hester Prynne's character develops because she does not adventure either into the wilderness or, until her ordeal is done, across the ocean. Her life on the outskirts of Salem village is an adventure not in activism but in passive surrender to her broodings and musings. Hawthorne takes the conventional association between passivity and feminine virtue and transforms it, through the character of Hester Prynne, into an inner adventure through labyrinths of the feminine mind.

Hawthorne locates Hester Prynne and her predecessor, "the sainted Anne Hutchinson," in Salem village, home of the witchcraft trials in a later generation. Through these associations Hawthorne connects witchcraft with both adultery and antinomianism. Hawthorne plumbs the conflict between feminine sexuality and Christian social order and shows the nature of passive compassion to be feminine sexuality turned inward and familiar with transgression.

Herman Melville brought the romantic fascination with female sexuality to still another level of consciousness, exposing the structure of the sexual mythology that sentimentalists and Hawthorne had elaborated. In *Pierre* (1852) Melville pursued the logic of sentimental conventions to extremes and exposed lust as insanity and marriage as incest. "The absolute effort to live in this world according to the strict letter" of convention involves protagonist Pierre Glendinning in "*unique* follies and sins, unimagined before." The agent of his lunacy is Isabel, a dark woman with a "face of supernaturalness," who claims to be his illegitimate sister, unknown to the family and raised in an insane asylum. She pleads for his recognition, and Pierre, breaking all other social ties to rescue her from despair, marries her. He comes to see Isabel as the embodiment of his own mystical vision: "She seemed moulded from fire and air, and vivified at some Voltaic pile of August thunder-clouds heaped against the sunset." Entranced by "her extraordinary physical magnetism," he becomes "locked in her spell" although increasingly aware that "interfusing itself with the sparkling electricity in which she seemed to swim, was an ever-creeping and condensing haze of ambiguities."[20]

In conventional mythology, wives were loved more as sisters than as partners in passion. In an outrageous recasting of convention, Pierre's sister becomes his wife and he becomes obsessed by his physical attraction to her. Pierre is driven to madness because he cannot learn whether Isabel is his muse, his devil, his sister, his wife, or his lover. When he suspects that she may not be his sister, the thought is more horrible than the incest he thought they were commiting, for she may have tricked and possessed him entirely, twisting his philosophical search for truth in a maze of falsely motivated good intentions. Through Pierre, Melville portrays the fate of the American male—though he longs for heroic originality, personal achievement, and integrity, Pierre is bewitched and unmanned by the ambiguities inherent in his own mythology and morality. Because Pierre believes that Isabel's beauty has a supernatural source, his religious consciousness and his sexual compulsiveness are interwoven. Because the power Isabel wields robs him of clarity and destroys his integrity, Pierre is as frightened of Isabel as he is drawn to her. The possibility that a woman might discover her own passion, and make sexual use of the power granted to her nature, darkens her attractiveness and blackens her power. At the end of *Pierre* Melville describes what happens when an American hero succumbs to a passionate woman: as he dies in prison, guilty as well as misunderstood, Isabel "fell upon Pierre's heart, and her long hair ran over him, and arboured him in ebon vines."[21]

Pierre is bewitched by the deadly combination of Isabel's sexuality and her spiritual awareness, which is a dark version of the sentimental combination of virginity and Christian piety. Isabel's feminine spirituality is demonic because she is a heatedly sexual creature; feminine spirituality is conventionally Christian when a heroine is indifferent to her sexual attractiveness and guards her chastity with righteous integrity. This pair of literary opposites, the intuitive whore and the steadfast virgin, had real effect on the lives of historical women. Literary characters are the essences, more or less creatively distilled, of perceptions about human characteristics. Perceptions about femininity expressed in literature are experienced in life, and analysis of the one yields understanding of the other.

Five

Women Under the World

ꙍ One may approach the history of femininity through the lives of women who dissented from conventional perceptions about femininity and who, like creative authors with freshly imagined characters, crafted new and bold insights through their own lives. The remainder of this book is concerned primarily with such unconventional women, women who amplified and transformed their culture's perceptions about femininity. This chapter considers the lives of two women who believed that sexual awareness belonged to feminine spirituality. This belief led them to become radically critical of conventional religious values and to speak out against the repression of the souls of women enforced by those values. The lives of these women were tragic, at least in part, because the belief that feminine sexuality was diabolical had so caught hold of the American imagination that these women were forced to live as anti-heroines, plagued throughout their lives by moralistic voyeurs and interpreters who caricatured their "evil" natures.

Frances Wright and Victoria Woodhull were nineteenth-century social philosophers whose life-styles, values, and careers were discussed avidly in the press, where they were perceived as unnatural and dangerous. Both were referred to by writers and preachers as if they were literary types rather than real women, and this rendered their public service ineffective and dislocated their personal lives. Both were mocked as witches: Wright was given the title "Priestess of Beelzebub" because she advocated free love and Woodhull was caricatured in a Thomas Nast cartoon as a beautiful hellion, with black robe and bat's wings, parading the motto "Be Saved by FREE LOVE." The caption read "Get thee behind me, (Mrs.) Satan."[1] Though both women advocated sweeping political and moral reforms, the press focused on their commitment to sexual freedom and paid little attention to the breadth of their visions, insinuating that their ideas were motivated and rendered ridiculous by sexual disorders.

Wright was born in Scotland in 1795, and received an exceptional education in a context of political liberalism. At eighteen she wrote *A Few Days in Athens,* an early expression of values that characterized her later philosophy. She portrayed Athens as an egalitarian utopia where human reason was educated without competition from organized religion. When she first visited America in 1818–1820, her published letters described how Americans were building a democratic utopia based on principles of reason. Measuring "the character of men" by "the condition of women," Wright symbolized the young nation's potential through her observation that American women were granted a degree of liberty and esteem that set them apart from women of other countries. She anticipated increased equality between American men and women and hoped women would soon "be taught in early youth to excel in the race, to hit a mark, to swim, and in short to use every exercise which could impart vigor to their frames and independence to their minds." As she became more familiar with American society and manners, and as her rationalism developed into a radical realism, Wright qualified her enthusiasm, remarking that she had first seen America through a "claud-lorraine tint." What she had first interpreted as "the energy of enlightened liberty" had only been "the restlessness of commercial enterprise."[2]

In 1824, Wright returned to America as a companion of Lafayette, an arrangement that inspired much public gossip and moral censure. Influenced by Robert Owen and others, she remained to found a colonization project in Nashoba, Tennessee, which evolved into an interracial communal experiment sanctioning sexual relationships based purely and freely on love. In 1828, having left Nashoba to write and speak on education and social equality, she began a lecturing tour in Cincinnati, where religious revivals were in progress. Disturbed by the nationalization of Protestantism, she attacked the Reverend Ezra Stiles Ely's call for a Christian political party, and delivered in response to it a scathing evaluation of organized religion and its manipulation of women. Outraged at the clergy's "taint[ing] every institution in the land," Wright argued that through their "influence . . . over the female mind" revivalists were engineering "a union of Church and State" that would "prostrate the independence of the people, and the institutions of the country." Because women were trained to be emotional creatures, while the education of their reason had been "lamentably neglected," they were particularly susceptible to the psychology of revivalism.[3]

Soon after this well-publicized slap at the American clergy, Lyman Beecher denounced Frances Wright as the "female expositer of atheistical liberty." Beecher, who made as close a connection between marriage and civil religion as Wright did, paraphrased her point of view: "Atheistical education must come, either by public suffrage or revolution." The American press and public became increasingly hostile to the ideas she publicized and turned the connection she made between the role of women and the state of society into an *ad hominem* attack. In 1829, the *New York American* described her as a "female monster" who had relinquished "every amiable attribute of her sex" and thus "ceases to be a woman."[4]

Wright's ideas were rendered ineffective by public perceptions of her perverted sexuality, a caricature that made her participation in reform movements a liability. Before the 1830 elections she left America, fearing that her presence would hinder the Working Man's Party she supported. The image forced upon her by the public also undermined her personal integrity. In 1831, she married William Phiquepal D'Arusmont, a Frenchman sixteen years her senior. After her marriage she broke off relations with Lafayette and Robert Owen and turned her attention to

domestic interests, almost as if she were attempting to transform herself from a female monster back into a natural woman.
Of her marriage, which later ended in divorce, Orestes Brownson wrote that it marked the central change in her life, for after
marrying "her charm was broken and her strength departed."[5]
She spent the rest of her life in the United States, finally settling
in Cincinnati, where, impoverished and isolated, she died in
1852. While her retreat into marriage suggests that she gave up
her attempt to broaden the opportunities available to American
women, her surrender must be attributed to the tenacity of
religious and social conventions that regarded women who demanded freedom as perverse creatures.

Victoria Woodhull lived as an anti-heroine even more thoroughly than Frances Wright. While Wright was a forthright
rationalist of the Jacksonian era accused of being a demonic
priestess, Woodhull was a melodramatic figure of the Victorian
era who—at least in part—enjoyed and encouraged perceptions
of her bewitching power. Born in frontier Ohio in 1838, Victoria
Claflin grew up surrounded by revivalist fervor. As a child she
imitated evangelical preachers by shouting "Sinners repent" to
outdoor congregations of children. Despite her lack of formal
education, she predicted a dramatic future for herself. In her
childhood a Greek man, whom she later learned to call Demosthenes, appeared to her in a vision prophesying: "You will know
wealth and fame one day. . . . You will live in a mansion in a city
surrounded by ships and you will become ruler of your people."[6]

Victoria Claflin married her first husband, Canning Woodhull, when she was fifteen and had two children by him, Byron
and Zulu Maud. Canning was a disappointing husband, and she
was the principal breadwinner in Chicago, San Francisco, and
New York, working as an actress and as a "spiritualist physician." The Woodhulls joined the Claflin clan in Cincinnati but
neighbors' complaints that the household functioned as a brothel
encouraged the family to move to Chicago. In St. Louis, after
another family move, Victoria Woodhull married Colonel James
Harvey Blood, the former president of the St. Louis Spiritualist

Society, a classicist, an advocate of free love, and the St. Louis City Auditor.

After fourteen years of itinerant life, Victoria Woodhull moved to New York City in 1868. There she took up permanent residence with her family. She entered New York business life with her sister Tennessee Celeste (later Tennie C.), who became mistress to Cornelius Vanderbilt. The sisters amassed enough capital from stockmarket tips to purchase their own brokerage house in 1870. Heralded as the "Bewitching Brokers," their charm and acumen brought financial success and public renown. Throughout her career Woodhull remained a religious woman; in her Wall Street office she hung the motto "Simply to thy cross I cling" and in her wealthiest days dressed soberly with words from Psalm 102 stitched in the sleeve of every gown: "Deliver my soul, O Lord, from lying lips and from a deceitful tongue."[7]

As a young adult whose morality was questioned by others, she turned against organized religion as hypocritical and focused her venom on Protestant views of prostitution. While Protestant men, even ministers, supported prostitution in practice, they publicly denounced prostitutes as evil women who threatened marriage, religion, and social stability. Woodhull was further offended by the hypocritical thinking that set prostitution and marriage in sharp opposition. In her economic philosophy, marriage was a popular and accepted form of prostituion. Woodhull argued that when sexual exchange took place within an economic relation, as it did in marriage, sexuality was purchased rather than given freely. She championed the practice of free love in which sexuality was openly expressed, independent of economic arrangements, and motivated simply by love.[8]

Woodhull's desire for public acclaim and her antagonism to the hypocrisy of those in power turned her toward social reform. In 1870, she announced her candidacy for president of the United States and published the first edition of *Woodhull and Claflin's Weekly*. The paper advocated spiritualism and the "single moral principle" of free love, published Marx's *Manifesto* for the first time in America, and argued for organized labor and women's rights. She called for "A United States of the World," a "Universal Church," a "Universal Home," a "Universal Canon of Art," and advocated "the Universal Language, Alwato." The millennium, she predicted, would be inaugurated "through Cooperation of the Spirit World."[9]

Many supporters of women's suffrage were horrified by Woodhull's stand on free love and perceived her as a danger to their cause. But more radical feminists like Elizabeth Stanton and Isabella Beecher Hooker defended Woodhull's right to hold her own opinions about the freedom of love and the slavery of marriage. Stanton argued that "this sentimental, hypocritical prating about purity" was a male technique for making women "hangmen" for each other. "We have crucified the Mary Wollstonecrafts, and Fanny Wrights, the George Sands, the Fanny Kembles, of all ages. . . . If Victoria Woodhull must be crucified let men drive the spikes and plait the crown of thorns."[10]

Isabella Hooker's sister Harriet Beecher Stowe spoke from a contrary—and more common—view of Woodhull's ideas and person. In a popular novel serialized in the *Christian Union,* Stowe caricatured Woodhull as Audacia Dangereyes. A woman "who *takes* her rights" and asks a gentleman to "come round and take a smoke with me this evening," Audacia spoke like an uneducated revival preacher who bullied the gentlemen: "that boy's in heathen darkness yet, and I'm going round to enlighten him." When the editors of *Woodhull and Claflin's Weekly* were charged with obscenity and blackmail, Stowe portrayed the event in her serial. One of Stowe's female characters found it "horribly disagreeable . . . to have such women around. It makes one ashamed of one's sex." Another attacked Audacia's right to call herself a woman and categorized her as "an amphibious animal, belonging to a transition period of human society."[11]

Stowe's *Uncle Tom's Cabin,* the nation's best seller, portrayed the evil of disrupted domesticity and celebrated an innocent child whose maternal compassion led other characters to salvation. In her caricature of Woodhull, Stowe presented Audacia Dangereyes as a woman with qualities antithetical to Little Eva's saintliness. Audacia openly offered sexual invitations, had an abrasive backwoods manner, and was self-centered rather than sacrificial. Little Eva's prayers led others to salvation; Audacia's invitations led men to hell. Woodhull was angered by Stowe's mockery and defensive about the portrayal of her lack of education. When Isabella Hooker arranged an interview between Woodhull and her older sister Catharine Beecher, Catharine's patronizing remarks about the sacrality of marriage provoked Woodhull to insinuate that Catharine's famous brother Henry Ward was an adulterer. Though Catharine threatened to "strike" her "dead," Woodhull publicly exposed Henry's affair with Elizabeth Tilton. As a result he was tried for adultery. As history would have it, Henry Beecher was vindicated, and the scandal worsened rather than redeemed Woodhull's reputation.[12]

In her confrontations with the Beechers, Woodhull aligned her own religious and social values against those of America's most esteemed spokespersons. In the eyes of Catharine Beecher, whose ideas and contributions we shall consider in the following chapter, Victoria Woodhull was an unnatural woman and an incarnation of evil. Woodhull idealized self-fulfillment rather than self-sacrifice, and her advocacy of free love epitomized the immorality Catharine Beecher urged women to guard against. Henry Ward Beecher had warned against "The Strange Woman" whose charms paved the road to hell and showed how self-sacrificing motherhood epitomized God's love. But in Woodhull's eyes Beecher represented the religious hypocrisy she spent her life combatting: he prated about the purity of romantic love and the holiness of the home while he carried on a love affair with a married woman. Woodhull wanted religious and sexual honesty, and she singled out the nation's most prominent preacher as the target for her honesty.

Escaping arrest for sending "obscene literature" through the mails, an accusation based on interpretation of her *Weekly*, Woodhull appeared as scheduled at Cooper Union, removed her disguise as an elderly Quaker woman, and delivered her lecture.

She described how she was persecuted and spoke on the more general theme of woman's persecution in the home, a theme she labeled "domestic damnations." A reporter described her spell over the audience as the charm of a "terrible syren." Soon after this unorthodox appearance, Woodhull collapsed, and the press reported that she was dying. After a partial recovery, she gave up political reform and embraced an occult form of pietism. She had once been visited by Demosthenes; now she was visited by apparitions of Jesus. Her mother, Roxana, once a fervid revivalist and now a dramatically emotional Catholic, influenced her daughter's search for personal religious fulfillment. Woodhull turned her attention toward a cabbalistic pursuit of the Elixir of Life. From being a political visionary who looked forward to a Universal Home, she turned inward and dwelt on "the holy temple" of the human body. The Garden of Eden was the human body, nurtured and bounded by the rivers of bodily fluids. She identified menstruation as the secret of life, the New Jerusalem as the "purified woman," and "improper physical habits" as the root of all evil. Defilement could be avoided and perfection achieved when men and women united in marriage with the sole intention of engendering undefiled children.[13]

Woodhull's early self-confidence allowed her bravely and boldly to argue for global institutional reform. Religious idealism had led her from a career as a backwoods clairvoyant to a self-determined social reformer whose universal vision affirmed sexual equality and passion. But instead of fame she acquired notoriety; instead of becoming a leader of her people she was jeered at as a lunatic and a whore. Though she remained a visionary, she looked backward to Eden rather than forward to the millennium and advocated the religious purification rather than the social revolution of marriage.

Like Frances Wright, in her public career Victoria Woodhull associated Christianity with the subserviency of women and argued that the free love she advocated would spring women from the confinements of domesticity and Christianity. As with Wright, the public evaluated her ideas by caricaturing her person

and in so doing restricted her social effectiveness. But unlike
Wright, Woodhull's personal integrity may not have been undermined. Turning her focus back upon herself and crafting a
theology of the human body, Woodhull indeed surrendered her
claims to social power and failed to fulfill her early ambitions.
But in her inward turning she may have succeeded in discovering
religious fulfillment in an occult version of the embodied spirituality vital to the tradition of feminine piety in America.

Six

Women Transform the World

W Victoria Woodhull made her peace with domestic pietism by interpreting the family, the home, and the female body in visionary imagery. She had once stood steadfast against reigning religious values and their implications for the lives of women. In later life she wrote about the spirituality of womanhood with a depth of vision that extended the horizons of conventional perceptions about femininity, figuring the body of woman as the Holy Land, the incarnation of the sacred places described in the Old and New Testaments. Woodhull never changed her mind about the positive relation between sexuality and spirituality. But in her later life she ceased arguing for free love and other social reforms and turned her attention to the celebration of the holiness and undefiled purity of the human body.

Victoria Woodhull could not destroy the conventions that associated Christianity and womanhood, but she did transform them, to her own satisfaction at least, by reimagining the nature of the connection between Christianity and womanhood. And she was not the only American woman who found satisfaction in the association between femininity and spirituality by extending it to new dimensions. But while Victoria Woodhull retreated from social reform to discover a new connection between womanhood and Christianity, other women embarked on their public careers with new versions of feminine spirituality already in mind. This chapter considers women who were more successful than Woodhull in implementing their social reforms, women whose recasting of feminine spirituality achieved popularity and earned them political support.

Elizabeth Seton and Catharine Beecher are two American women who intuited the power Christianity granted to femininity and actualized it. In their visions of a better society, they tapped the spiritual authority of women and applied the values of family pietism to larger communities. Seton and Beecher differ from one another in how they internalized their femininity, in how they described the purposes of their lives, and in how they expressed the power of their femininity. Seton fused her own suffering with Mary's suffering for Jesus, becoming the Mother Superior of America's first female religious order and, more recently, the first native-born American to be canonized as a saint; Beecher celebrated woman's capacities for moral integrity and self-sacrifice and called women to a national activism as professional educators. Elizabeth Seton and Catharine Beecher are taken here to represent two ends of a spectrum of feminine religious power. Seton represents the grace of saintliness; Beecher the virtue of moral energy.

The debate between grace and virtue provides a simple typology that helps distinguish among modes of religious consciousness throughout American history. In theory, the New England Puritans understood the experience of grace and the practice of moral virtue to be mutually reinforcing. But even among first-generation settlers there was debate about the nature of a balanced relation between individual religious experience and social order. Then and ever since, mystically inclined Americans have criticized the moralistic tendencies in American religion. And, on the other hand, Americans concerned with the preservation or reform of social order have criticized the antinomian tendency of religious enthusiasm or felt uncomfortable with the intense personalism demanded by those who cultivate grace.

Mystically inclined Americans have argued that grace spawns virtue and that holy people are good people who contribute to social order. Jonathan Edwards argued this point when he described his wife's ecstasy within the context of her reputation as an energetic contributor to moral life in her community. Her conversion to Catholicism notwithstanding, Elizabeth Seton's mysticism falls within the tradition represented by Sarah Edwards. Seton's personal religious experiences motivated her social work. Furthermore, like Sarah Edwards, she craved moments of grace and when she received them they filled her soul with movement and love. But Seton is different from Sarah Edwards in her style of grace. Elizabeth Seton experienced grace more as the ecstasy of anguish than as the joy of swimming in sunlight.

Born in 1774, Elizabeth Bayley was raised an Episcopalian and from her childhood was attentively pious and thoughtful, and at times wishful, of heaven. Her mother died when she was four, and with her father's remarriage she became an unwelcome stepchild who spent much of her adolescence depending on the support of other relatives. Her father, Richard Bayley, was Columbia's first professor of anatomy, New York City's first health officer, and a pioneer researcher of croup and yellow fever. His commitment to the sick and dying estranged him from his second wife but endeared him to his idolizing daughter Elizabeth.[1]

This sensitive and lonesome girl married William Seton in 1794, and bore three daughters and two sons. William Seton assumed responsibility for his family's failing export business, and as he suffered bankruptcy he succumbed to consumption. In an effort to give him the therapy of a peaceful interlude in a warm climate, Elizabeth took William and their oldest daughter to Italy. Their landing was intercepted, and they were confined in quarantine for a month in dark quarters. William suffered exceedingly, and Elizabeth, in a journal written for her sister, reported that "you would find me a lioness, willing to burn your *lazaretto* about your ears, if it was possible, that I might carry off my poor prisoner to breathe the air of heaven in some more seasonable place." Though able to write fiercely about the situation, she also welcomed it as the occasion to encourage William's conversion. Like a Puritan who gratefully accepted affliction as God's opportunity for mercy, she wrote that "in the dungeon of this *lazaretto*, I should bless and praise my God for these days of retirement and abstraction from the world, which have afforded leisure and opportunity for so blessed a work."[2] Throughout her life Elizabeth Seton "worked" to transvalue suffering as grace.

William died shortly after their release from quarantine, and Elizabeth, stranded and penniless, was consoled and provided for by Catholic acquaintances. On her first visit to their church she was fascinated by the sensual warmth of the Catholic house of God. She was pleased by the ornate interior, the candles and the organ music—"a foretaste of heavenly pleasures"—and found "delight in seeing. . . all sorts of people kneeling promiscuously about the altar." She too "sank" to her "knees . . . and shed a torrent of tears."[3]

Elizabeth responded to the indulgence of the Catholic esthetic, admiring the sumptuousness of the rituals as well as of the space itself. Catholics could indulge their piety with much greater freedom and frequency than Seton was used to: "here they go to church at four every morning, if they please. And you know how we were laughed at for running from one church to the other, *Sacrament Sundays,* that we might receive as often as we could." Catholic ritual was more lavish, more concrete, visual, and sensual than Protestant ritual, and Seton was struck by what she took to be the central belief and essential practice of Catholicism—the literal embodiment of God in the sacramental mass. Realizing that Catholics believe "they *possess God* in the Sacrament" caused Seton to "feel the full loneliness and sadness of my case, I cannot stop the tears at the thought: My God! how happy I would be, even so far away from all so dear, if I could find You in the church as they do."[4]

What most attracted Seton in her first encounters with Catholicism was the holy personality and power of Mary. After reading St. Bernard's prayer to the Virgin, Seton found herself talking to Mary. In Mary she found the maternal presence she had been deprived of for years: "I felt really I had a Mother—which you know my foolish heart so often lamented to have lost in early days." As early as she could remember Seton had

"looked . . . to the clouds for my mother." Now "it seemed as if
I had found more than her. . . . So I cried myself to sleep on her
heart."[5]

Seton not only found a mother in Mary but a model for how to
be a mother as well. "I am a *mother*," Seton wrote in a meditation
that was to become a central theme in her spiritual life. "How
was my God a little babe in the first stage of his mortal existence
in Mary? But I lost these thoughts in my babes at home, which I
daily long for more and more."[6] The Catholic sacrament made
Christ a living presence, and Mary had literally incarnated his
mortal presence in her womb. The biological concreteness of
Mary's mothering of Christ came so intimately alive for Seton
that she "lost" the Mary-Jesus relation in thoughts of her relations with her own children.

Mary bore Christ in a second sense as well. She carried his
suffering in her compassion. The month spent in the *lazaretto*
made Seton responsive to images of Mary's anguish over the
suffering and death of her son. One of the first images of the
virgin mother to deeply impress Seton was a picture of Christ's
descent from the cross. She wrote that the painting "engaged *my
whole soul*—Mary at the foot of [the cross] expressed well that the
iron had entered into hers, and the shades of death over her
agonized countenance so strongly contrasted the heavenly peace
of the dear Redeemer that it seems as if His pains had fallen on
her. How hard it was to leave that picture, and how often, even
in the few hours' interval since I have seen it, I shut my eyes and
recall it in imagination!"[7] Mary perfectly embodied the suffering
of Jesus, taking his agony upon herself, mothering his death and
his immortality as she had mothered his birth.

After Seton's return to America and reunion with her children, the memory of the warmth of the Catholic mass and the
intimate, actual presence of God in the sacraments made Protestantism seem cold and rationalistic. Although she was torn by
indecision and ostracized by friends and family, her confidence in
the truth of Catholicism grew steadier, her attendance at St.
Peter's—"the Church . . . with the cross on top, instead of a

weathercock"—became frequent, and in March of 1805, she received her first communion. That event, like Sarah Edwards' intercourse with the sun, was a moving experience. Seton's first communion brought her a spiritual expansiveness as sensual and as privately dramatic, if not as publicly alarming, as the leaps of joy inspired by Sarah Edwards' baptism of light. Seton danced before her God, at least in her desire: "Now, then, all the excesses of my heart found their play and danced with more fervor—no, must not say that—but perhaps, almost with as much as the royal prophet's before his ark."[8]

Seton's sensitivity to suffering prepared her for the remarkable ecstatic experiences that, from her first months as a convert to her last as a revered mother superior, satisfied her longings for grace. To elicit these satisfying experiences of spiritual ecstasy Seton dwelt on the sufferings of Jesus. In her words, Catholicism was "the way of suffering and the Cross," and the God present to her in the sacraments was a suffering, sacrificed God. The vivid sacramental presence of Christ encouraged Seton to find the nature of God in the mirror of her her own experience of suffering and sacrifice. Engaging in holy communion was tasting Christ, a filling and sharing of his sacrificial body with hers: "the *Blessed Sacrament* is *my Jesus,* the daily sacrifice, the opening of the pained and suffering heart to a guide and friend."[9]

The ritual of holy communion became the most palpable reality of Seton's life. The hours, days, and months of her life were ordered by this ritual of womanly intimacy with the sacramental body of Christ. Especially during her last illnesses, the ritual of tasting the body of Christ and drinking his blood provided the meaning as well as the calendar of her life. Death brought the purpose of her life as a woman religious into focus. In November, 1818, in a letter to her close friend and spiritual advisor Gabriel Bruté, Seton described how "we talk now all day long of my death and how it will be just like the rest of the housework." As she confessed to Bruté, her spiritual housework assumed cosmic proportions and ecstatic dimensions: "I see the everlasting hills so near and the door of my eternity so wide open that I turn too wild sometimes." Near death one night in October of

1819, she refused water despite extreme thirst so that she could take communion the next morning. The priest who brought the sacrament to her recorded that "her joy was so uncommon that when I approached . . . she burst into tears." When he asked if she wanted confession, she responded, "No, no! Only give Him to me!" The "ardor" of her desire so impressed the priest that his own soul was stirred by the event. He described "her whole face so inflamed that I was much affected."[10] Like Anne Bradstreet's anticipation of death, in Seton's near experience of it she surrendered her mortal body to the presence of God.

In the last weeks of her life, Seton wrote that "it seems as if Our Lord stood continuously by me in a corporeal form, to comfort, cheer and encourage me in the different weary and tedious hours of pain. Sometimes sweet Mary, also, gently coaxing me—but you will laugh at my imagination." When she died on January 4, 1821, a sister who had been present recorded: "I do not know if you will give . . . the name of superstition to that which I felt at this moment. It seemed to me that Our Lord was there, near to her, very close, awaiting this good soul. I do not know when His Presence made a livelier impression upon me."[11] The sheer force of Seton's femininity made the Presence of the Bridegroom come alive. With her saintly receptivity, Seton begged for Him and unceasingly prepared for His coming. The sister who watched her die experienced the living Christ.

At death Seton was fully and finally united with Christ. In her lifetime she never had enough of Him. In a meditation characteristic of her sensibility she cried: "My Jesus—have pity give at least full grace *for the moment.*" Impatient in her desire for grace she reminded Jesus that in her moments of suffering she resembled his own mother. She could persevere as a mother who took the sorrows of the world into her heart if Christ would pity her with his grace as he graced his own mother. "Pity a Mother, a poor Mother that she may persevere with you in the garden or nailed to the cross, given up perfectly resigned in her long agony."[12] Suffering was her approach to Christ and she needed grace to bear the pain she cultivated.

Like the Holy Mother Mary, Seton had so great a capacity for suffering that she could feel the pain of others as her own. Because of this special receptivity, her life was mingled with the lives of others in a radically literal way. As Mary bore the agony of her son as literally as she had born his infant body, so Seton could feel the pain of others as if it lived inside her. Seton felt this union with other personalities most dramatically in experiences with her natural children. In 1812, while she was Mother of the Sisters of Charity in Emmitsburg, Maryland, Seton nursed her dying daughter Annina. Seton portrayed their communion as a reciprocal sacrifice: "The child offering the mother, the mother the child." Each offered her pain to the other, and each offered up the pain of the other to God. Each felt a joy in sharing herself that transcended the pain: "The sweet half-hour of love and peace with Jesus between us, as she sits on her bed of pain and I kneel beside her."[13]

At Annina's death, Seton identified her own sorrow with the sorrow of Mary: "Begging crying to Mary to behold her son and plead for us, and to Jesus to behold his Mother—to pity a Mother—a poor poor Mother—so uncertain of reunion."[14] In Seton's prayer sorrowing mother and dying son have interchangeable functions: both embody sacrificial love. In death lies the fulfillment of that love, and both Mary and Jesus are dying of grief—Mary for her son, Jesus for the whole human race. As the mother of a dying child, Seton shared Mary's holiness; she is like Mary and Mary is like Jesus. Through her suffering and sacrifice the boundaries of Seton's religious subjectivity became mystical horizons of divine life. As in more conventional domestic theology, femininity, sacrifice, and death are elided in Seton's soul. But unlike the commonplaces of domestic pietism, Seton's identification with Mary at once elevated her experience of divine maternity and grounded her grieving in a bottomless passion.

Seton's youngest daughter, Rebecca, also died in Emmitsburg. In the last months of a tortured dying, Rebecca spent most of every day and night in her mother's embrace. "Most of her time is passed in my arms or on my knee. We wet each other pretty often with tears." In this Pieta-posture Elizabeth suffered as

well—her "left arm lost all sensation, becoming almost atro-
phied, and her legs grew so still that she limped when she
walked."15

Elizabeth Seton's attraction to Catholicism, however singular
in its circumstances, intensity, and fruits, was not an uncommon
attraction among nineteenth-century American women. In *Gates
Ajar* Elizabeth Stuart Phelps explained Aunt Winifred's theology
of "spiritual materialism" as New England Protestantism infused
with the warmth and literalism of Catholicism.16 Like Seton,
Phelps gravitated toward the sensuality of Catholic ritual and
doctrine. But while Seton dwelt on the literal presence of Christ
and on Mary's embodiment of her son's agony and joined her
own suffering with theirs in an experience that challenged and
transformed her life, Phelps appropriated the concreteness of
Catholicism as justification for a perpetually *status quo* economy
of conventional domesticity. In *Uncle Tom's Cabin,* Harriet
Beecher Stowe identified St. Clare's mother with the sensual
esthetic of Catholicism. Accompanying herself at the organ to
the "fine majestic music of the Catholic Church," St. Clare's
mother caused her son to collapse in her lap, dissolved in emotion. While Stowe used St. Clare's mother as an indecipherable
symbol that functioned to keep St. Clare from falling into "utter
disbelief,"17 Seton internalized the image of Mary as if the Holy
Mother were a vortex with a centripetal force that absorbed all
of her experience and a centrifugal force that transformed and
reactivated her life.

It is important to remember that *Uncle Tom's Cabin* and *Gates
Ajar* were written five and eight decades after Elizabeth Seton's
conversion to Catholicism. Sentimental romanticism laced the
culture that nurtured Stowe and Phelps and the piety to which
they gave expression. Sentimental romanticism fostered a certain style of feminine cuteness, totally absent in Seton's writing,
which worked against sustained introspection, tended to make
suffering a tableau of pretty images, and avoided both the discontinuity and the transcendence of pain. Most tellingly, romanticism offered Stowe and Phelps the device of sentimental fic-

tion. While Seton possessed, as her meditations document, an extraordinary imagination, her imagination delved inward unrestricted by the conventions that censured womanly passion. Seton, Stowe, and Phelps were all religious women whose piety focused on familial ties and the self-sacrifice that linked Christ with motherhood. But Stowe, and Phelps to a far greater extent, objectified their religious imaginings through literary conventions that were stereotyped and finally impersonal.

Although Seton's religious imaginings were subjectively directed and uniquely intimate, she was neither a solipsist nor a recluse. In fact, her religious life found strong objectification in her career as a mother superior and as a religious organizer. As foundress of the American Sisters of Charity, Seton became the religious mother of a community of sisters. In 1809, after taking vows and laying plans for a sisterhood in Emmitsburg, she wrote to her daughter Cecilia that "the tender title of *Mother* salutes me everywhere." As a religious mother Seton assumed an extended family: "I can give you no just idea," she went on, "of the precious souls who are daily uniting under my banner which is the cross of Christ."[18]

The nuns who lived under Seton's guidance prepared for active careers and, most commonly, to be teachers. The American Sisters of Charity was founded as a community devoted to the training of Catholic educators. Seton and her Sisters of Charity were renowned, and sometimes vilified, for their pioneer work in establishing America's first free parochial schools. During Seton's lifetime her community of women educators grew strong enough to diversify its organization in the establishment of orphan asylums in Philadelphia and New York.[19] As an organizer, a teacher of teachers, and America's first Mother Superior, Seton objectified and actively built on the spiritual power she experienced in her personal life.

Elizabeth Seton's success as an organizer of women was envied and imitated by American Protestants who believed that education was the key to social reform and that women were the natural educators of the human race. Mother Seton's success at institutionalizing feminine spirituality, by creating schools where nuns educated future citizens and mothers, captured the imagination of Catharine Beecher (1800–1878), daughter of re-vivalist theologian Lyman Beecher and eldest sister of Harriet Beecher Stowe and Henry Ward Beecher. Catharine Beecher argued for a national educational system supervised by Protes-tant "Sisters of Charity." Her program would be implemented by an organization of American women with the moral commit-ment and communal cohesion of a Catholic sisterhood. Beecher contested the view that Protestant women should limit their charity to one home. Encouraging Protestant husbands to loosen their purse strings to aid women in their benevolent enterprises, she pointed out that Catholic women had an ecclesiastical hier-archy "to counsel and sustain" them, "a strong public sentiment . . . in their favor" and "abundant funds . . . laid at their feet."[20]

Beecher advocated a cooperative system of self-sacrifice among Protestant women. She identified self-sacrifice as the essence of Christian virtue, and in an early theological essay mounted an elaborate defense of free will in an effort to give religious centrality to her theory. She took exception to Jona-than Edwards' theory that people always choose what they de-sire, arguing that Edwards' psychology did not admit the possi-bility of self-denial, which she understood to be the identifying characteristic of true Christians. Beecher understood religious virtue as the sacrifice of one's self-interest, the voluntary choos-ing against what one wants. In her later and more secular philo-sophy, she expanded self-denial into cosmic law: "We are now come to the *grand law* of the system in which we are placed, as it has been developed by the experience of our race, and that, in one word, is SACRIFICE!"[21]

Beecher shared the popular convictions that women's mater-nal qualities skilled them at self-sacrifice, and that virtuous mothers made representative Christians. But she departed from convention in her bold application of domestic pietism to the political future of America. Taking moral virtue to be the sacri-fice of self to the building of a Protestant nation, she extended her belief in woman's capacity for self-sacrifice into an argument that women ought to unify and institutionalize themselves as public representatives and teachers of moral culture. Catharine Beecher envisioned America as an extended family, held together by the sacrifice of individual self-interest for the public good, and indirectly governed by women educators like herself.

Beecher drew support for her program of moral education from the expansive spirit of social reform spawned by the revivalism of the second Great Awakening.[22] Revivalists like her father envisioned Protestant Americans cooperating together in benevolent societies and missionary enterprises in a grand effort to reform and unite America as a Protestant nation.[23] Lyman Beecher, and many of the revivalists who succeeded him, were militant evangelicals who asserted a providential correspondence between Protestantism and American democracy. These defenders of the "righteous empire" of American Protestantism argued that religious and political voluntarism, which encouraged individuals to exercise the virtues they freely chose, was an effective principle of social cohesion.[24] The religiously motivated reform movements of the nineteenth century enlisted the voluntary energies of women, and Catharine Beecher was not alone in recognizing that the promulgation of public virtue appealed to America's Christian mothers.[25]

Catharine Beecher introduced women into the equation between Protestantism and American democracy by showing that they, far more willingly than men, served their nation as volunteers. Beecher believed that, as wives and mothers, American women voluntarily relinquished their claim to be paid for their work and their right to participate directly in political government. Women in America chose instead to devote their lives to caring for others.

As moral educators, women exercised power indirectly. Women did not govern America by direct political authority, but their "superior influence" was inevitably exercised "in all matters relating to morals or manners." And Beecher believed that American culture was uniquely sensitive to the moral power of women. As "in no other nation," she wrote, the American "woman holds a commanding influence in the domestic and social circle." Catharine Beecher envisioned American women as queens of their families. Her dictum, "Educate a woman, and the interests of a whole family are secured," would trace every man's success and virtue to a woman's influence: "Let the women of a country be made virtuous and intelligent," she argued, "and the men will certainly be the same." Perhaps the noblest element in Beecher's vision was her appeal to the *communitas* of American democracy. She encouraged women to extend their moral leadership to all classes and places, to look through such divisions among themselves. Perceiving women as the power behind the home, she worked to establish the sisterly union of all American women as the power behind the nation. In a statement that revealed the theological backdrop of her vision of American womanhood, Beecher promised that if the "wishes and efforts" of American mothers could be "united for a benevolent and patriotic object," maternal authority would become "almost omnipotent."[25]

Placed in this context, Catharine Beecher's vision of a Protestant Sisters of Charity should be seen as a Protestant effort to exceed Catholic reliance on the cooperative moral strength of women. Her father had no love for Catholics. He pitted America against Rome and planned for the day when the truly Christian power of democracy would vanquish the corrupt power of Catholicism. In 1830, in a letter to Catharine, he worried that Catholics would organize the West before they could. Lyman was anxious over the Catholic schools already established, arguing that education was the most powerful weapon of any religion, and "Catholics and infidels have got the start of us." And he predicted, with the crusaderism characteristic of his ministery, that "the moral destiny of our nation, . . . and the world's hopes, turns on the character of the West." In the strategy of his millennialist campaign, the religious and political future of the world hung on Protestantism's victory over Catholicism in the battle for the American West.[27] In his daughter's strategy, this meant that Protestant women had to out-teach their Catholic sisters in the competion for the west.

In Boston in 1835, Lyman Beecher delivered *A Plea for the West*, in which he drew the battle lines between Protestantism and Catholicism and, as if ordering ammunition, summoned Protestants to establish "the requisite intellectual and moral culture" for a Republican Christian Empire. That same year, Catharine stepped to her father's defense with *An Essay on the Education of Female Teachers*. Like her father, she argued that the West could only be saved from infidelity by a national system of moral education. By singling out "energetic and benevolent women" as best fitted to implement this national education, she called women to the job of teaching virtue in America.[28]

Although the "wishes and efforts" of evangelical Protestant women bear a sisterly resemblance to the integration of pietism and activism achieved by contemporary American Catholic nuns, many evangelical Protestants overdramatized the threat and intentions of Rome. Anti-Catholic incidents and literature of the period disclose a fear of Catholicism far out of proportion to the actual power and motivations of American Catholics. This fear was often linked with an obsession with Catholic "perversions" of womanhood. Numerous anti-Catholic novels, tracts, and tales of horror ostensibly related by escaped nuns exposed the sexual scandals of convent life. Imaginative Protestants perceived convent chastity as an escape from the Christian responsibilities of marriage and as an excuse for sexual promiscuity between monks and nuns. The popular Maria Monk's *Awful Disclosures of the Hotel Dieu Nunnery of Montreal* described a nunnery's ghastly and elaborate system of infanticide, the Catholic solution to "criminal intercourse" between priests and nuns.[29]

American Protestants believed that something in Catholicism pushed feminine piety over into sexual perversity—a reaction that reveals fear of women wholly dedicated to religiousness and recognition of a relation between intense piety and feminine sexuality. In the fears they projected onto Catholic sisters, righteous Protestants associated the "perversions" of Catholic brides of Christ with the sexual hunger they imagined "witches" like Victoria Woodhull to have.

Catholicism offered women seemingly unlimited opportunities to cultivate the spirituality of grace and to feel the satisfactions of virtuous social activism. The rewards of Catholic discipline could be achieved without the constraints of marriage and motherhood. Although Catholic sisters accepted obedience to priestly fathers and ecclesiastical hierarchies, at a fundamental level they depended only on God. In Elizabeth Seton's case, this radical dependence on God was wedded to the adoration and imitation of Mary. Such a spiritual situation could certainly encourage a sister's intimacy with God. With Christ as their spouse—and Son of their Holy Mother—Catholic nuns were freed for an intensely subjective and empowering spiritual life.

In contrast, the promise of subjective intimacy with God was not how Catharine Beecher beckoned women. In her calls for a Protestant sisterhood, Beecher never stressed the emotionalism of feminine piety. She carefully and rather insightfully distinguished Catholicism and Protestantism by arguing that Protestants sacrificed themselves for the public good whereas Catholics actually cultivated the self through rituals of denial. Catholics practiced "a selfish and ascetic self-denial, aiming mainly to save *self* by inflictions and losses."[30] Although here she confused the Catholic desire for grace with the desire for assurance of salvation characteristic of evangelical Protestantism, Beecher came close to acknowledging that self-denial and suffering, if directed inward, could magnify the soul. But Catharine Beecher was opposed to selfish, subjective time spent in enlarging one's soul. She preferred to turn herself outward and devote herself entirely to the moral growth of America.

In urging women to extend their maternal virtue through a national system of moral education, Catharine imitated her father's aggressiveness but far exceeded his emphasis on moral energy as the measure of virtue. In 1823, in her twenty-third year, Catharine painfully discovered just how much she resisted undergoing the process of conversion. To her father's despair, she drew away from the conversion psychology that dominated her heritage. She removed herself from religious subjectivism and emotionalism, and by 1829 she had ceased encouraging conversion experiences among her students.[31] Her own personality was characterized by a rebellion against emotional surrender. The moral activism she substituted for emotional surrender enabled her to promote education and celebrate the organizational aptitude of American women. Although in her theories and organizations Catharine Beecher certainly drew on the emotional sensitivity perceived to characterize women, she did not dwell on it.

In addition to her educational vision and the teacher-training schools that helped implement it, Beecher reconceived of the cult of domesticity as a science. Her writings on domestic economy and health promoted motherhood as a profession. In *A Treatise on Domestic Economy* (1841), Beecher outlined the complex applied science of homemaking and showed how the homemaker could most healthfully nurture and structure the enormous range of human experience that she supervised in her domain—food, clothing, disease, mental health, environment, education, and domestic plants and animals. In her program for national education she encouraged women to extend the profession of motherhood beyond the home into institutions of public education. Although Beecher's ideas were rooted in religious assumptions about femininity and shaped by the religious context of social reformism, as her ideas evolved they redirected maternal qualities toward a secular professionalism.

Catharine Beecher was not alone among her contempories in her commitment to the professionalization and institutionalization of feminine spirituality or in her perception of motherhood as a science. Transcendentalist Elizabeth Peabody worked to create an educational "science" out of "mother love" and established the field of kindergarten teaching in America. Dorothea Dix used her womanly powers as a "moral autocrat" in her national campaign to separate asylums for criminals from those for mental patients and to reform the treatment of both types of inmates.[32] The contributions to public virtue sponsored by these two Unitarian women show how the energy of feminine spirituality cut across denominational lines. Over issues of theological doctrine and political agenda evangelical ministers like Lyman Beecher attacked Unitarianism with almost as much venom as they attacked Catholicism, but the mythology of maternal love that linked Catharine Beecher and Elizabeth Seton, despite their differences in doctrine and personality, also characterized Peabody and Dix. The nineteenth-century commitment to the professionalization of maternal virtues, and the devotion to social reforms based on those virtues, established a venerable tradition of social service that has continued to motivate American women to the present day.

The social programs envisioned and implemented by women like Catharine Beecher, Elizabeth Peabody, and Dorothea Dix grew out of religious assumptions about femininity and drew public support from the religious energies behind social reformism. But the tendency toward secular professionalism could undercut the very assumptions about female religiousness that had inspired organized female benevolence and enlisted the support of religious women. Other nineteenth-century women whose careers represent the middle of the spectrum defined by Beecher and Seton kept their reformism within a thoroughly religious context and worked to achieve and promulgate a dynamic reciprocity between grace and moral virtue. With this integration of piety and public service, women could retain their religious expertise and attain social authority as teachers, reformers, and missionaries. In the expanded domesticity envisioned by these religious women, the world was to become a Christian home. In school rooms, benevolent enterprises, and foreign mission societies, public mothers hoped to guard their nation and convert the world. With the religious mandate to free people in every land from the thralldom of pagan superstition and to liberate all women from religious persecution, the Christian adventure carried women not only outside their homes but across oceans as well. *The Young Lady's Guide* (1870), a publication of the American Tract Society, asserted that Christ had declared women the religious equal of man by his birth through Mary and by his "personal conduct" toward women "during his sojourn on earth." The dignity of women measured a culture, and in foreign lands "woman has been cruelly and wickedly sunk below her proper level in social and domestic life." A Christian woman had two obligations: "*piety*—the only sincere expression of female gratitude to God," and responsibility to women "degraded and oppressed" by heathen religions. Christian women would usher in the millennium and would take joy in freeing all humanity, but especially other women, from religious cultures oppressive to women. In this evangelical fantasy, women from on top of their husbands' funeral pyres, women from under veils and behind grilled windows, women in every heathen country were stretching their arms toward their American sisters, "piteously imploring, 'Come over and help us!'"[33]

The missionary zeal at Mount Holyoke Female Seminary struck a balance between the cultivation of religious experience and the preparation for moral activism. The religious intensity of life at Mount Holyoke offered a correction to Catharine Beecher's movement away from the religious assumptions about womanhood that legitimated her program of moral reform. Founded in 1837 as America's first publicly endowed institution for women's higher education, Mount Holyoke established a classical curriculum that offered an alternative to the domestic science taught at Beecher's seminary in Hartford. Unlike Beecher, Holyoke's foundress Mary Lyon maintained her enthusiasm for the emotional dimensions of Christian life: a conversion experience was reported to be part of a Mount Holyoke education, and alumnae agreed that "it is harder to be a Christian anywhere than at Mount Holyoke." One alumna wrote that "the seminary outranked every church in the land as a seat of divine grace. Its almost annual revivals were a topic of interest to religious circles everywhere; many a student enrolled in the express hope of finding salvation."[34]

Lyon tutored the minds and hearts of her students in preparation for careers of public service. As both disciplinarian and visionary, Lyon governed an institution that encouraged women to fulfill themselves as intellectuals, submit themselves as Christians, and organize themselves as missionary-teachers committed to purifying the nation and saving the world. Lyon's original vision focused on the American West, where she sent young women to teach and then marry. Her "hope" rested on "young ladies scarcely out of their teens, whose souls are burning for some channel into which they can pour their benevolence, and who will teach two, three, or four years and then marry and become firm pillars to hold up their successors." With "such a circulating system" teachers-*cum*-wives would become a national support community for piety and social reform.[35]

Resounding Lyon's battle call to "go where no one else will go, do what no one else will do," Holyoke women turned their attention to foreign countries. One such far-seeing Holyoke woman was Fidelia Fiske, one of America's first unmarried female missionaries. She opened a "Little Holyoke" in Oomoo, Persia, that became a model for mission schools as widely separated as Africa, Turkey, India, Ceylon, China, and Hawaii. Fidelia Fiske's career and charisma illustrate the glory that a foreign mission offered a New England maiden. At her departure for Persia, students reveled in her impending martyrdom: everyone knew she "chose to go cherishing no expectation of again seeing friends or native land." She received each of her students for a separate farewell interview. One student recalled "her sweet face with the soft holy light upon it, as looking out to us." Fidelia Fiske was more than simply a religious model; she had the presence of a saint and even mediated the salvation of her students. One student, preparing to give up Miss Fiske to foreign fields, wrote her a letter that requested, "When your eye glances over these lines on the broad waters, will you not offer one petition for me, that I be not lost forever." Fidelia's departure left a religious revival in its wake. Confident in her faith and power, on her arrival in Persia she asked for only one thing—the translation of the English words "give me your daughters."[36]

Fidelia Fiske combined the grace of saintliness with the moral energy of Christian virtue. To this was added, at least in the eyes of those who worshiped her, the glow of a romantic heroine. Her piety of character and her adventures in an exotic land would have made her a fine heroine in a contemporary novel. But Fidelia Fiske was more than an ideal in the minds of others, she also had a mind of her own. Despite the fact that her admirers venerated, romanticized, and objectified her, she wrote her own life and encouraged others to do the same—in the name of Christ, of course.

Seven

Emily Dickinson

In the fall of 1847, at the age of sixteen, Emily Dickinson enrolled at Mount Holyoke Female Seminary. At the beginning of fall term it was Mary Lyon's custom to interrogate each of her students about their relation to Christ, to take "the names of the professors of religion, those who have hope, and those who have not," and to schedule counseling sessions for each group. In her year Dickinson was classified as "impenitent." Lyon focused her attention on Dickinson's group during December and January, following a series of morning lectures on the "great doctrines of the Bible, as Total Depravity, the Nature of Sin &c," with meetings for the impenitent held in her room. On January 11, Emily Norcross, a professed Christian who felt called to help her Dickinson cousin, wrote that "Emily Dickinson appears no different. *I hoped I might have good news to write with regard to her.*" Norcross added somewhat optimistically that her cousin "says she has no particular objection to becoming a Christian and she says she feels bad when she hears of one and another of her friends are expressing a hope." Good news seemed as if it might be in store when another schoolmate wrote six days later that "seventeen attended a meeting in the evening for those who felt unusually anxious to choose the service of God that night . . . Emily Dickinson was among the number."[1]

Shortly after, Lyon assembled the seminary and asked those who simply "wanted to be Christians" to stand. Emily Dickinson was "the only one who did not rise," explaining later, with characteristic sharpness, "they thought it queer I did not rise—I thought a lie would be queerer." Without apology to Miss Lyon, she stopped attending meetings for the "impenitent" and at the end of the spring term she left school forever. In the years following her return to Amherst she confirmed her stance as a religious rebel and took some delight in herself as a result. Soon after her nineteenth birthday, she announced, "I haven't changed my mind yet—either, I love to be surly—and muggy—and cross—." A few months later she called herself "one of the lingering *bad* ones." She sometimes closed a letter in testimony to her lasting impenitence: "Your very sincere, and *wicked* friend, Emily E. Dickinson," or "I am never ready to go—Reluctant Emily."[2]

Though sentimentalists and evangelicals would have called her impious, Dickinson worshiped their God on her own terms. In the demands she made on God's justice and existence and in the independence she cultivated, she hunted for God with passion and played with him with wit.

Dickinson chose to "stand alone." The dependent posture common among women seemed weak to one who "love[d] to buffet the sea." She commanded God to "keep me from what they call *households,* except that bright one of 'faith' " and leveled her irony at the institution of marriage: the notice "she is to be sacrificed in October" was her way of announcing a friend's wedding.[3] She gathered her contempt for conventional femininity in a poem that portrayed the matrons of America:

> *What Soft—Cherubic Creatures—*
> *These Gentlewomen are—*
> *One would as soon assault a Plush—*
> *Or violate a Star—*
>
> *Such Dimity Convictions—*
> *A Horror so refined*
> *Of freckled Human Nature—*
> *Of Deity—ashamed—(401)[4]*

The angelic femininity that sentimental Americans celebrated seemed from Dickinson's perspective a sweet flattery that denied the powers of femininity and of God.

Dickinson's decision to reject the institution of marriage, like her decision to rebel against Christianity, was an act of will that brought her pain and required persistent courage. "To put this World down, like a Bundle—," she wrote, "And walk steadily, away,/Requires Energy—possibly Agony—/'Tis the Scarlet Way"(527). Although the patterns of conventional life may have been but a bundle of dimity convictions, to put that bundle down required the courage to face herself and the courage to bear the separation. If she resisted the conventional sacrifice of marriage, she chose a sacrifice more singular. The Scarlet Way into herself was a solitary road. Speculating about what lay at the end of her journey, she once hoped that "Maybe—'Eden' a'n't so lonesome/As New England used to be!" (215).

Dickinson sacrificed social intercourse to pursue an inward dialogue, and she put the bundle of the world down in order to be a poet. Her choice to be a poet was a momentous decision, and the business of her craft became a religious vocation. She believed that the circumference of her imagination enclosed the power of God. Her gamble was that history would affirm the special status she realized within herself.

> A solemn thing—it was—I said—
> A woman—white—to be—
> And wear—if God should count me fit—
> Her blameless mystery—
>
> A hallowed thing—to drop a life
> Into the purple well—
> Too plummetless—that it return—
> Eternity—until—
>
> I pondered how the bliss would look—
> And would it feel as big—

When I could take it in my hand—
And hovering—seen—through fog—

And then—the size of this "small" life—
The Sages—call it small—
Swelled—like Horizons—in my vest—
And I sneered—softly—"small"! (271)

Like many of Dickinson's poems, this one is about herself. And also, like many of her poems, this one suggests that the poet is God. In the first stanza Dickinson says that if she suits God, she will wear blameless mystery as the dress of her divine election. The color of her dress is white—the color of sheer brightness and extraordinary glory and the color of ambiguity as well—at once powerfully pure and mysterious in meaning. In later life, indeed, Dickinson had a habit of wearing white, perhaps as her way of ritualizing the religious mysteries of her femininity and of celebrating her religious vocation. Risking life for Life, the woman in the poem has dropped self into a divine and purple well on the chance that a royal immortal may return. Like a bride, her purity will take the purple dye. Her gamble for immortality promises success when she recalls that she is the measure of herself and she swells in her vest as no man can. God is perhaps a woman in this poem; if so, the poet has dropped her life well: she has been God all along. Her whiteness absorbs all colors.

An all-absorbing independence defined her triumphs, but the victories never lasted. Like other women she was brought to accept dependence. But where others submitted to conventional perceptions about femininity, Dickinson acknowledged her dependence and her femininity after a private struggle with God.[5] Dickinson's greatest problem with God was the death he inevitably dispensed. She fastened the eyes of her soul on death and in its gaze she met obliteration. Death's stare was terrible, final, and unjust. God's indifference to the death he decreed contrasted with her preoccupying sensitivity to death. She pitted her feminine creativity and her sense of compassion against the cold power of God's justice. In all her thoughts about the future of her life, death was continually victorious over her. But to portray the deadening victory was an imaginative rejoinder.

> *Like Eyes that looked on Wastes—*
> *Incredulous of Ought*
> *But Blank—and steady Wilderness—*
> *Diversified by Night—*
>
> *Just Infinites of Nought—*
> *As far as it could see—*
> *So looked the face I looked upon—*
> *So looked itself—on Me—*
>
> *I offered it no Help—*
> *Because the Cause was Mine—*
> *The Misery a Compact*
> *As hopeless—as divine—*
>
> *Neither—would be absolved—*
> *Neither would be a Queen*
> *Without the Other—Therefore—*
> *We perish—tho' We reign (458)*

In this poem, Dickinson sees Eyes viewing reality as a Blank. The Eyes are incapable of mercy and the poet will not forgive that incapacity. Although the vision of the Eyes and the vision of the poet are antagonistic, they are dependent on each other. Each antagonist requires the other to exist: Dickinson will perish under the power of indifference, but her vision communicates the terrible stare. "Neither would be a Queen" suggests that the omnipotent Eyes refuse to be feminine and refuse to accept the viewpoint of the poet. Were she allowed to fulfill her nature and become Queen, Dickinson would rule reality with compassionate vision and poetic justice.

Characteristic of Emily Dickinson's personality is her acceptance and often her enjoyment of surrender. Her will to become independent of the world led her to realize that she finally depended on a power greater than herself. This recognition

parallels Sarah Edwards' realization that only when she became
independent of other people's perceptions and expectations
could she experience her full dependence on God. Just as Sarah
Edwards found that holiness and humility coexisted in her experience of swimming in the light that swallowed her, so Dickinson learned that the exercise of power required her submission
to it.

As the Puritans used sexual imagery to describe their submission to God's power, so Dickinson used the imagery of sexual
passion to portray religious sanctification. Her frequent association of religious and sexual passion places her poetry as an
expression of the embodied spirituality characteristic of feminine mysticism in America.

> He touched me, so I live to know
> That such a day, permitted so,
> I groped upon his breast—
> It was a boundless place to me
> And silenced, as the awful sea
> Puts minor streams to rest.
>
> And now, I'm different from before,
> As if I breathed superior air—
> Or brushed a Royal Gown—
> My feet, too, that had wandered so—
> My Gypsy face—transfigured now—
> To tenderer Renown—
>
> Into this Port, if I might come,
> Rebecca, to Jerusalem,
> Would not so ravished turn—
> Nor Persian, baffled at her shrine
> Lift such a Crucifixal sign
> To her imperial Sun. (506)

In this poem, religious and sexual imagery are intertwined and
both involve submission. The woman searching with her body
across her lover's breast is stilled by his touch, just as streams are

silenced when they reach their sea. With his touch she finds new birth and in his air she finds poetic breath. The experience described in this poem finds its prototype in the Old Testament story of Rebecca, who was saved by Isaac from rape by the Philistines. Isaac loved and protected Rebecca, and she left her family to wed him. The willing sacrifice of her virginity was fruitful; the birth of Jacob made her a link in the geneological motherhood of Christ.

As in the poem about Eyes, in which the vision of the Eyes and the vision of the poet reciprocate services, so in this poem the tributary stream feeds the sea she is consumed by. Similarly, Rebecca's imperial Sun is also her son. And the Crucifixal sign denotes the sacrifice not only of the Son, but also of the holy women who surrendered themselves to the pleasures of love and the responsibilities of motherhood. Like nineteenth-century women, Dickinson's Rebecca was deified by motherhood, but in distinction from the tacit canons of domestic pietism, Rebecca's submission brought her ecstasy. The poet predicts even greater delight for herself. Out of her own esthetic sensitivity is born a beautiful poem. The metaphor of motherhood suggests her poetic fertility and the labors of her imagination recall the ecstatic moment of her religious surrender. At that moment she gave herself to his power; she was not raped. She relaxed her will and learned tenderness; she did not loose her voice.

Nor did she lose her strength. In another poem in which the interchange of submission and power is at once a religious and a sexual event, she took the interchange between her submission and his power one step further.

> I rose—because He sank—
> I thought it would be opposite—
> But when his power dropped—
> My Soul grew straight. . . .
>
> And so with Thews of Hymn—
> And Sinew from within—
> And ways I knew not that I knew—till then—
> I lifted Him— (616)

Dickinson holds and lifts her lover and discovers, to her own surprise, a male power in her woman's embrace. Her love mingles the tenderness of woman with the strength of man in the slow motions of erotic gentleness.

In a number of her "Wife" poems, Dickinson recorded religious experiences in which she sacrificed herself and received the power of God.

> Title divine—is mine!
> The Wife—without the Sign!
> Acute Degree—conferred on me—
> Empress of Calvary!
> Royal—all but the Crown!
> Betrothed—without the swoon
> God sends us Women—
> When you—hold—Garnet to Garnet—
> Gold—to Gold—
> Born—Bridalled—Shrouded—
> In a Day—
> Tri Victory
> "My Husband"—women say—
> Stroking the Melody—
> Is This—the way? (1072)

Her life is a religious ordeal and through that Calvary, Dickinson is a match for Christ. Like Christ, she has laid down her life in a spirit of devotion; for the love of one thing she has sacrificed all else and realized her own death. The suffering she has endured entitles her to divine status. Like a virgin prepared, she is betrothed to God and waits only the final sign of death to wear the Crown of immortality as his Wife. But although she is without the final sign or heavenly Crown, in a sense she is already The Wife—even now she is Royal Empress and the owner of Title divine. In fact, Dickinson may not need the conventional signs of immortality just as she does not swoon with the faintness common among brides. She has made a singular marriage, a marriage with herself. Her bridal passion is only the cold embrace of stone but that embrace is preciously jeweled and lasting in strength.

In the experience of religious solitude recorded in this poem, Dickinson feels death as well as power. The royal life she celebrates offered her the consummation of her imagination but required the bridle of religious discipline and the shroud of living out the experience of her own death. In the difficult privacy of facing herself and in the achievement of her poetry, Dickinson integrated sexuality and sanctification and relished both her mischief and her ecstasy. The deep potential of poetic fiction engaged her subjectivity and encouraged her to fancy her own divinity. She explored, alone, what it meant to be a woman of magical power, passion, and creative receptivity.

Dickinson identified her life with her work. She chose against "life" as her culture defined its circumference and conventions, choosing to live as a recluse in her father's house in Amherst. "Life is over there—," she wrote, "Behind the Shelf . . . Like a Cup—Discarded of the Housewife." As housewife to her own soul alone, Dickinson discarded the cup of convention for poetic "Porcelain" (640). As she gave her life to her work, her work assumed the fullness and personal character of her life. There is perhaps no other American poet whose personality is so thoroughly disclosed as Dickinson's is in her poetry. The privacy she chose as a life-style gained for her readers the revelation of her soul. The corpus of her poetry, her "letter to the World" (441), is unsurpassed for the consistent intimacy of its insights into her personality. Dickinson won a "personal" immortality that, by contrast, consigns Elizabeth Stuart Phelps to relative oblivion as only a half-hearted religious heroine.

As Elizabeth Seton and her sister nuns took religious vows, so Dickinson committed her life to religious poetry.

> Only a shrine, but Mine—
> I made the Taper shine—
> Madonna dim, to whom all Feet may come,
> Regard a Nun. (918)

The images in this stanza are the religious realities important to Elizabeth Seton. Emily Dickinson regards herself as a nun. The nun prays for the Madonna's approach, prepares a shrine, and makes her taper shine. The nun has worked to make this shrine and the work is at once a supplication and the shrine itself. Just as Elizabeth Seton's humble supplications to Mary effected her own holiness, and her identification with Mary, so Emily Dickinson's shrine is "but Mine," a little thing but well capitalized. Seton "possessed" her sacred images as religious "presences" and did not doubt their corollary objectivity. The inner life recorded in her meditations found objective confirmation in the doctrines, institution, and history of her Church and in the sacramental presence of Christ's body. By contrast, the context of Dickinson's soul was her own soul; her inner life was not moored in any institution or truth outside herself. Unlike Seton, Dickinson did question the objective status of God, though she never doubted the presence or passion of her own subjectivity. As if she were God, Dickinson objectified her own subjectivity in the sacrament of her poetry. The dim Madonna is illumined by the shrine of the taper; the holy Virgin Mother comes alive in the subjective life that shines through the poem.

Dickinson's life is her poetry and religious subjectivity was her life and work. And as Dickinson did her work at home, she frequently imaged her subjectivity as a house.

> Just so—Jesus—raps—
> He—doesn't weary—
> Last—at the knocker—
> And first—at the Bell. (317)

In a singular appreciation of the pietism of domesticity, Dickinson figures Jesus as a patient caller at the home of "the lady's soul." With a coyness characteristic of her style, Dickinson appropriates, even exaggerates, the diminutive conventions of domestic sentimentality. She aggrandizes the minimal and diminishes the grand with a playfulness that balances everything out as seriously innocent. Domestic pietism becomes charming enough to be taken seriously, and the poet, as Dickinson put it elsewhere, "Distills amazing sense / From ordinary Meanings" (448):

> *Papa above!*
> *Regard a Mouse*
> *O'erpowered by the Cat!*
> *Reserve within thy kingdom*
> *A "Mansion" for the Rat!*

In this poem about domestic animals, religious life is a cat and mouse game and God is a householder. He owns and probably admires the cat who is such a devil to the unwelcome rat. But the rat would like to be remembered for her mousey soul, to be saved from the game that for her has grown far too serious, and to be adopted into the heavenly home as an angelic pet.

> *Snug in seraphic Cupboards*
> *To nibble all the day,*
> *While unsuspecting Cycles*
> *Wheel solemnly away! (61)*

In this miracle of hierarchical reversal the meek will be regarded as cute and the mice will inherit the house. Dickinson uses her wit to affect innocence and her mouse is innocently witty about its loss of innocence.

The image that provides a context for these inversions of large and small, serious and silly, innocence and wit, is the home. Dickinson has taken the pietism of domesticity as a "supreme fiction."[6]

> *The Soul should always stand ajar*
> *That if the Heaven inquire*
> *He will not be obliged to Wait*
> *Or shy of troubling Her*
>
> *Depart, before the Host have slid*
> *The Bolt unto the Door—*
> *To search for the accomplished Guest,*
> *Her Visitor, no more— (1055)*

Although robbery is a worrisome image in a number of her house poems, in this one the door of the soul is enjoined to "stand ajar." This heaven who comes visiting does not petition but inquires and then only if he is welcomed. Despite his accomplishments he is too timid even to rap—this is not the persistent Jesus who is last at the knocker and first at the bell. While in both poems the soul is a house shut, in this poem heaven is a welcome intrusion and the bolt may be slid from the door.

In another mood,

> The Soul selects her own Society—
> Then—shuts the Door—
> To her divine Majority—
> Present no more—

Here Heaven lives inside the home of the soul. Filled with and satisfied by the divine society of herself, the soul positively refuses admittance to any guest, no matter how accomplished.

> Unmoved—she notes the Chariots—pausing—
> At her low Gate—
> Unmoved—an Emperor be kneeling
> Upon her Mat—
>
> I've known her—from an ample nation—
> Choose One—
> Then—close the valves of her attention—
> Like Stone— (313)

In the seclusion of her self-selection, the soul spurns all visitors and withdraws from all society except her own. The concentration of her inward focus is unmovable. With the strength of stone the soul seals off "the valves of her attention" against the world. This poem celebrates the fullness of solitude and suggests the sheer strength required for such self-confidence. The two lines that close the poem convey the silence and weight of a tomb and suggest that the achievement of solitude also carried with it an experience of living burial, an experience that brings to mind the fantasies of premature burial that haunted Edgar Allan Poe. But while Poe's characters are drawn toward hysteria by the fear of being trapped into suffocation, Dickinson chooses her self-enclosure and shuts her own door. In the power of her own will she has made a self like stone and turned deaf ears to the human noise outside.

As we have seen, domestic pietism was characterized by the association between home and heaven and that association celebrated the home as a sacred space but also acknowledged the home's separation from this-worldly life. Portraying heaven as home-like was a way of suggesting that there was life after death. In a less conscious way, portraying home as heaven-like suggested that being secluded at home could be an experience that felt like death. In her poetry, Dickinson thoroughly internalized the association between home and heaven and rendered the experience of death ingredient in that association with frightening explicitness and self-consciousness. In her deep animation of domestic imagination, she documented its costs as well as its rewards.

While the poem "The Soul Selects her own Society" considers the relation between the self and the world and focuses on the soul's separation from exterior reality, other poems describe the experience of self-enclosure from a perspective inside the circumference of the soul. At times Dickinson championed the internal gaze that solitude gave her as the precondition for ecstasy and self-fulfillment: "Exhilaration—is Within—/The Soul achieves—Herself" (383). And she claimed that the best moments of her life were moments alone. "The Soul's Superior instants/Occur to Her—alone—," she wrote, "When friend—and Earth's occasion/Have infinite withdrawn" (306). But solitude claimed the worst moments of her life as well as the best. In other poems written about events that occur within the soul's interior, enclosure is a terrible ordeal in which the soul lives out the experience of her own death.

> I felt a Funeral, in my Brain,
> And Mourners to and fro
> Kept treading—treading—till it seemed
> That Sense was breaking through—

And when they all were seated,
A Service, like a Drum—
Kept beating—beating—till I thought
My Mind was going numb—

And then I heard them lift a Box
And creak across my Soul
With those same Boots of Lead, again,
Then Space—began to toll,

As all the Heavens were a Bell,
And Being, but an Ear,
And I, and Silence, some strange Race
Wrecked, solitary, here—

And then a Plank in Reason, broke,
And I dropped down, and down—
And hit a World, at every plunge,
And Finished knowing—then—   *(280)*

The poem begins with a funeral service held within the room
of the brain. The dark parlor of the soul strains under the
pressure of mourners' leaden footsteps crossing and recrossing
the floor. A drumbeat picks up the rhythm and transforms its
pressure into pure sound. Sensation inside the space of the mind
grows numb from the ritual beating. The mourners rise again,
gather, and lift the coffin across the floor. Pressure and sound
concentrate and fill the room, expanding the space within the
soul to a circumference that contains all the Heavens, merging
space with sound as if all of space were a tolling bell. Some small
version of herself is wrecked and left alone inside the gigantic
sound-space of her soul. Some part of the soul holds out against
the loud monotone of her madness; she is a small silence cor-
nered within the larger space of her sounding soul. Then the
bottom of the soul drops away, the floor across the brain gives
way to pressure, and the last surface of reason snaps like a
broken plank. The soul, finally at one with her death and her
madness, plunges downward through bottomless spaces. Her

fall is broken only by the worlds she hits on her downward hurl. She falls through everything there is to know, and when she finishes, she knows nothing at all.

The poem documents and communicates an experience. It is not a literary conjecture about what madness or death might feel like nor is it a metaphorical meditation on funerals. It is simply— and powerfully—a record of an event. The event occurred, as the first line states, within the poet's brain. That situation does not diminish the reality of the event. Dickinson's poems record the life of her soul. She chose poetry as her mode of documentation because poetry suited and conveyed the reality she experienced. Prose did not reflect her experience of the world. The causal explicitness that prose demanded restricted the motion of her thinking and did not communicate the motion of her world:

> They shut me up in Prose—
> As when a little Girl
> They put me in the Closet—
> Because they like me "still"—
>
> Still! Could themself have peeped—
> And seen my Brain—go round—
> They might as wise have lodged a Bird
> For Treason—in the Pound—
>
> Himself has but to will
> And easy as a Star
> Abolish his Captivity—
> And laugh—No more have I— (613)

The poem implies that conventional household discipline could circumscribe human experience and reduce it to a prosaic formula. Domestic space could function like a prison. Yet a poetic reality was lodged in those interiors just as poetry moved in the brain of the little girl in the closet. The poetry in her brain could not be shut up any more than a bird could reasonably be impounded because his freedom was treason. The bird—and the poet—need only the will to fly to accomplish an escape. The flight of a bird and the movement of poetry are both like laughter—sudden, free, and never quite captured in prose.

Like liberal theologians and sentimental writers Emily Dickinson located religious virtue in life at home. But while they celebrated the religion of family life, Dickinson shrunk domestic consciousness to solitary proportions. As she withdrew from public life and as she drew domestic life inside the circumference of her soul, her solitude intensified the ordinary experiences of her life and the limits of her imagination expanded to cosmic dimensions. In these "liminal" experiences[7] she endured the agonies of Calvary and encountered the royalty of God; she suffered the tortures of the damned and tasted the tenderness of love; she lost her reason in the infinite spaces of madness and found the universe in the celebration of herself.

At the limits of her consciousness Dickinson encountered deep pain or great joy: the pattern of her subjective intensity oscillated between extremes of terror and ecstasy. In the times of terror her soul was bound, damaged, and accosted:

> The Soul has Bandaged moments—
> When too appalled to stir—
> She feels some ghastly Fright come up
> And stop to look at her—
>
> Salute her—with long fingers—
> Caress her freezing hair—
> Sip, Goblin, from the very lips
> The Lover—hovered—o'er—

At one end of her inner life the soul felt frozen and still, with Fright against her like a Goblin drinking her warmth and movement in a chilling, ghoulish imitation of a lover's tender caresses. At the other end of inner life her soul filled her body with dance and her body expanded in tune with the time of life itself.

> The soul has moments of Escape—
> When bursting all the doors—

> She dances like a Bomb, abroad,
> And swings upon the Hours.   (512)

   Solitude preconditioned her moments of ecstasy, just as with-
drawal propelled her moments of escape and seclusion gave her
doors to burst. As she put it elsewhere, "Captivity is Consciousness / So's Liberty" (384). Similarly, submission to the power that
terrorized her soul gained her an intimacy with power that
activated the explosive dance of her soul and inspired her poetry.
The poetry that burst the soul open on paper, like the bird-brain
that flew round in the closet of prose until it abolished captivity
with a laugh, expressed an exuberance that had its source and
found its balance in constraint.

   Restraint and explosion were the complementary opposites
that determined the range and the arrangement of Dickinson's
consciousness. The polarity between restrained isolation and
explosive ecstasy is manifest throughout her work, even to the
dynamic of juxtaposition that characterizes her style. In a
number of poems Dickinson used polar tension to express the
nature of religious experience. She characterized religious epi-
phany as the sudden reversal of states of mind.

> I think I was enchanted
> When first a sombre Girl—
> I read that Foreign Lady—
> The Dark—felt beautiful—
>
> And whether it was noon at night—
> Or only Heaven—at Noon—
> For very Lunacy of Light
> I had not power to tell—
>
> The Bees—became as Butterflies—
> The Butterflies—as Swans—
> Approached—and spurned the narrow Grass—
> And just the meanest Tunes

I could not have defined the change—
Conversion of the Mind
Like Sanctifying in the Soul—
Is witnessed—not explained—

'Twas a Divine Insanity—
The Danger to be Sane
Should I again experience—
'Tis Antidote to turn—

To Tomes of solid Witchcraft—
Magicians be asleep—
But Magic—hath an Element
Like Deity—to keep—   *(593)*

With a sorcerer's charm the ordinary world is converted into
an extraordinary one: the small things of nature dance grandly
and a sombre Girl is overwhelmed by the rush of religious
power. The transformation of nature is a change of mind, and
the change of mind not only sanctifies the soul but also modifies
the conception of what sanctification entails. In this conversion
experience, the enchanting writings of a Foreign Lady initiate
the change. And the manuals that preserve and are used to
recollect the experience are Tomes of solid Witchcraft. Books of
magic words and lessons will help this convert avoid sanity—
should that bland state of mind reappear—with counter-charms
more powerful than any spell of common sense. In this poem, the
art of black magic initiates a somber girl to the powers of womanhood.

In Dickinson's consciousness, nature has the magic art and
beauty of a woman. Nature is a witches' world, a world of
miraculous events. What enchants her most about nature is the
wonderful way she reverses herself. As dramatic swings of
mood characterized her own superior moments, so Dickinson
delights in nature's capacity to upset herself and reveal supernatural power in her drastic changes. The seasons, for example,
transform themselves against reason: "If Summer were *an Axiom*

—/ What sorcery had *Snow?*" (191). Dickinson regarded the now-
you-see-it-now-you-don't of summer as a trick as marvelous as
transubstantiation and a habit as feminine as changing fashions.
"The Wild Rose" will "redden in the Bog—"

> *Till Summer folds her miracle—*
> *As Women—do—their Gown—*
> *Or Priests—adjust the Symbols—*
> *When Sacrament—is done—*   *(342)*

Night metamorphosizes into day with as much display as
Summer:

> *The Day came slow—till Five o'clock—*
> *Then sprang before the Hills*
> *Like Hindered Rubies—or the Light*
> *A Sudden Musket—spills—*
>
> *The Purple could not keep the East—*
> *The Sunrise shook abroad*
> *Like Breadths of Topaz—packed a Night—*
> *The Lady just unrolled—*

The Day approaches stealthily until, in an ambush of jewels and
light, he springs upon the hills in surprise attack. The Purple
night cannot hold command of her eastern position and she
shakes out her colors, like a Lady who has spread a midnight
picnic shakes out her cloth and packs up her supper. The ambush
that ends the picnic, and the Musket that hurries the Lady, are
images that depict the encounter of day and night as a battle of
the sexes. The Lady, of course, does not think of confrontation
and retreats, leaving room for Day's full achievement. Then she
reappears with the tactical charm of orderly brightness and
domesticates her Day:

> *How mighty 'twas—to be*
> *A Guest in this stupendous place—*
> *The Parlor—of the Day—*   *(304)*

The purpling of the night's end is one of nature's changes that most captivated Dickinson, who watched nature's beauty and waited on her power. Nature's capacity to mix her colors in a moving spectrum of tonal variations corresponds to the facility with which Dickinson's own consciousness changed mood. This correspondence between color and consciousness[8] was one of the magical relations Dickinson used in her poetry. The hues of nature became the material of her own craft.

> Purple—
>
> The Color of a Queen, is this—
> The Color of a Sun
> At setting—this and Amber—
> Beryl—and this, at Noon—
>
> And when at night—Auroran widths
> Fling suddenly on men—
>
> 'Tis this—and Witchcraft—nature keeps
> A Rank—for Iodine—   (776)

Dickinson especially favored purple, a color that conjured up royal self-consciousness and, more particularly, Queenliness. As we have seen, Dickinson celebrated her own religious Queenliness in poems that immortalized her agony as well as her excellency. She was Empress of Calvary as well as the divine Majority of her own Society. To be a religious personality of such stature required this breadth of consciousness, a capacity to mix her moods with grandeur, and a talent for dramatizing the reversals of her fate.

Purple is the Color of a Queen whose majesty encompasses the Iodine of suffering as well as the widths of dawn. And further, Iodine is not only the mark of suffering, it is a curative chemical as well. Witchcraft—like the art of nature and the craft of poetry as Dickinson experienced them—knows the lore of suffering and the secrets of healing.

> *Witchcraft was hung, in History,*
> *But History and I*
> *Find all the Witchcraft that we need*
> *Around us, every Day—*   *(1583)*

When the nature religion of witchcraft competed with Christianity, witches suffered capital punishment for their heresy. Despite the fact that the Salem trials in 1692 were a late, isolated, and minor episode in the contest between Christianity and paganism, nineteenth-century Americans kept witchcraft alive in their literature, as we have seen. Like other nineteenth-century authors fascinated by witchcraft, Dickinson used witchcraft as a metaphor for religious devotion and for the sexual power of femininity. Dickinson was unique in her unified and self-conscious practice of the arts of metaphor, witchcraft, religious naturalism, and sexual passion. In this concentrated combination, she found all the witchcraft she needed, around her, every day.

Dickinson's religious devotion to the natural world and her practical cultivation of natural arts were, she reported, motivated by the extraordinary power of every day. She believed that witchcraft was accessible to all; first in birth and always in death, everyone experiences the marvels of natural reversal.

> *Witchcraft has not a Pedigree*
> *'Tis early as our Breadth*
> *And mourners meet it going out*
> *The moment of our death—*   *(1708)*

Although encounters with nature's witchcraft may be common and accessible, the conscious imitation of nature and the exercise of magic set witches apart from other people. From Dickinson's point of view, her witchcraft was as much of a complex discipline and heterodox alternative to the dominant religion of Christianity as it had been two centuries earlier. Dickinson used the imagery of witchcraft to describe her own consciousness and to express her rebellion from the institutions and conventions of Christianity. At twenty she had called herself "very sincere, and *wicked*"; in her maturity she applied the symbol-system of witch-

craft to her independent vocation. Witchcraft offered her the
symbolism of an alternative religious tradition in which she
could practice the fullness of her personality, indulge the skepticism others perceived as wicked, and live intimately with spiritual powers that others feared or disbelieved.

Just as Dickinson appropriated domestic consciousness and
transvalued it through solitude, so she assimilated the symbolism of witchcraft and redefined it through her own point of
view. She took the indoor life of domesticity to describe the
experiences of her soul's interior; she took the nature religion of
witchcraft to describe her communion with life outside.

As we have seen in many of her poems, the intense solitude of
her interior life could encompass the universe in feeling. In a
similar move, illustrated in her poem about the encounter of
night and day, Dickinson could take domesticity outdoors. She
enjoyed the miracles of nature for their homeliness and she felt
primly at home in her celebration of a witches' sabbath:

> Some keep the Sabbath going to Church—
> I keep it, staying at Home—
> With a Bobolink for a Chorister—
> And an Orchard, for a Dome—
>
> Some keep the Sabbath in Surplice—
> I just wear my Wings—
> And instead of tolling the Bell, for Church,
> Our little Sexton—sings.
>
> God preaches, a noted Clergyman—
> And the sermon is never long,
> So instead of getting to Heaven, at last—
> I'm going, all along.   (324)

One of the four poems published during Dickinson's lifetime out
of the 1,775 she preserved, "My Sabbath" may have been accepted for publication in 1864 because the coyness of its voice
and conclusions lent itself to the sentimentalism of popular
romanticism. But as her publisher may not have seen, Dickinson

domesticated her world with a mischievous if disarming mixture of irony and sincerity.

It was one thing to refer to an orchard as home and to have the pleasure of God's presence there on a Sunday when more narrow-minded Christians expected him in church—such play at the expense of undomesticated Christianity was a commonplace among sentimental romantics. It was quite another thing to refer to God as a noted clergyman. Dickinson recommended God. She even approved of the brevity of his sermons.

Dickinson's singular achievement as a religious personality was to diminish the conventions of domestic pietism to the proportions of her solitude and then to expand her uniquely domesticated self to the world of nature. This juxtaposition of contraction and expansion not only characterizes her poetry but also suggests a notion of spiritual transformation that may transcend, encompass, and add to our appreciation of the religious experiences characteristic of conversion psychology. If Dickinson's poetry suggests a rule, spiritual transformation is the collision of nature and solitude, of world and home, and of reality and imagination.

Dickinson may have been going to heaven all along, but the nature of her heaven was ambiguous and the way there full of reversals and next to impossible to find.

> *I saw no Way—The Heavens were stitched—*
> *I felt the Columns close—*
> *The Earth reversed her Hemispheres—*
> *I touched the Universe—*
>
> *And back it slid—and I alone—*
> *A Speck upon a Ball—*
> *Went out upon Circumference—*
> *Beyond the Dip of Bell—* (378)

Emily Dickinson's work offers the profoundest illustration of the poetics of feminine spirituality. It is Emily Dickinson who saw clearly that the development of personality was at once an esthetic and religious achievement and who immortalized in poetry the dimensions and development of her own self.

In numerous poems, Dickinson wrote about her encounters and relations with God. Like other women of her time she wrote about love and marriage, home and garden, but her fiction differed from theirs in that her husband, lover, father, son, and minister was God. And in complement to this homely display of divine authority, she canonized her various responses to God as exemplary religious personalities. She included in her gallery of feminine characters her perverse intelligence, her sexual passion, and her desire for authority, portraying a relish for the demonic, for sexuality, and for power that sets her apart from all but a few contemporaries—such as Victoria Woodhull, the anti-heroine, "Mrs. Satan"—and connects her work with the artistry of notable twentieth-century women. The central religious problem of Dickinson's life and the principle source of her creativity was her relation to God, the author and sometime victim of her personality. She wanted both to be God and to be chosen and taken by God and she assumed every role she could imagine in her approach to his authority. As we have seen, the multi-faceted personality revealed in Dickinson's poetry reflects and connects all the exemplary women in this history of feminine spirituality.

Emily Dickinson is the principal personality in a parade of immortal American women. She succeeds those exemplary, black-gowned women who followed their God and men to America and she leads the way for a variously costumed, modern class of esthetically sensitive women. As a recluse in Amherst, Dickinson dressed in white during her mature life, in the symbolic costume of wife of God and holy, virgin mother. As the human mother-God of modern daughters, her personality has been transmitted through a mysterious family of the spirit by a kind of immaculate conception. But her conception of the future is not without spot or color. In the prism of her future, Dickinson's spirit is refracted in a multitude of shades—witches, prostitutes, and suicides; nurses, mothers, and educators; as well as painters, dancers, and poets. Behind these modern daughters of feminine spirituality stands the consummate achievement of Dickinson's personality and, behind that, the bride-consciousness of Puritan saints. To view this colorful succession is to suspect that within the hearts of those distant black-robed women lurked traits of demonic as well as moral beauty. As much as contemporary women practice charms and share dark secrets, so did they. And as much spiritual authority as they commanded, so have their heirs.

Eight

Science, Social Work and Sociology

W Emily Dickinson, Elizabeth Seton, and Victoria Woodhull, each in her different way, stand within the tradition of religious deviancy initiated by Anne Hutchinson. Hutchinson taught that experiences of grace lay at the heart of Christianity. She further believed that her biblical visions were direct revelations from God. The disapproving ministers and magistrates objected to her highly personal interpretation of the Bible and to her assurance of her own authority. Although not all of the mystically inclined deviants in American religious history have been women, there is good reason to link the femininity of Hutchinson, Seton, Woodhull, and Dickinson with their departure from the main-streams of Christianity. The receptive piety associated with femininity could easily take the posture of social submissiveness. But when religious receptivity was filled with an experience of God, social submissiveness might be overturned, replaced by an authoritative point of view that claimed the truth.

Such is the case with Mary Baker Eddy (1821–1911), foundress and charismatic leader of the Church of Christ Scientist. Like other women we have considered, Eddy based her religiousness upon her femininity, cultivating through her suffering and spiritual sensitivity a receptivity to religious experience. Like other women who deviated from conventional Christianity, Eddy claimed for her mystical experiences the power of divine revelation. She stands apart as the most successful religious deviant in American history, as a woman who single-mindedly conceived and constructed a religion of lasting appeal and an institution of remarkable wealth and organization. Her career is particularly instructive because her revelations became authoritative for her community and her mysticism was successfully institutionalized. Early in her career, Eddy's religious practices were perceived as a form of occult spiritualism. Their acceptance, one might say their neo-orthodoxy, was due in part to her legitimation of those religious practices as a science. Eddy established her church during a period of significant cultural transition, and the movement of her career, from a deviant spiritualism to her establishment of Christianity as a scientific religion, indicates one direction that feminine spirituality would take in twentieth-century America.

In their final expression, Eddy's metaphysical doctrines and her practical instructions centered on the affirmations that God is life and that life is a state of mind. The belief that life is Mind offered believers direct participation in the life of God and a perspective that subsumed and explored all other states of mind. In Eddy's theology, God represented the power of love as well as the truth that Mind was all-powerful: Mind is love and nothing but Mind exists. These principles led Eddy to the conclusion that anything contrary to the spirit of love is a mistaken idea. Evil, a false product of minds alienated from God, resulted from the pervasive but erroneous idea that anything other than love is real. Arguing that the idea of evil was always accompanied by belief in the independent existence of the material world, Eddy believed that once matter was granted objective reality, pain and death inevitably followed. Because believing in matter was a mental illness that debilitated its victims with pain and fears of death, Eddy treated sickness and death as symptoms of incorrect thinking. When the delusion that matter was more than mind was dispelled, health and immortality prevailed.[1]

In *Science and Health,* Eddy did not explain why false ideas originate but she was prolific about the nature and recovery of truth. Eddy magnified and connected the sentiments of domestic pietism in a theological system that betrays its origin in both senses of that word. Eddy philosophized and institutionalized the domestic sentiments that God was more mother than father and that women were supremely qualified as mediators of divine inspiration. But in the aggressiveness with which she pursued the logic of feminine religiosity and in the authority she claimed for her revelations and powers, her theology represents a radical departure from the canons of nineteenth-century domestic pietism.

Eddy understood gender as a quality of mind and broadened the Christian definition of God to include femininity. God was Truth and Love: Truth, which corresponded to an idealized paternity, signified that Mind was all-powerful; Love, which corresponded to the nature of motherhood, symbolized the compassion of Mind. In Eddy's theology, Love was the consort of Truth, and Love had more effective power than her spouse: "We have not as much authority for considering God masculine, as we have for considering Him feminine, for Love imparts the clearest idea of Deity." In the glossary of *Science and Health* Eddy defined Mother as "God; divine and eternal Principle; Life, Truth, and Love," an indication that religious life was demonstrated in motherhood and that maternal love sustained and revealed religious truth.[2]

Just as Eddy emphasized the love of God as the maternal and superior aspect of deity, so she stressed Mary's role in Christianity: "The Christ dwelt forever an idea in the bosom of God . . . and woman perceived this spiritual idea." While, on the one hand, Jesus was a "corporeal man," Christ on the other, is an idea—the idea that corporeality is an idea in the Mind of God.[3] It is crucial that Mary was virgin, for her conception was a mental conception. It is also crucial, if paradoxical, for Eddy's theology that Mary's body became a vehicle of divine inspiration. Mary bore the Christ idea in the pure form of the female body: the undefiled body of woman mediated the power of Mind.

The coincidence of Eddy's stress on Mary's sexual purity with her affirmation of the maternal aspect of God shows that mother-love represented the nature of God in a way that linked religion with gender but not with sexuality. The paradoxical, but familiar, equation of religious femininity and sexual chastity shows how Eddy built her religion on the tacit values of domestic pietism. The equation also suggests a resemblance between her theology and the Catholic association of Mary's holiness and her virginity. In addition to these influences, Eddy's religious thought certainly shows the imprint of the Shaker religion, which she came in contact with during her girlhood in New Hampshire. Mother Ann Lee, foundress of the Shaker sect, located the root of human evil in sexual intercourse, and in the communities that lived according to her religious vision, men and women lived celibate and relatively segregated lives. Mother Ann Lee also directed her worship to the feminine dimension of God and regarded herself as the female counterpart to Christ, as the second and final incarnation of God.[4]

Like Mother Ann Lee, but with far more popular and lasting success, Eddy founded a religion based on her own revelation of the feminine principle of God. Eddy compared *Science and Health* to the book of final revelation prophesied at the end of the New Testament. In her reading, "the revelation of divine Science" was foretold in the tenth chapter of Revelation, where a "mighty angel came down from heaven . . . had in his hand a little book open." In Eddy's personal revelation, her book *Science and Health* is the bible within the Bible, the final book of revelation promised in the final Book of *Revelation.* In this fusion of Christian inspiration and her own writing, Eddy carried the intimate association of religion and literature to its logical extreme. Harriet Beecher Stowe had claimed that God wrote *Uncle Tom's Cabin;* Mary Baker Eddy went one step further in her claim that *Science and Health* was the final book of biblical revelation. In this aspect of her religious consciousness, as in so many others, Eddy brought a tendency within feminine spirituality to a final conclusion.

Just as the angel's "little book" is *Science and Health,* St. John's apocalyptic woman represents Eddy herself. In her interpretation of St. John, Eddy called attention to the passage in Revelation 12 in which a woman wonderfully encircled in light "appeared . . . in heaven; a woman clothed with the sun, and the moon under her feet, and upon her head a crown of twelve stars." In Eddy's interpretation this radiant apparition heralds the final integration of divine and human life, "the coincidence of God and man as the divine Principle and divine idea." The woman incarnates the divine principle of motherhood: "As Elias presented the idea of the fatherhood of God, which Jesus afterwards manifested, so the Revelator completed this figure with woman, typifying the spiritual idea of God's motherhood."[5] The principle of motherhood signified that humanity was born as an idea contained within the Mind of God; the apocalyptic revelation of God's motherhood heralds the human realization that the Divine Mind has always contained humanity and promises final reunion.

Mary and the apocalyptic woman were, in Eddy's imagination, the prototypes of her own personality. She incarnated the motherhood of God that had been veiled in the feminine figures of the New Testament. The events prophesied in Revelation offered Eddy an allegory of the history of her revelation of Christian Science, and she believed that Christian theology was consummated in her own life. The woman in Revelation, who conceived a "sweet promise," suffered greatly for her perception. After much "travailing in birth," the woman "brought forth a man child, who was to rule all nations" but who must first escape a ten-horned red dragon that waited to devour him as soon as he was born.[6] Like the woman of Revelation, Eddy herself endured extreme suffering before the birth of her divine idea and battled to protect the life of her idea after it had been revealed to her.

During the first forty-five years of her life, Eddy suffered debilitating back pain, chronic invalidism, economic destitution, a traumatic childbirth experience, the death of one husband, and the adultery and divorce of a second. Eddy experimented with a variety of therapies and medicines and sought out spiritualist solutions to her problems. She became a disciple of Phineas T. Quimby, the brilliant mesmerist who was the foremost American pioneer in the field of mental health and in the philosophy of what came to be called New Thought. Quimby helped Mary Baker Eddy in 1862, healing her severe mental and physical distress and imparting his knowledge to her. Eddy took Quimby's teachings and techniques and interpreted them in the context of Christian images and stories about the healing power of Jesus. Her ideas crystalized when she realized that she had the spiritual power to heal herself. In 1866, she took a severe fall and the medical prognosis was that she would never walk again. Two days later, while reading of Jesus' healings, the power of Mind revealed itself to her. She felt this power directed to her own ailments and she recovered her health—to the astonishment of those around her—within a few days. As the woman in Revelation gave birth to a divine child who was to command all people, so Eddy's mind gave birth to the idea that Mind is life. The physical healing that accompanied the experience revealed the loving power—the maternal compassion—of Mind. Through this momentous childbirth of the spirit, Eddy formulated her conception of God and experienced the full assurance of its truth.[7]

After her integration of the principles of truth and health, Eddy met difficulties that she felt corresponded to the allegorical red dragon with ten horns. During the second forty-five years of her life she faced many obstacles as she struggled to promulgate her faith and institutionalize her authority, as she battled to defend the originality of her theology and to maintain control over her disciples. Most of these disciples were women. In 1895, 80 percent of Christian Science practitioners were women and, as one biographer generalized in 1929: "Mrs. Eddy and her doctrines held few men of outstanding qualities. All of the personal leadership ever exercised in her church was exerted by women." For female disciples of Christian Science, as for Eddy herself, a religion that promised the end of physical suffering and affirmed the wholly spiritual nature of reality offered an avenue to personal and social fulfillment that "the world" did not. But problems arose out of this concentration on women's spiritual leadership. Many of her most gifted followers were, in Eddy's

evaluation, "two-faced" creatures who learned under her tute-
lage to exercise the power of mental healing and then asserted
their own independent authority.[8]

Christian Science attracted many converts because it promised and produced health. Eddy believed that, in their practice of
healing, Christian Scientists had rediscovered the essential spirit
of early Christianity. As a demonstration that Christian Science
offered the healing power of faith, the last hundred pages of
Science and Health present a catalogue of first-person testimonies
of diseases cured and deaths prevented. The power of God's
feminine love resided, in part, in its effectiveness: faith really
healed—as no other medicine could. True Christianity was
pragmatically effective and the motherhood of God could be
scientifically applied.

With spirituality counting for everything, Eddy subsumed
health, wealth, the techniques of bureaucratic organization, and
the practice of scientific objectivity into her religion. By the turn
of the century Christian Science had become a mammoth and
highly centralized denomination in which funds as well as spiritual leadership were effectively recruited and carefully por-
tioned.[9] Eddy erected a church as her successor, her guarantee
that Christian Science would outlast her own lifetime and never
require a second charismatic leader. The imposing architectural
structure of Boston's Mother Church stood as the grand hearth
to a home of national scale. The organizing principles of single-
family stability burgeoned under Eddy's leadership to ecclesiastical proportions. The Church of Christ Scientist grew into a
gigantic house, its organization as efficient and conservative as
its smaller model, the heavenly ideal of the Victorian home.

With the values of maternal religiousness not only on her side
but in her possession, Eddy moved into the world as she moved
against it, appropriating for her church the values and benefits
of science, pragmatism, and organizationalism. Although Eddy
drew on the values of domestic pietism, as she extended them in
the theology and practice of Christian Science she created an
alternative to domestic pietism, a hybrid of absolute idealism and

effective practicality, of maternal power and scientific ingenuity.

Eddy did not introduce American women to the arts of organizational efficiency or healing; since the Puritan era housewives had exercised managerial skills and provided for the most basic wants of their families, including, of course, their health. Following in the path of Catharine Beecher's work to professionalize maternal benevolence and to canonize domestic economy as a practical science, Eddy contributed to feminine spirituality the bureaucratic exercise of organization and practicality and the transformation of healing by womanly faith, prayer, and nursing into an applied science. But while Beecher sought recognition for women by encouraging them to apply their talents beyond the range and legitimation of devotional piety, Eddy created a new religion that subsumed and justified women's professional and scientific skills.

We find Beecher's closer counterpart in Jane Addams (1860–1935), an immensely and deservedly famous woman whose social settlement work combined maternal benevolence with pragmatic professionalism. Where Eddy subsumed organizational techniques into her divine science, Addams translated Christian idealism into the secularized practice of social activism.

From 1877 to 1881, Addams attended Rockford Seminary in Illinois—the Mount Holyoke of the West—where she pursued her education with a zealous idealism. Speaking of her ambition for herself and her world in a graduation oration, she argued "that social evils could only be overcome by him who soared above them into idealism, as Bellerophon, mounted upon the winged horse Pegasus, had slain the earthly dragon."[10] Once out of school, however, Addams discovered that the secular world offered few opportunities to newly educated women who wished to utilize their idealism. Consumed by a sense of her uselessness, she became severely depressed and chronically ill. In 1888, a visit to the London settlement houses of Toynbee Hall and People's Palace sparked her enthusiasm and encouraged her to launch a similar reform experiment in America. In her social thought and in her self-understanding Addams began to realize a "Christian movement toward Humanitarianism."[11] In September of 1889, she became a full member of the Presbyterian Church and moved to Chicago and Hull House.

Reflecting on her season of disillusionment, Addams asserted that a career of social reform was both an objective and a subjective necessity for American college women. The plight of the thousands of immigrants who clogged American cities and lived in substandard conditions presented an objective imperative for reform. The industrial poverty that determined "the objective value of a social settlement" coincidentally provided an outlet for the "subjective necessity" of benevolent activism. The subjective imperative had its source in feminine socialization: from "babyhood" parents encouraged "altruistic tendencies" in their daughters, teachers "deliberately expose[d]" them "to knowledge of the distress of the world," and in the morally intense atmosphere of college, young women learned "the desire for action, the wish to right wrong and alleviate suffering." But once young women left college, parents asserted "the family claim," a claim of "exclusiveness and caution" that contradicted the expansive charity that newly educated women had been prepared to implement. In Addams' analysis, "young girls suffer[ed] and [grew] sensibly lowered in vitality in the first years after they [left] school" because they had no way to express the compassion they had been educated to feel. Addams believed that a "sense of uselessness is the severest shock which the human system can sustain." She argued that widely available opportunities for social usefulness were the only deterrent to the "atrophy of function" prevalent among women.[12]

By 1893, when Addams diagnosed this problem, college education for American women had expanded greatly since the founding of Mount Holyoke in 1837. Although women since Abigail Adams had longed for broader educational opportunities, higher education became widely available to women only in the late nineteenth century. After the Civil War, when female seminaries became accredited colleges, Vassar, Smith, Wellesley, Bryn Mawr, and Radcliffe were established. The first generations of these college women faced unique challenges and their careers transformed women's self-expectations. While the pre-war seminaries were established to train teachers and missionaries, later education focused less insistently on teacher-training and on the transmission of denominational values. Changes in women's education changed women. A Holyoke graduate of 1850 would be expected to become a missionary-teacher; a Vassar woman of 1900 might become a professional, political, feminist woman.

During her career Addams struggled with the relation of idealism to practicality. In college she accepted the definition of woman as one who provides for others, and she aspired to embody her class motto, "The early Saxon for lady, translated into breadgiver."[13] Set apart from the mother-daughter apprenticeship system of the home, and temporarily freed from the practical restraints of maternity and marriage, college women embraced an abstract definition of womanhood. But by definition a lady did not exist in the abstract: the lady was an ideal of practicality. The women who learned the nature of femininity in classrooms and dormitories learned about motherhood as a metaphor. The sanctity of the ideal was not diminished—it was abstracted and expanded. But the college woman found herself unable to fulfill one essential ingredient of the ideal—the imperative to practice. A complex consciousness characterized women of Addams' generation and vision. They inherited the sacred ideal of motherhood and were driven by a subjective necessity to practice it. They reapplied the mother metaphor to political contexts and in doing so helped create a new breed of woman and a secularization of the maternal ideal.

During her career as director of Hull House, Addams reconceived her ideas about the function of a social settlement and the pattern of her revisions reflected her increasing social realism and political pragmatism. Hull House opened with lectures on art to immigrant women but soon after changed its educational emphasis to health and housekeeping. Later, the settlement achieved neighborhood power when residents successfully pressured the city for improved sanitation services, and finally, Hull House attained international recognition when it became known as a center of labor-reform lobbying and political support for workers in unions and on strike. The more Addams accepted political bargaining as her context, the more astute and successful she became as an organizer and political realist. In fact, her tendency to compromise her ideals rather than lose a battle occasionally distanced her from more radical colleagues.[14] To succeed in practice Addams in part dispensed with the mythology that had characterized her early life and motivated her career. Would the cultural idealist have given up teaching art classes? Would Bellerophon have compromised with a ward boss?

Addams' pragmatism transformed her religiousness. Christian compassion and classical idealism had motivated her social philosophy and defined her personal identity. As her objectives became more political and her organizational skills more adept, she secularized her ideals in order to realize them. Addams' mature gospel was a social one, a gospel that transported Christ to city slums and translated the New Testament into a program of social reform. Skeptical of the elitism of private religiosity, Addams dissociated Christian humanitarianism from exclusiveness: "all that is noblest in life is common to men as men." She was impatient with the self-indulgence of pious devotionalism and maintained that Christianity was not "a set of ideas which belong to the religious consciousness, *whatever that may be,* that is proclaimed and instituted apart from the social life of the community." By the canons of Addams' moralism, the gospel "must be put into terms of action" and "Christianity has to be revealed and embodied in the line of social progress."[15]

The first years of the new century were, in the broadest sense of the term, an era of progessivism. For two and a half centuries Americans had seen their land as the rebirthplace of the best of European civilization and now the philosophy of science added a new objectivity to that idealism. Pragmatism, the distinctively American philosophy that achieved explicit articulation at the turn of the century, affirmed an evolutionary idealism in which truth and justice were progressively manifested through history. Here was an objective, practical idealism: as philosopher William James put it, "If we do *our* best, *and* the other powers do *their* best, the world will be perfected."[16] When joined together with the will to believe, the bright light of objectivity promised to diminish injustice and evils. Pragmatism was not a blind optimism; rather its light exposed social inequities. Revolutionaries, feminists, social gospellers, Progressive Republicans and Democrats saw injustice and set to scrub it out.

Despite the fact that her Christian faith was more political than pious, Addams was heralded as "The Only Saint America has ever produced." Journalists compared the women of Hull House to nuns and located the source of their goodwill toward others in "the God-given feminine impulse to help the less fortunate." To be sure, Addams was admired for her practicality and political shrewdness as well as for her dedicated self-sacrifice. As one reporter put it in 1910: "Jane Addams is a blend of the saint and the statesman. . . . She had the purity of life and character and immense capacity for self-sacrifice of the one combined with the facility of looking at things in the large and the knack of securing results of the other."[17]

Addams' popularity epitomized the link between Victorian and progressive values. Whatever her claims to sainthood, the fact of her gender meant that her reform efforts were perceived as expressions of religious self-sacrifice. Essentially religious conventions about the nature and limits of femininity determined Addams' public image until her death in 1935. The story of her fall from popularity after 1915 indicates the power and persistence of those conventions.

When Addams pressed the cause of peace after war broke out in Europe, she exceeded the previously invisible limits of her authority and her public image reversed itself. Her press became uniformly bad and suddenly she became "a silly, vain, impertinent old maid, who may have done good charity work at Hull House, Chicago, but is now meddling with matters far beyond her capacity." Addams had trespassed too far in her practical activism, and in their displeasure with her, Americans reasserted the family's claim on women. The former paragon of American womanhood was now admonished to get herself a "strong, forceful husband." Addams had been America's symbol of Christian harmony, but peace, like piety and womanhood, was an ideal to be extolled as long as its context and impact was confined. As a reporter for the *Nation* interpreted her involvement in a world peace conference, there was a difference between "Jane Addams, of Hull House," and "Jane Addams, of the World." Addams' public virtue seems to have hung on the fact that her sphere of real activity and influence was clearly circumscribed. While only a few years before she had been lauded for her "facility of looking at things in the large," she was now chastized for having lost "her definiteness of vision."

The *Nation's* reporter defined the limits of Addams' usefulness: "Hull House and the work she knew from centre to circumference."[18] In one short phrase the reporter put Addams in her place: the words House, centre, and circumference established the limits of Addams' womanhood. While Emily Dickinson had celebrated precisely those words as she explored the dimensions of her own imagination, selecting her own society and then shutting the door, Addams took the political world as her circumference and attempted to politicize the values of domesticity. In Addams' case, the American public made it clear that it was unnatural for a woman not to confine her ideals. Like Anne Hutchinson and Victoria Woodhull, Jane Addams lost her authority by asserting it publicly.

In the Red Scare that followed the war, Addams' name headed a list of sixty-two "dangerous, destructive, anarchist" Americans submitted to a Senate subcommittee. Her name often figured centrally in the spider-web charts that mapped out American Bolshevism by drawing lines between columns of dangerous public figures and dangerous institutions. On the War Department's first chart there appeared the statement from Lenin that "if Bolshevism fails it will be because we could not get enough women interested."[19] Political conservatives of the 1920's worried over women's susceptibility to Bolshevism for reasons similar to those that had prompted "liberals" of earlier eras to worry that women would succumb to the excessive emotionalism of revivalism or Catholicism.

Jane Addams was far from being either Bolshevist or excessively emotional. She would have no part of the socialist ideologies favored by more radical reformers, and she defended American democracy and capitalism throughout her career. And as an upholder of moral order, Addams was unimpeachably dedicated. At the basis of her sensitivity to the abuses of industrialism lay a concern for the moral welfare of the nation. Her interest in social reform was motivated by her perception that America's urban poor had no opportunity to develop the stable family life from which moral culture sprang.[20]

Addams hardly deserved being attacked for leanings that, if acted upon, would have destroyed the family, sapped women's maternal instincts, and nationalized children. She shared with the anti-suffragists and superpatriots an ultimate commitment to preserve traditional family structures and a deep belief in the social value of maternal sensibilities. Like other social feminists who spoke in favor of women's suffrage—and Addams did so only with much prodding and not until 1897—she believed women's votes would be a means to reform, particularly in the areas of protective legislation for women and children. The real dissent from conventional wisdom was voiced by the militant minority of women who fought for the vote because they demanded political equality, and who, after women's suffrage was established, lobbied and voted for equal rights and against protective legislation.[21]

Hull House was essentially a home, a home where immigrants were integrated into American culture. Although Addams relinquished the pietism of her domesticity, her activities and ideals carried with them the old maternal avenues and obstacles to power that only a generation before had linked Christianity with femininity. Hull House had many rooms and laid many paths to city offices but it remained a home presided over by a matron of moral virtue.

Addams contributed to the home-ideal a scientific interest in the active integration of environment and ideals. In "A Function of the Social Settlement" she argued that a settlement was an environment in which community could take shape, and community was compassionate love for others realized through a structure of social harmony. Borrowing from the pragmatic philosophies of John Dewey and William James, Addams defined a social settlement as "an attempt to express the meaning of life in terms of life itself," which was "forms of activity." Hull House was applied science, "the coalescence of theory and life, the application of the moral code to the material life, the transforming of the economic relation into an ethical relation until the sense that religion itself embraces all relations, including the ungodly industrial relation, has become common property."[22] Addams wedded the spirit of love to an organizational program of environmental reform. The integration of spirit with body, morality with environment, and theory with life was Addams' idea of a social settlement. With great brilliance and vision, she reapplied domestic values to the twentieth-century industrial world.

For women who followed Addams in careers of social service, secular techniques finally outmoded and replaced maternal idealism. During the 1920's and 30's professional social work competed, with increasing success, with settlement work. As with the older-fashioned settlement work, women dominated the field of social work. But social work became a "magnificent and thoroughly perfected machine" with little room for the compassionate volunteer "to indulge her own idiosyncracies at the expense of the work."[23]

Social work became externally unified through a national organization and through professional schools that trained and accredited members. Scientific procedures unified the field internally: case work structured a worker's relation to her "client" and psychological terminology became her specialized language.

Organizational and procedural homogeneity encouraged a professional categorization of both worker and client and discouraged emotional attachment. By emphasizing worker expertise and client psychology, the new profession isolated the worker-client relation from the rest of society. A highly structured individualism replaced the ideal of community that had been so dear to the hearts of earlier reformers. The scientific techniques and bureaucratic organization of a "professional subculture"[24] replaced the religiously motivated, maternal pragmatism of the settlement idea.

Social feminists like Addams advocated equal suffrage on the assumption that the woman's vote would hasten social reform. More radical women activists wanted suffrage because they believed in sexual equality and because they wanted equal vocational opportunities for women like themselves. Radical feminists desired work and recognition outside the home not on the basis of any maternal concern but in the terms of the professions to which they aspired. The problem these women faced was how to be both citizens and women. As attorney Crystal Eastman put it in 1920: "If the first feminist program goes to pieces on the arrival of the first baby, it is false and useless."[25] Though Eastman, and others like her, believed and participated in marriage and motherhood, her statement suggests the tension between radical feminism and common cultural perceptions about femininity. The radical feminists of the progressive era were, like Mrs. Carter in Charles Brockden Brown's *Alcuin*, rationalists. They resisted symbolic interpretations of womanhood, including those that associated spirituality with femininity. In their struggle for vocational equality they disregarded Christian expectations for wives and mothers. They rejected any "feminine mystique" that supposed fundamental differences—beyond the obvious biological ones—between men and women.[26]

Henrietta Rodman, teacher and organizer of the Feminist Alliance, shared Eastman's concern about resolving the tension in values and identity between being a feminist and being a mother. Rodman argued that feminists could be mothers, and mothers feminists, if the spaces and functions of the home were reimagined to streamline maternal responsibilities. In 1914, Rodman designed an apartment building for professional women with families in which living spaces were designed for maximum efficiency and easy cleaning. Professional cooks and launderers, located in a fully mechanized basement, would dispatch food and clean clothing to each apartment by electric elevator and children were to attend classes at a Montessori school on the upper floor.[27]

Rodman's scheme for modern, feminist living was one result of the subjective necessity for social reform that had troubled Jane Addams' college generation. Addams' womanly idealism drove her into the arena of urban reform and she politicized maternal effectiveness in terms of the philosophy of pragmatism and the secular idealism of progressivism. The subjective necessity for active usefulness led Eastman and Rodman to question, which Addams never did, any sex-linked understanding of women's business. Radical feminists like Rodman and Eastman appropriated organizationalism and professionalism not only as techniques for implementing political goals, but as ends in themselves.[28]

Henrietta Rodman planned her apartment house in the progressive spirit of secular efficiency and intelligence. She designed housing space for serious-minded people. She could hardly have anticipated the technological leap that followed World War I—the mass consumption of frozen and packaged food, compact bathrooms, vacuum cleaners, radios, the rituals of installment buying, or the manipulations of massive advertising. Rodman certainly did not foresee the desert of interpersonal intimacy represented by individual frozen dinners eaten before televised images. She wished to throw out the antimacassars and knickknacks that caught dust and diverted a woman's attention, to demythologize the feminine mysteries of cooking and washing, to air out and lighten the overheated and draped temples of maternity, to release the priestess. "Intelligent mothering"[29] would replace the primitive religion of maternal nurture and sentimental romanticism.

Charlotte Perkins Gilman was the philosopher queen of this

movement to free women from the slavery of domestic pietism. Her seminal work, *Woman and Economics* (1899), traced the evolutionary history of women's work. In her analysis of contemporary culture Gilman found that domestic work was gender-specific for conventional rather than biological reasons. She argued that men could perform domestic tasks as well as women and that archaic definitions of gender-specific work retarded the progress of civilization.

In *The Home* (1903), Gilman applied her sociological expertise to contemporary family life and found the ideal of single-family bliss at the core of the self-perceptions of most Americans. She specified the content of that ideal in a sarcastic vignette aimed directly at the values of domestic pietism:

> A beautiful, comfortable house meeting all physical needs; a happy family, profoundly enjoying each other's society; a father, devotedly spending his life in obtaining the wherewithal to maintain this little heaven; a mother, completely wrapped up in her children and devotedly spending her life in their service, working miracles of advantage to them in so doing; children, happy in the home and growing up beautifully under its benign influence—everybody healthy, happy, and satisfied with the whole thing.

Gilman also found that the realities of domesticity contradicted the ideal, although that disparity was "studiously concealed from casual observation." The actual conditions of domestic life involved financial anxiety, inadequate sanitation, unhealthy children, and psychologically distressed parents, in short" a degree of unhappiness to which the divorce and ciminal courts, as well as insane asylums and graveyards, bear crushing testimony."[30]

In Gilman's analysis, religion was to blame for this mystification of the facts. The religious power of the myth of happy home life exerted such enormous power over the minds of Americans that it prevented them from admitting to the disappointments and unhealthy conditions that actually characterized family life. In her sociological evaluation, the essential functions of domesticity were simply to maintain health and comfort and to provide a stable context for reproduction. These functions, common to all animal life, had acquired religious status during the course of human history. Unfortunately, archaic religious concepts remained operative in contemporary home life even though they were undemocratic and unsuited to modern civilization. The "home-sanctity idea" perpetuated ancient rituals of ancestor worship. "Sex-seclusion" and the primitive "harem-idea" shrouded the modern home with the "feeling of mystery and 'tabu,' of 'the forbidden'—a place shut and darkened—wholly private." The cult of domesticity centered on the "dogma of 'the maternal instinct,'" a "nature-myth," Gilman commented, "far older than humanity."[31] But "milk and eggs" merited no special religious aura: Gilman was convinced that the deification of maternity prevented women from exercising the full range of their capabilities as human beings.

Gilman defined instinct as "inherited habit" and assumed that the habits that structure human behavior and perception were open to scientific scrutiny and reform. Just as the "great phallic religions" of ancient nations had been left behind, contemporary culture should overcome its blind worship of motherhood. Gilman did not dispense with religion; she only suggested that it be modernized along with the rest of civilization. Christian love might have its origins in the home, where a child begins life, but to remain Christian and avoid falling into selfishness and ignorance, religion must journey out of the home and fully enter the modern world. Changes in religious practices and beliefs should accompany the evolution of Truth, and the future success of Christianity—and democracy—demanded unflagging commitment an enlightened society. Gilman called for an "erect and open-eyed" worship of the future.[32]

To the epigram of her book—"Shall the home be our world— or the world our home?"—Gilman answered that the world was our home. Like her great-aunt Catharine Beecher, Gilman encouraged women to enter professional careers, and she worked to restructure the home as a full-fledged member-institution of democratic civilization. But Gilman's scientific feminism took her far beyond her great-aunt's domestic science. Gilman wished to thoroughly expunge the home-sanctity idea and debunk all beliefs in the religious superiority and privileged moral perspective of women.

The developments we have traced—from the sentimental belief that home was like heaven and more religiously authoritative than a church, through Eddy's maternal science and Addams' maternal politics, to Rodman's feminist apartment and Gilman's sociology of the home—show how sacred qualities were attributed to domestic space, then abstracted in an application of domestic values to more public spaces, and finally subtracted from domestic space altogether. For sentimental Christians the home had functioned as the private church of each family. In Eddy's theology mother-love was not confined to single-family dwellings, but the home did symbolize the sacred space in which the idea of love was actualized: to Eddy, home was "the dearest spot on earth, and should be the centre, though not the boundary of our affections." Eddy simply institutionalized domestic pietism on an ecclesiastical scale, establishing her church as a home large enough to accomodate her extended family. In her "Temple"—"the shrine of Love . . . where mortals congregate to worship"[33]—Eddy not only expanded the space of the home but transformed its functions as well, incorporating her religion as a business organization and an educational institution that instructed members in the science of healing.

Taking domestic pieties one step further, Jane Addams established Hull House as a "Cathedral of Humanity."[34] Like Eddy she constructed a public institution modeled on the spaces and functions of private homes, but in her institutionalizing of domestic pietism, religious sentiments bowed to the priorities of political programs. As a home for Chicago's immigrants, Hull House transmitted the values of American culture and provided an outlet for the exercise of maternal virtue. But as her career and her institution became recognized in the public sphere, Addams found herself at once a moral critic and a professional representative of the values of her culture. This proved to be a contradictory situation; when she used the success of Hull House as a platform for her moral indignation, her authority was discredited. The professional responsibilities of the women who followed Addams into careers of social work were simplified—and restricted—to facilitating their clients' socialization. The sacred space of the settlement home was secularized as was the purpose of social service. Insofar as social workers were concerned, the dilemma Jane Addams faced between being a reformer or a representative of American society was resolved in favor of the latter. The relation Jane Addams revealed between educated American women and the moral energy of social reform was a spiritual relation, depending on the recognition that both femininity and moral virtue were grounded in religious experience and values. The tragedy of Jane Addams' story is that the success of the settlement idea involved the loss of the spiritual context out of which it originated, a loss that diminished the lives of women social workers as well as the prospects for social reform in America.

Henrietta Rodman, interested in easing the domestic responsibilities of professional women, reconceived the spaces and functions of the home as a maximally efficient and fully serviced apartment building. In Rodman's design, home life was not only stripped of any religious implications but restructured to require a minimum of attention. Although one might well be sympathetic to the wish to free women from work they find oppressive, the reductiveness of Rodman's domestic psychology offered a dull alternative to sentimental elaborations. One need only recall Emily Dickinson's imaginative cultivation of sacred space to appreciate the spiritual potential of domestic consciousness.

Charlotte Perkins Gilman shared many of Rodman's feminist assumptions, and she was accurate in her assessment that religious mythology was responsible for the domestication of woman and the femininity of home life. In her "erect and open-eyed" worship of the future she saw no need for sacred spaces that offered room for the mysteries of grace. But the product of her imagination was not, as it was with Rodman, a design for an unholy apartment building, but rather a piece of fiction that told the story of a woman driven mad when her home became a prison of meaninglessness. The next chapter discusses Gilman's short story of madness and the psychological traumas that followed the secularization of home life. Gilman's story about madness will illustrate the painful cultural transition into the twentieth century in which Christianity lost much of its feminine power. In our new age, American women have recovered sacred space, grace, and feminine spirituality apart from Christian theology.

Nine

Changing the Space Inside a Room

In the short story "The Yellow Wall Paper" (1891), Charlotte Perkins Gilman created a nameless heroine who suffers from "temporary nervous depression—a slight hysterical tendency." She has just given birth to a child, and her husband, a physician, prescribes rest. He arranges a summer retreat to "ancestral halls" enclosed by "hedges and walls and gates that lock," where he assigns his wife to an upper room, once a nursery, with barred windows and a bedstead nailed to the floor. The room grows on the woman, merging with her consciousness, and her nervous symptoms increase. But the more hysterical she becomes, the more often she is sent to her room to rest.[1]

The room is hideously yellow, even to its smell. Outdoors "everything is green instead of yellow," but the woman's room excludes that "delicious" color. The bedroom is her prison, the room where she grows to identify with the yellow of rottenness—not the yellow of buttercups, but of "old, foul, bad yellow things." The sex-seclusion idea has overripened the maternal instinct and the fertility of femininity has become fetid. Shut up in an ancient nursery, the woman becomes hysterical with decay. She is as far away from productive accomplishment as she is alienated from nature's greenery. There may once have been a time when domestic consciousness offered contentment, but this woman's feminine sensibilities have been spoiled by overcultivation and the deeper passions of her soul have been ruined by neglect. "Greenhouses" had once been built on the grounds, but "they are all broken now."[2]

177

Just as the woman feels suffocated by the color of her room, in the designs of the wallpaper she finds busyness—the cruel delusion of work. The "sprawling flamboyant patterns committing every artistic sin" obsess her imagination and consume her time. The woman's daily pattern-tracing is the housework of meaninglessness, "dull enough to confuse the eye in following, pronounced enough constantly to irritate and provoke study." The woman's work becomes a mirror of herself, and in her mirror she studies her self-destruction: the "lame uncertain curves" of the pattern repeatedly and "suddenly commit suicide—plunge off at outrageous angles, destroy themselves in unheard of contradictions."[3]

Upon reflection the woman discovers body parts in the design, "a recurrent spot where the pattern lolls like a broken neck and two bulbous eyes stare at you upside down." As her attention moves from the design itself to the meaning of the design, from surface pattern to deeper reality, she detects, ever more clearly, another woman "skulk[ing] about behind that silly and conspicuous front design," and she is drawn deeper inside the pattern. The hidden woman, like a crazy baby locked in a nursery, "crawls around fast, and her crawling shakes [the pattern] all over." The woman behind the walls demands increasing attention and soon she lurks everywhere, like the fog that "creeps all over the house" and "gets into my hair." One day she appears outdoors, where the first woman identifies her immediately—"most women do not creep by daylight." The first woman is not yet brave enough to parade herself openly inside out—"I always lock the door when I creep by daylight."[4]

When the once-hidden woman takes to crawling all day, returning by moonlight to shake and move through the pattern, the first woman sleeps during the day and awakens at night to help the other move through and inhabit her own body. As they develop the ability to change the space inside the room, the two women become one. The hidden woman, a figure of the imagination, becomes the only woman. On her last day in the country house she locks the door, throws the key out the window, finishes tearing the paper off, and wonders "if they all come out of that wall-paper as I did?" To be finally free, she ties herself to the bed with a rope. When her husband threatens to enter with an ax, she knows "it would be a shame to break down that beautiful door!" and directs him to a single green leaf that lies outside on the ground covering the key. When he returns with the key and opens her door she tells him from the floor where she is crawling, "I've got out at last . . . And I've pulled off most of the paper so you can't put me back!"[5]

Gilman's story portrays the familiar connection between a woman's subjective life and the space she inhabits. But if the connection is familiar, the horror of it is not. In Gilman's story a family home no longer establishes a woman's vocation but simply, and meaninglessly, her confinement. The space inhabited by Gilman's protagonist at once imprisons her soul and mirrors its very nature. A conventionally agreed-upon characteristic of woman's nature was her depth of soul—her access to instincts and feelings, images, and her empathy for others—but for Gilman's protagonist, feminine subjectivity is as small and tight as her yellow room. The dimensions and elements of her soul are as flat and repetitive as her wallpaper's designs. Her insanity is a mockery of spiritual depth. In the mad movement of her subjectivity she is a pathetic creature—not because she lives out a fantasy, but because her fantasy is at once so mean and so self-destructive.

When domesticity was experienced religiously, women could enjoy the practice of moral virtue and find grace at home. But when the religious dimension of home life had drained away, as it had for Gilman, the spiritual depth assumed to characterize femininity became a false expectation veiling the emptiness of a woman's lot. In the name of realism and in a desire for freedom, Gilman believed it essential to expose and discredit the environmental determinism that victimized women.

During her own marriage Gilman suffered nervous depression, an unspecified but not uncommon ailment among middle and upper-class women, and after the birth of her child she became severely withdrawn. Whether or not she experienced the same radical dissociation as the woman in "The Yellow Wall Paper," one may fairly conclude that she drew on her own experience of depression to create the portrait of a woman gone mad. Gilman emerged from her ordeal fit enough to write a short story, and when that was written and her marriage ended, she moved toward an aggressive and pragmatic feminism. Her subsequent sociological work reflected an objective perspective on her old domestic world. The scientific detachment of sociology must have offered a welcome alternative to the self-destructive prison of subjectivity and, in the context of her own depression and will to recover, the dedication with which she exposed and discredited the pietism of domesticity seems admirable. Gilman found emotional health and vocational fulfillment in a discipline that freed her from the closed intuitive living associated with femininity and enabled her to debunk the myths and rituals of domestic pietism.

Imprisonment in the values and spaces of home life is a central theme in the fiction written by Gilman's contemporaries. Female protagonists created by Edith Wharton, Kate Chopin, Neith Boyce, and Susan Glaspell long for a self-knowledge they cannot attain and live with despair (or die on account of it) because their lust for freedom cannot effectively counter their domestication. Edith Wharton merits particular attention because of her persistent use of domestic space to structure her fiction and to describe herself.

Interior spaces are the root metaphors of Wharton's fiction. She portrayed the personalities, self-reflections, and development of her female characters in terms of their responses to the space they inhabit. With the finely tuned language characteristic of her style, Wharton detected and conveyed the subtle domestication of the feminine psyche. And the brilliance of her work reflects the sharpness with which she examined and the ease with which she indulged the inner spaces of her own consciousness. In a passage that merits quotation, her biographer, R. W. B. Lewis, suggests that a preoccupation with domestic space identifies and connects the woman and her work.

> Wharton had a profound addiction, sometimes
> amounting to an obsession, with enclosed as against
> unbounded spaces; with houses themselves . . . ,
> the arrangement of rooms within houses,
> the make-up of properly designed gar-
> dens. . . . Elements like these were habitual
> sources of metaphor in her fiction. When it is added
> that those metaphors were almost invariably used to
> describe the inner nature of women . . . we reach a
> point of speculation: Edith Wharton's intense, con-
> tinuing interest in enclosures may quite likely be
> another register of her alertness to her own de-
> veloping nature as a woman.[6]

Like Gilman and other creative women, Wharton experienced debilitating periods of depression. During a nervous collapse early in her career as a serious fiction writer, she regained some of her energy by collaborating with architect Ogden Codman on *The Decoration of Houses* (1897). Their book offered descriptive models for room design in an expensive, urban house and advised readers how to blend esthetic with functional decorating. *The Decoration of Houses* aimed to reform the "exquisite discomfort" of dark and cluttered townhouses like the one presided over by Lucretia Jones, the mother of the exquisitely sensitive and unhappy child Edith.[7] Although Wharton's philosophy of interior design did not correspond to Henrietta Rodman's notion of household efficiency, it did center in a functionalism that abhorred distractions and clutter. As an upper-class artist interested in pleasure as well as convenience, Wharton's theories wedded beauty to use. By paying attention to the relation between space and light she showed how one might decorate a home to encourage both social intercourse and self-reflection.

Wharton's first major fictional success, *The House of Mirth* (1905), revealed that houses decorated by the rich could have the gaiety of a nightmare. The book takes its title from the verse in Ecclesiastes, "The heart of fools is like a house of mirth." In this masterfully structured novel, the heroine identifies herself with her opulent, artifical surroundings, and when she is forced to leave them she finds she has no heart of her own and little capacity to establish a new living space for herself. In novels since *Charlotte Temple,* heroines have faced the sad choice between beauty and freedom, their beauty shining or deteriorating according to the spaces they inhabit, their beauty set off or sunken by the people they mirror, their hearts never managing to be really free. Wharton pursues this theme with an artfulness that penetrates the heroine's beauty to her heart and finds it small, shallow, terrorized, and suicidal. *The House of Mirth* portrays a funhouse where the mirrors of other people's perceptions distort beauty and burn the soul; it is a house of velvet horrors where self-reflection is put off until it is too frightening to be attempted and too late for integrity. Wharton's *House of Mirth* explores the end of Victorian politeness and the realization that the adulation of feminine beauty could deny women the experience of a soul.

As the story is told, the beautiful, impoverished, and socially ambitious Lily Bart is given room and allowance by her Aunt Peniston, whose Fifth Avenue townhouse externalizes her dreary, wealthy, and maximally secure self. Complacently satisfied by her virtue and wealth, Mrs. Peniston "keeps her imagination shrouded, like drawing-room furniture," and she is as uninterested in freedom as she is displeased by sunshine and spontaneity. Her house is a house of prose—as in Emily Dickinson's poem about the bird in the cage and the girl in the closet—where laughter and freedom, and poetry and imagination, are treated as treason. Though she is surely not a creative homemaker, Mrs. Peniston's diligence and scrutiny are exemplary. Fall cleaning provides her with "the domestic equivalent of a religious retreat.":

> She "went through" the linen and blankets in the precise spirit of the penitent exploring the inner folds of conscience; she sought for moths as the stricken soul seeks for lurking infirmities. The top-

most shelf of every closet was made to yield up its
secret, cellar and coalbin were probed to their dark-
est depths and, as a final stage in the lustral rites,
the entire house was swathed in penitential white
and deluged with expiatory soapsuds.[8]

Mrs. Peniston cleans her house as if it were a guilty soul and
she the stern examiner. She is the conscience who keeps her
house in order. Wharton uses this housecleaning language in the
spirit of her contemporaries who crusaded for political reform.
In her anger at dirty politicians, Frances Willard, president of the
American Women's Christian Temperance Union, threatened
that "women would come into government and purify it, into
politics and cleanse its Stygian pool, for women will make home-
like every place on this round earth."[9] Wharton returns the
metaphor to the home, and in Aunt Peniston's case, the fall ritual
assumes the moral force of a crusade against evil.

Mrs. Peniston and her niece are quite a twosome. While the
aunt finds satisfaction in the moral security of her parlor, Lily
has a "streak of sylvan freedom" as if "she were a captured dryad
subdued to the conventions of the drawing room." Lily is beautiful, graceful and vain. She finds her aunt's house claustrophobic
and her aunt's moral energy rigid, over-demanding, and bother-
some. Mrs. Peniston wants to be clean, Lily Bart wants to be free.

Through the character of Lily Bart, Wharton shows how
tragic the connection between heart and house could be. Lily's
admirers perceive her beauty as at once the perfection of decoration and the mysterious essence of loveliness itself. Lily adds
natural grace to the opulent artifice of the interiors she inhabits.
But, as the male protagonist Lawrence Seldon puts it, "she must
have cost a great deal to make." Her natural beauty, the symbol
of what money cannot buy, only blooms in the affluence of her
surroundings. Even Lily "could not figure herself as anywhere
but in a drawing room diffusing elegance as a flower sheds
perfume."[10]

Lily is like a bird kept in a "great gilt cage," and she knows it.

She realizes that her soul has been captured and some part of her longs to escape: "How alluring the world outside the cage appeared to Lily, as she heard its door clang upon her!" She knows that, if she wills it, she is free to escape: "In reality, as she knew, the door never clanged: it stood always open." But she also recognizes how difficult it is for a woman to abandon the environment that contains her, even if it is unnatural and restricting: "most of the captives were like flies in a bottle, and having once flown in, could never regain their freedom."[11]

Lily's charm enchants others but she cannot act on the freedom that haunts her own soul. Although her soul longs for freedom, her will is weak. She has no access to inner strength and "gasp[s] for air in a little black prisonhouse of fears." Lily "can't bear" reflecting on her emptiness or on the ugly fears that inhabit her soul any more than she could "imagine looking into [her] glass some morning and seeing a disfigurement." Without realizing it until the process is accomplished, she has allowed herself to become the product of other people's imaginations just as she has identified herself with her mirror image. Confronted with the disgrace of having spurned too many suitors, lost heavily in gambling, and displeased wealthy friends on whom she depends even as she disdains them, she is as helpless and frightened as if her mirror had shown her ugliness. Having seen that she has become an object of displeasure, "Lily went up to her own room and bolted the door." But Lily has no real room of her own. Solitary for the first time, she finds only a small, sad space. "The last door of escape was closed—she felt herself shut in with her dishonor."[12]

Lily endures a pathetic retreat down the social ladder, finally finding employment as a decorator of ladies' hats. Before she takes a fatal overdose of sleeping medicine in her spare boardinghouse room, she visits Seldon and asks him to keep the Lily Bart who was fascinated by freedom. She assures him "she'll be no trouble, she'll take up no room."[13]

As the creator of Lily Bart, Edith Wharton is not to be confused with her heroine. Wharton was born to wealth and social rank. She retained her wealth despite a manic husband who tried to spend it all and, later, she retained her social position despite a divorce. Also in contrast to the sad history of Lily Bart, Wharton achieved literary fame and found in her art a vocation that was spiritually engaging and fulfilling. Her art gave her both the freedom to explore many rooms of herself and the security to establish an unassailable serenity.

In *A Feast of Words,* her biography of Wharton, Cynthia Wolff considers the relation between Wharton's development as an artist and the history of her characters and plots. Wolff shows how Wharton became an accomplished writer of credible fiction as she learned to separate herself from the characters and plots in her books. To create characters who were different from herself, who had experiences and ideas other than her own, she had to learn to formulate those characters as distinct personalities observed by her mind's eye.[14] Wharton's own personality included one or two characteristics represented in Aunt Peniston as well as others represented by Lily Bart. Wharton urged her characters to completion and probed their failures much as a religious soul might set her spiritual goals and work to accomplish them, then count up her failings and mete out compensating punishments. But Wharton created her characters as much as she experienced them. She is an accomplished author because she transcended and controlled the characters she crafted in her own image.

Wharton imagined her environments as she imagined her characters. Throughout her life she managed the spaces she inhabited as a way of visualizing moods and controlling depressions. Wharton characteristically packed up and moved during times of stress and creative barrenness. She built, bought, or redecorated houses as if to help satisfy her need for the rearrangement or acquisition of mental furniture. And, conversely, she used domestic imagery to confess her own states of mind. When she portrayed herself as a house, she visualized her soul as constructed of solid walls that secured her privacy. She also imagined herself as having hospitable outer rooms built to receive visitors and to enjoy and entertain friends. In a letter written in 1918 to a friend suffering depression, Wharton offered the decoration of psychological interiors as a panacea for emotional health:

> I believe I know the only cure, which is to make one's centre of life inside of one's self, not selfishly or excludingly, but with a kind of unassailable serenity—to decorate one's inner house so richly that one is content there, glad to welcome any one who wants to come and stay, but happy all the same in the hours when one is inevitably alone.[15]

In the living of her own life, Edith Wharton's own experiences of freedom and spiritual power far exceeded those she allowed Lily Bart or Mrs. Peniston. And like some of her predecessors in feminine spirituality, Wharton was not unfamiliar with the freedom of ecstasy. In a poem she called "Terminus," Wharton recorded a distinguished moment of her life, a night spent in a railway station hotel with her lover. In this poem Wharton imagines her environment as the expression of her heart. She speaks within the tradition of domestic consciousness and follows this feminine consciousness of space to its mystical depths. The ordinary space of a railway station hotel is transformed by her heart into a temple of religious love.

> *Wonderful was the long secret night you gave me, my Lover,*
> *Palm to palm breast to breast in the gloom. The faint red lamp*
> *Flushing with magical shadows the common-place room of the*
> *   inn,*
> *With its dull impersonal furniture, kindled a mystic flame*
> *In the heart of the swinging mirror . . .*
> *And the low wide bed, as rutted and worn as a high-road,*
> *The bed with its soot-sodden chintz, the grime of its brasses,*
> *   . . . —perchance it has also thrilled*
> *With the pressure of bodies ecstatic, bodies like ours,*
> *Seeking each other's souls in the depths of unfathomed caresses,*

> *And through the long windings of passion emerging again to*
> *the stars . . .*
> *And lying there hushed in your arms, as the waves of rapture*
> *receded,*
> *And far down the margin of being we heard the low beat of the*
> *soul,*
> *I was glad as I thought of those others, the nameless, the many,*
> *Who perhaps thus had lain and loved for an hour on the brink*
> *of the world,*
> *Secret and fast in the heart of the whirlwind of travel . . .*
> *Thus may another have thought; thus, as I turned, may have*
> *turned*
> *To the sleeping lips at her side, to drink, as I drink there,*
> *oblivion.* [16]

In "Terminus," Wharton becomes involved in a kind of mystical democracy as she thinks of the travelers who had slept in the same bed before her. The poem is sympathetic to the spirit of Walt Whitman, whom Wharton regarded as America's greatest poet.[17] The coincidence of sexual and mystical ecstasy in the worn and grimy room of an inn offers an experience of embodied spirituality far removed from the great gilt cage and precious drawing rooms that imprisoned Lily Bart. The fusion of sexuality and spirituality, and the portrayal of an ecstatic oblivion, hark back beyond Whitman to Anne Bradstreet's poem that associates the moment of death with the ravishing power of a divine lover. Wharton's lover, Morton Fullerton, functions in this poem as Christ functioned for Anne Bradstreet, enabling her spiritual transformation as a glorious body in "the long secret night" he "gave" her.

The power of the poem involves the spiritual transformation of the room that accompanies the transformation of a woman's self. The "magical shadows" from the "faint red lamp . . . kindled a mystic flame/In the heart of the swinging mirror." Hearts of fire are reflected everywhere. In a night of passion, a "common-place room" is transformed into a sacred space. This sacred space has become an *axis mundi* where heaven and earth meet,[18] where the stars become accessible and "the low beat of the soul" can be heard "far down the margin of being."

In a variety of different mediums, other twentieth-century artists experimented with techniques to help them express such collisions of extraordinary and ordinary reality. The explosion of modern art in America can in part be understood in terms of the vision in Wharton's "Terminus" in which a common experience in an even more common space vibrates with the color, form, feeling, and movement of the whole cosmos.

Ten

Modern Grace

W Across the range of modern art in America no medium was more responsive to Wharton's experience of the relation between one's heart and one's space than the medium of dance. The new art form of "modern" dance carried the spatial consciousness characteristic of feminine spirituality to a new level of expression.

America's early modern dancers aimed to recover the spiritual awareness of ordinary reality that they believed characterized primitive cultures. These artists perceived a primitive element in modern life and they celebrated it in their work. They imagined that the modern world could be rejuvenated if dance, and other related arts, were recognized for their ancient and original religious power. In primitive cultures, spaces that are holy are often places where sacred dancing is performed; in the search for the space that spirituality required for self-awareness and for clarity of expression, the pioneers of modern dance found that the confined space of a studio or theater offered a room that could be transformed with imagination, passion, and power.

In the philosophy of pioneer choreographer Martha Graham, modern dance aimed to provide what was most essential and most neglected in contemporary life, "to send the spectator away with a fuller sense of his own potentialities and the power of realizing them, whatever the medium of his activity." She invested the new art with the responsibility of reviving the spiritual vitality of America: "The dance can and must be a powerful

189

influence. . . . We must look to America to bring forth an art as powerful as the country itself. We look to the dance to evoke and offer life." In Graham's neo-primitive eyes, the dancer had a special, priestly role to play in mediating this new spirituality. She considered the true dancer "a divine normal" whose vocation was to offer viewers a performance of their own humanity.[1]

Modern dancers offered their art as the epitome of life, as an art that communicated not only meanings and moods but the nature of life itself. Dance gave time to space, mind to body, and self to others. Embodying rhythm in space gave structure to space without ever letting space stand still. The confined space of a theater or studio contained an infinite potential for form and transformation, and the dancing soul commanded a freedom that moved that space. Further, dance gave body to soul, not transcending emotion or abandoning intellect, but embodying both. Every step or turn taken, every head movement, arched foot, or arm's reach was at once a feeling and an act of knowledge. A dancer's soul was, exactly and literally, a sensitive, intelligent body. Finally, dance gave self to others. As Graham put it, "A dancer's world is the heart of man with its joys and hopes and fears and loves." Although a dancer's performance was far removed from the self-sacrifice associated with moral virtue, a dancer's gift of grace extended the self toward others in an effort to communicate the heart of life.

Modern choreographers proclaimed as truths that the soul is embodied and that movement through space expresses personality and creates community. To realize these claims, and to claim the attention of their culture, they revolted against the formulas and fairy tales of ballet. The creators of modern dance strove for an esthetic that probed for the essence of vitality in a reflection of the stark realities of contemporary life. Graham attributed the primitivism of her style to her desire to experiment with the bare essentials of human existence. "Like the modern painters and architects, we have stripped our medium of decorative unessentials. Just as fancy trimmings are no longer seen on buildings, so dancing is no longer padded. It is not 'pretty' but it is much more real."[2]

In her revolt against the sentimental elaborations of ballet, Graham worked against cloying decoration. In her own mode she shared this enterprise with Henrietta Rodman, Charlotte Gilman, and Edith Wharton. Rodman wanted living space cleared of disfunctional distractions; Gilman wanted living space stripped of mythical sentimentality. Wharton's philosophy of interior design stressed the beauty of simple functionalism, and, as we have seen, she experienced the relation between space and freedom in a multiplicity of ways. In her effort to isolate and motivate the most primitive physical and psychological building blocks, Graham approached the relation between space and self-expression at a different level. Regarding the body as the condition of human freedom, she asked her dancers and her audiences to recognize the body as the geography of the soul. Although self-expression was only achieved by disciplining the body and structuring space, the goal of dance was neither structure nor discipline but freedom. "No animal," she remarked in 1926, "ever has an ugly body until it is domesticated."[3]

Submission to discipline for the sake of freedom summarizes Graham's philosophy of dance. She insisted that it took ten years to make a dancer: "It takes the pressure of time so that [a] body can hold its divine tenant." If Graham's dance theory is finally a theology, it is a theology brought firmly down to earth: "The dancer is realistic. His craft teaches him to be. Either the foot is pointed or it is not. And no amount of dreaming will make it so." In the years spent in the studio the dancer was trained to "submit [the self] to the demands of [the] craft," a craft dedicated simply and concretely to "the material of the self." When the material of the self was finely tuned and "a dancer is at the peak of his power," Graham believed that there were "two lovely, fragile . . . things at his disposal, spontaneity . . . and simplicity." The discipline that prepared for spontaneity and cultivated simplicity—"the state of complete simplicity costing no less than everything"—could yield a performer whose heart was at once submissively receptive to deep currents of feeling and confident enough to communicate personality to others: "You dance for the first time when you are able to hold the stage and dance with clarity the deep matters of the heart." Dance, like life itself, was "the privilege of the instant—but," she added, "we have so little time to be born to the instant."[4]

The ecclectic expressionism of Isadora Duncan and Ruth St. Denis preceded the modern dance created by St. Denis' students, Martha Graham and Doris Humphrey. Both Graham and Humphrey developed new vocabularies of dance, new techniques of movement, and new principles of balance. Graham based her movement style on pelvic tension and muscular contractions that sculpted the body in angles of power and in curves that cradled space. Humphrey, whose personality was less demonstrative and whose influence on the devleopment of modern dance was more subtle, built her technique out of natural falls, rises, and circles and found new ways to embody a sensitivity to the correspondence between humanness and nature, new ways to express the world of the body and to experience the body of the world.[5]

In 1932, Humphrey wrote that "there is only one thing to dance about: the meaning of one's personal experience and this experience must be taken in its literal sense as action. . . . Art, like religion, is based on events: physical manifestations which have been lived through and therefore represent action, emotion."[6] In her consideration of the relation between art and religion, Humphrey stressed the experiential nature of both. What modern dance offered Americans was ritual, a form of cultural expression that acted out in public performance the personal experiences of its viewers. Many religions, especially "primitive" ones, have found ritual expression through dance. The choreographers of modern dance gleaned meaningful patterns in the personal lives of their contemporaries and worked to formalize those patterns in the art of dance.

In a sense a dance performance is not what modern Americans commonly understand to be a religious ritual. Although a dance may be performed many times by the same dancers and qualify as a ritual for them, viewers may be expected to see a dance only once and this seems to disqualify modern dance from being any kind of ritual for viewers. And yet, in a more fundamental sense, ritual refers to the formalization of human activity and emotion. A choreography interprets ordinary life in formal patterns invested with symbolic weight and performed as if they could be repeated. A particular dance might be seen only once and still qualify, in the eyes of a viewer, as a religiously significant formal expression of human activity.

Modern dance offered a reformulation not only of ritual but of grace. The critic who predicted that if Graham were to give birth "it would be to a cube" may have been insensitive to her modern style of grace. As Graham explained herself, "Grace in dancers is not just a decorative thing. . . . Grace means . . . the beauty your freedom, your discipline, your concentration and your complete awareness have brought you."[7] Her definition of the beauty of complete awareness echoes Jonathan Edwards' philosophy of the beauty of holiness. And for Graham as for Edwards, grace was always accompanied by an arduous discipline. Grace was something one prepared for with the material of the self. But even after years spent in a dance studio or pouring over Scripture, it came as a gift. When Edwards and earlier Puritans spoke of the radical freedom of grace, they meant that no amount of work could compel grace and that an individual could never manufacture grace but only prepare for the experience of it. Grace was like the energy of light, available to all, possessed by no one. The radical freedom of grace also meant that to receive grace was to be free, to experience freedom from self-analysis as well as from self-alienation. In its privileged instant, grace was being at home in the universe in a state of complete awareness and integration. In this state of embodied spirituality an individual could exert tremendous power over others. The recipient of grace communicated grace much as a performer at the peak of power speaks with clarity the deep matters of the heart.

Grace means beauty. Martha Graham said it and so did Jonathan Edwards. Graham redefined beauty, releasing it from the cliche's and confinements of prettiness, and exposed its power. Edwards redefined religion, releasing it from the conventions of moral virtue, and exposed its beauty. Edwards' theology was finally an esthetic. Graham's esthetic was finally a theology. Despite the differences in their lives and languages, Graham and Edwards are joined across centuries by their celebration of the *experience* of grace.

Religious images and dilemmas dominated Graham's work. Descended from Miles Standish, she described her "people" as "strict religionists who felt that dancing was a sin." One might well interpret Graham's work as introducing the art of dance to her Puritan heritage. Critics described the stark strength of Graham's early dance group as puritanical. Her focus on the power and centrality of the will, and the determinism that shaped the narratives of her major choreographies, parallelled Puritan psychology. A center episode in "American Document" (1938) was titled "The Puritan," a duet for Graham and Eric Hawkins accompanied by lines from Edwards' sermons and the Song of Solomon. "Death comes hissing like a fiery dragon with the sting on the mouth of it" preceded the biblical phrase "Let him kiss me with the kisses of his mouth / For thy love is better than wine." Graham's biographer interprets the conjunction of Edwards and the Song of Solomon as "New England Puritanism versus lusty abandon," but as the early part of this work has suggested, a bridal attitude toward death and the confluence of religious and sexual passion epitomized the embodied spirituality of Puritan religiousness.[8]

Virtually all Graham's choreographies had religious themes, from her first important work, "Heretic" (1929), to her later choreographies based on Greek and Hebrew mythology. Her religious themes were typically dominated and interpreted by a forceful feminine lead, danced by Graham herself. Graham presented religious dilemmas in her choreographies, and the development of her work reflects her changing attitudes toward feminine spirituality and toward herself. "Heretic," which pitted an outsider against the orthodox, may be fairly interpreted both as a dance about religious deviancy and as the performance of Graham's own heresy in the dance world. Her early work explored a spectrum of feminine intensity as it ranged from "Lamentation" (1930) to "Ekstasis" (1933).

Graham's first performance groups included only women, and not a cluster of *Sylphide* ballerinas but rather an "Amazonian world of vestals." With these instruments of virgin strength, Graham focused on the religious power of feminity in the major group work "Primitive Mysteries." This dance was inspired by her observation of religious rituals in New Mexico in which Catholic and Native American mythologies were combined in cults and rituals of penitence. "Primitive Mysteries," a dance of three parts, dealt with Woman's compassion, sacrifice, and deification—the same themes of feminine religiousness that had inspired, intrigued, and angered religious women throughout American history. In the first part of the dance, "Hymn to the Virgin," a "white-clad Madonna . . . epitomizes the native concept of a Virgin Mother whose tender compassion embraces them"; the second part, "Crucifixus," depicts "the anguish of the Passion as felt by the Mother"; the third part, "Hosanna," portrays "that glorification which amounts to deification of the Queen of Heaven in simple hearts."[9]

In her early choreographies Graham surveyed the emotional depths and celebrated the divine powers associated with femininity. Her work took new direction when Eric Hawkins joined her company in 1938. Despite resentment among Graham's women, Hawkins assumed classroom leadership, stepped into leading roles in "American Document," which was then in progress, and became Graham's lover in life as well as in her dances. Together they danced "The Puritan," in which the words of Edwards and the Song of Solomon intermingled in gestures of death and love. Graham titled her next major work after Vachel Lindsay's poem, "Every Soul Is a Circus" (1939). She performed the soul and Hawkins, whip in hand, danced her ringmaster.[10]

As she redirected her attention from the integrity of feminine power to the entanglements of passion, Graham danced about the relationship between religious and sexual power. She explored the religious dimensions of sexual ecstasy that had characterized the embodied spirituality of Puritanism and that had been buried in the sentimental Christianity that regarded sexual passion as religious evil. She also recovered the complementary agonies of finitude, dependency, and jealousy, the same dark forces that had captured Sarah Edwards and confronted Emily Dickinson. As her focus shifted from the totemic feminine strength expressed in "Primitive Mysteries" to the passions of a woman enmeshed in her own history, Graham turned to American history for choreographic material. In "Appalachian Spring" she drew on legends about American frontier revivalism and set the passions of religious enthusiasm within the context of sexual relationships.

In her "Letter to the World" (1940) Graham recreated Emily Dickinson. For her set, Graham chose a "dreamlike" summer house "with a Bridge-like thing I walked over into reality."[11] Using the home on the stage as a spatial metaphor for the artist's imagination, Graham's Dickinson danced back and forth across the bridge between a social space and the private space of her home. Dickinson, who had accorded her imagination the status of a world and was pleased to call it home, worked inside the spaces of her imagination with the help of biblical imagery and Calvinist logic. Dickinson's understanding of the relation between her own imagination and religious symbolism was similar to Graham's: both artists appropriated religious symbol-systems and imagery to inspire, structure, and represent their own souls. Like Dickinson, Graham moved from a rebellious feminine solitude to a passion that deepened aloneness as it brought recognition of final dependence. Both women moved from chaste strength to the pain and passion of a love engagement with death. In her American choreographies Graham moved from virgin mother to religious lover, exploring in her own medium the passion, gaiety, and terror experienced by Emily Dickinson.

In the third period of her art, Graham's choreographies involved feminine personalities drawn from ancient mythology. This redirection of her creativity again paralleled changes in her personal life. By 1945, the relationship with Hawkins brought her more pain than fulfillment and both of them sought psychi-

atric help. Graham's Jungian therapist Frances Wickes may have
encouraged her to search for choreographic and personal inspiration among the stories of classical and biblical mythology. In
"The Cave of the Heart," Graham danced the Medea story. Her
biographer, Don MacDonagh, perceived that in the Medea dance
Graham "created one of the most venomous parts of her reper-
tory." In her solo Graham "extracted a long red ribbon from
herself, simulat[ing] the spewing up of a vile liquid."[12] Medea's
violence had its source not only in jealousy and revenge toward
Jason—danced, as one might guess, by Hawkins—but also in a
lust for freedom. In "Night Journey" (1947) Graham reworked
the Oedipus myth to make it Jocasta's story. "Clytemnestra"
(1958), "Phaedra" (1962), and "Legend of Judith" (1962) constructed universal meaning out of woman's capacity to hate and
her lust for freedom. In this part of her career, Graham presented her audiences with the venom, vanity, madness, and
passion perceived to characterize witches.

In 1963, Frances Wickes published *The Inner World of Choice,*
which included a dream that may well have been Graham's.
Wickes identified the dreamer as a dancer threatened by loss of
love and support. The theme and titles of Graham's 1946 works,
"Dark Meadows" and "Cave of the Heart," may have this dream
as their source:

> "The tide is out. I am walking on a seemingly end-
> less strip of white sand, carrying in my hand a chal-
> ice? a casket? On one side is the withdrawing ocean,
> on the other an unscalable cliff. I see far out across
> the waters a great wave gathering in towering, men-
> acing force. It approaches with incredible swift-
> ness. I throw myself upon the sand just as it is
> about to break over me. It encloses me in a cave of
> clear jade. Then there is utter unfathomable dark-
> ness." When the wave recedes she sees a narrow
> opening in the cliff where the wave broke through.
> Beyond the rocky passage is a meadow with a green
> and leafy tree in the center.[13]

The beauty of the dream lies in the way its spaces, and the forms that structure those spaces, are transformed. The spaces in this dream succeed one another with a force of movement that is clear and marvelous. Sacred space is not only discovered in the dream but changed again and again, each time with a different kind of power.

The final scene of the dream is soft and centered in strength. It is a place of fertility, where a living tree stands in the middle of a meadow. The spaces in this dream, and the images that structure them, are as sexual as they are sacred, but here again the sexual force of the dream lies in its moving transformations. The dream, like the religious experiences of Sarah Edwards and Emily Dickinson, is a vivid and moving dramatization of the creative power of feminine receptivity.

The achievement and pleasure of expressing the shapes and color and movement of her soul prompted Graham, as it had Dickinson, to feel that she deserved immortality. Dickinson, like Graham, entitled herself to divinity because she applied the discipline of immortality to the privacy of her heart. Dickinson's enemy was death. She survives as the poet she is because she accepted the approach of her enemy as the movement of a lover. Among her later poems she wrote:

> Death is the supple Suitor
> That wins at last—
> It is a stealthy Wooing
> Conducted first
> By pallid innuendoes
> And dim approach
> But brave at last with Bugles
> And a bisected Coach
> It bears away in triumph
> To troth unknown
> And Kindred as responsive
> As Porcelain.   (1445)

Dickinson found grace in the approach of death and the movement of age, and although she may have wished for warmer reward, she submitted to the porcelain consequences of her poetry.

Graham may not be so fortunate, perhaps because in her own lifetime she achieved such public renown and found disciples who adored her genius. While Dickinson was never given the opportunity for such vanity, Graham was forced to live with the mirror of her reputation. In her own eyes and in the eyes of her worshipers, Graham's agile, embodied imagination established a role for herself not only as a modern interpreter of religious ritual and mythology but as the goddess of modern dance. "I must be adored," she once insisted. When told, "You must admit your mortality," she responded, "That's difficult when you see yourself as a goddess and behave like one."[14] This modern style of religious deviancy suggests why Graham's public has often perceived her as demonically vain; her vanity suggests, in turn, how closely her personality resembles Sarah Edwards'. In the eyes of her audience a model of grace could easily become a witch.

Martha Graham danced many of the dimensions of feminine spirituality experienced by religious women in American history. She performed the passion of Puritanism, the adoration of Mary, and the witchcraft of sexual power. And like other American religious women, she could turn her attention to the reputation of her virtuosity and fall into patterns that took grace for granted and preferred idealization to realism. Taken together, Graham's dances reflect the moving relations of many feminine personalities that emerge from one another. Graham's dances offer a mirror for feminine spirituality in America.

In the dancer's dream, even the final image, the meadow and its tree, contains a principle of movement. This final interior, the last closet in the home of the dreamer's soul, may be associated with the symbolic landscape of Eden. The principle of movement, potential even in the tree of paradise, is the movement of falling. Graham and Emily Dickinson and Sarah Edwards have shown that women have imagination and courage to fall gracefully. They have also shown that religious power objects—like God in heaven or like the broom in a closet—can be flown through the sky by a woman.

To illustrate feminine spirituality at the distant end of a historical spectrum I have focused on Sarah Edwards, a Puritan woman renowned for her husband, her virtue, her intelligence, her beauty, and, one suspects, her pride. At the contemporary end of the spectrum I have seen Martha Graham as the representative of feminine spirituality in modern art. Edwards and Graham are connected through Dickinson's poetry, which mediates the conceptual change between the religious and the artistic and the historical change from Puritan to modern consciousness. Edwards and Graham also belong together as women who devoted their lives to the cultivation of the same experience, namely, the experience of grace. Grace for Sarah Edwards was feeling and communicating to others the beauty of God. Grace for Martha Graham was a being dancing beautifully in space. The languages that describe grace for Edwards and Graham are as different as Calvin from Copland, but the experiences cultivated and performed by these two women are intimately related.

I have seen Graham as Dickinson's most illustrative daughter not only because Graham herself realized the connection, and recreated Emily Dickinson in her dance "Letter to the World," but also because Graham concretized an identifying characteristic of feminine spirituality. Graham presented spiritual awareness through movements of the body, carrying to full expression the capacity to embody beauty characteristic of feminine spirituality. Graham located grace in the flesh, carrying to resolution the Puritan tension between God and humanity, between the truth of the spirit and the beauty of the flesh.

In her dance "American Document," part of which was set to the words of Jonathan Edwards and an Old Testament psalmist, Graham recreated the religion of Puritanism by connecting the beauty of dancing with the sins of the flesh. "American Document" presented the opposition between the power of the Puritan God and the passions of humanity as a coherent work of art.

In Graham's modern art, the body's capacity for beauty is large enough to encompass all the passions and all the personalities known to man. In the spectrum of feminine personalities she danced in her choreographies, a spectrum that ranges from a benevolent Virgin Mary to a hellish Medea, Graham interpreted the attitudes of femininity as a sisterhood of the spirit.

An embodied spirituality characterizes all the women in this history and may even reach far behind them to the oldest professions and most ancient religious arts. In modern art, the medium of dance stands out as an embodied form of expression that expands upon the awareness of space characteristic of feminine spirituality. Graham's work stands out from all other contemporary choreography in its explicitly religious subject matter and exploration of feminine personalities. The grace with which she danced through the dimensions of her personality is a symbolic illustration of the movement of feminine spirituality through history.

Notes

Chapter One

1. The thesis of William A. Clebsch's *American Religious Thought: A History* (Chicago, 1973) is that belief in the universe's hospitality to the human spirit connects the work of Edwards, Emerson, and James and defines a major tradition of religious thought in America. My work on feminine spirituality depends on his insights as I am indebted to his teachings.

2. In ecstatic prose, Annie Dillard's *Pilgrim at Tinker Creek* (New York, 1975) defends and elaborates the thesis that nature is splendidly, violently, and fundamentally extravagant. Dillard's work as a poetic naturalist is the modern daughter of Emily Dickinson's nature poetry.

3. William James, *The Varieties of Religious Experience* (1902 Gifford Lectures; New York, 1961), p. 45.

4. See William A. Clebsch, *Christianity in European History* (New York, 1979), esp. pp. v–viii, 3–19, 25–27, for discussion of a historical approach to religion informed by James' *Varieties*.

5. Sacvan Bercovitch, *The Puritan Origins of the American Self* (New Haven, 1975). For a psychological approach to theology different from Bercovitch's historical work but influential on mine see David L. Miller, *The New Polytheism: Rebirth of the Gods and Goddesses* (New York, 1974).

6. Kathryn Kish Sklar, *Catharine Beecher: A Study in American Domesticity* (New Haven, 1973). For another, equally remarkable example of a biography that is also the cultural history of an era see Allen F. Davis, *American Heroine: The Life and Legend of Jane Addams* (New York, 1973). As the reader will see, I am indebted to Sklar and Davis for the stories they tell as well as for their methodological insights.

7. Ann Douglas, *The Feminization of American Culture* (Avon, 1977), and Betty Friedan, *The Feminine Mystique* (New York, 1964).

8. For discussion of the process of "counter-conversion" see the chapter "The Divided Self and the Process of Its Unification" in James' *Varieties*, esp. pp. 146–149.

9. I have based these brief theoretical remarks about conversion on the psychology of Jonathan Edwards, especially as it is presented in *A*

Treatise Concerning the Religious Affections in Three Parts (Boston, 1746). I have tried to make my comments here general enough that they also ring true for a diverse collection of nineteenth-century revivalists, such as Lyman Beecher, Peter Cartwright, Charles Grandison Finney, and Dwight Lyman Moody.

Chapter Two

1. Sarah Edwards' first-person narrative is preserved in Sereno Edwards Dwight, "Memoirs of Jonathan Edwards," *The Works of Jonathan Edwards, A.M.*, ed. Dwight (2 vols.; London, 1840), I, civ–cxii. Jonathan Edwards' edited version of her narrative appears in *Some Thoughts Concerning the Present Revival of Religion in New England*, which is reprinted in *The Great Awakening: The Works of Jonathan Edwards*, IV, ed. Clarence C. Goen (New Haven, 1972), 331–341.

2. Edwards, *Some Thoughts*, pp. 331–332.

3. Dwight, "Memoirs," pp. cvii, lxxxi.

4. Jonathan Edwards, *A Treatise Concerning Religious Affections, in Three Parts*, in *The Works of Jonathan Edwards*, II, ed. John E. Smith (New Haven, 200–205, and Jonathan Edwards, "A Divine and Supernatural Light" (1734), *Jonathan Edwards: Basic Writings*, ed. Ola E. Winslow (New York, 1966), p. 126.

5. Jonathan Edwards, *Images and Shadows of Divine Things*, ed. Perry Miller (New Haven, 1948), pp. 135–137 ("The Beauty of the World").

6. *Ibid.*, p. 61.

7. *Ibid.*, p. 137.

8. For a succinct discussion of the Puritan sacraments see Perry Miller, *The New England Mind: From Colony To Province* (Boston, 1961), pp. 83–84. Essential to Puritanism is the assertion that the sacraments were signs of but not means to a relation with God.

9. As quoted by Thomas Shepard, *The Parable of the Ten Virgins, Opened and Applied: Being the Substance of Divers Sermons on Matthew xxv. 1.–14: The Difference between the Sincere Christian and the Most Refined Hypocrite, the Nature and Character of Saving and Common Grace, the Dangers and Diseases Incident to Most Flourishing Churches, or Christians, and Other Spiritual Truths of Greatest Importance, Are Clearly Discovered, and Practically Improved* (2 vols. in 1; Falkirk, Mass., 1797; orig. pub. 1659), I, 9.

10. The betrothed longs for a full union with Christ, but she waits her time. She "may see his beauty here" by enjoying his ordinances; a

faithful virgin obeys Christ's commands because she "sees and beholds" in them a "hidden glory." Christ disclosed something of his loveliness to those who follow him on earth; that loveliness irradiated this life and illumined the way of heaven (Sheppard, *Parable*, I, 11, 26, 36, 57–58, 221–227; also see Jonathan Mitchell, "To the Reader," *ibid.*, p. vi).

11. Benjamin Colman, *Practical Discourses upon the Parable of the 10 Virgins, Being a Serious Call and Admonition to Watchfulness and Diligence in Preparing for Death and Judgment* (London, 1707), pp. 15, 26.

12. *Ibid.*, pp. 11–13. The covenant of marriage was familiar to Puritans as an interpretive analogy for the covenant of grace, and the covenant of grace stood at the center of New England religiousness. Puritans conceived of God as an omnipotent sovereign whose power was arbitrary and finally inscrutable. He partially disclosed his will in his relation to men and women by entering compacts of agreement. Under the covenant of works, God had promised salvation to those who perfectly fulfilled his laws, but all men and women inherited Adam's sin and inevitably transgressed God's commands. The coming of Christ inaugurated the covenant of grace, in which God freed humanity from the covenant of works by offering them salvation through faith in Christ. Those whom God elected as Christians were responsible for salvation through a life of faith. Though the contractual theory may have bound God to his agreements, an intense piety characteristically accompanied Puritan legalisms. At the heart of Puritan spirituality lay an awful gratitude for God's graciousness. Despite the unworthiness of humanity, God poured out mercy on those who believed in him.

Behind the covenant of grace was an agreement between God and Christ—the covenant of redemption. Christ freed humanity from the covenant of works by fulfilling that covenant himself. God allowed Christ's merit to be imputed to those who believed in Christ. For a discussion of the Puritan covenants of grace and redemption see Perry Miller, *The New England Mind: The Seventeenth Century* (Boston, 1961), pp. 365–397.

Edmund S. Morgan, in *The Puritan Family: Religion and Domestic Relations in Seventeenth-Century New England* (New York, 1966), outlines how the Puritan notion of a covenant between lovers was structured by Ramist logic. "Relation" was a technical term meaning "affectionate contraries of which the one exists out of a mutual affection of the other." "Relatives" were defined by what they were related to, and relation was always one of causal opposition. For example, buyers and sellers, or husbands and wives, cause—exist only in relation with—each other. In terms of the covenant of marriage, husband and wife were contraries, he the superior, she the inferior. A wife's role was defined as something other than and derivatively caused by her husband's. As John Cotton put it, a wife's identity was to "keep at home," attending to the "education of her children, keeping and improving what is got by the industry of man." But the "contrary" relation of husband and wife was "affirmative," that is, defined by mutual love. Benjamin Wadsworth described the equality of affirmation between husband and wife in the *Well-Ordered Family:* "This duty of love is mutual, it should be performed by each, to each of them. They should endeavour to have their affections really, cordially, and closely knit, to each other. . . . The indisputable Authority, the plain Command of the Great God, required Husbands and Wives, to have and manifest very great affection, love and kindness to one another. They should (out of Conscience to God) study and strive to render each others life, easy, quiet and comfortable; to please, gratifie and oblige one another as far as lawfully they can" (*Puritan Faimily,* pp. 21, 23, 42, 36, 47–48). Morgan's *Puritan Family* is one of the great studies of American life. In a number of places this chapter relies on his analysis of the relation between Puritan theology and interpersonal relations.

13. Thomas Johnson published a first selection of the "Poetic Workes" in the *New England Quarterly* in 1937, from a manuscript in the Yale Library. See Donald E. Stanford, "Introduction," *The Poems of Edward Taylor,* ed. Stanford (New Haven, 1960), pp. lvii–lviii. For a discussion of autobiographical writing in New England, see Daniel Shea, *Spiritual Autobiography in Early America* (Stanford, Calif., 1966).

14. Taylor, *Poems,* pp. 5, 39.

15. *Ibid.,* p. 15.

16. Edwards understood the natural universe as a harmonious composition of shadows and images of divine things. The shadow-body world of nature owes its visibility, color, and animation to the movement of light. In my reading of Edwards, "divine things" are not abstract forms but the warmth and movement of "mere light" itself.

17. Quoted in Edmund S. Morgan, *The Puritan Dilemma: The Story of John Winthrop* (Boston, 1958), pp. 53, 13.

18. Robert C. Winthrop, ed., *Life and Letters of John Winthrop* (2 vols.; Boston, 1869), I, 135, 261, quoted in Morgan, *Puritan Family,* pp. 50–51.

19. Edward Taylor, "A love letter to Elizabeth Fitch, dated Westfield,

8th day of the 7th month [September], 1674," quoted in Morgan, *Puritan Family*, p. 50.

For another quotation and discussion of Taylor's love letter to Elizabeth Fitch, see Stanford, "Introduction," in Taylor, *Poems*, p. xlii.

20. Thomas Shepard, *God's Plot: The Paradoxes of Puritan Piety; Being the Autobiography & Journal of Thomas Shepard*, ed. Michael McGiffert (Amherst, Mass., 1972), p. 53.

21. *Ibid.,* p. 55.

22. *Ibid.,* p. 70–71.

23. John Davenport, *Letters of John Davenport*, ed. Isabel MacB. Calder (New Haven, 1937), pp. 58, 77, quoted in Morgan, *Puritan Family*, pp. 49–50.

24. *Poems of Anne Bradstreet*, ed. Robert Hutchinson (New York, 1969), p. 41.

25. *Ibid.,* pp. 74–75 and "July 8, 1656, Appendix A," p. 183.

26. *Ibid.,* pp. 89–91.

27. "As weary pilgrim, now at rest," *ibid.,* p. 78.

28. See "Examination of Mrs. Anne Hutchinson," *The Antinomian Crisis, 1636–1638: A Documentary History*, ed. David D. Hall (Middletown, Conn., 1968), pp. 326–327.

29. Quoted in Morgan, *Puritan Family*, pp. 19, 45.

30. Dwight, "Memoirs," p. lxxxi.

31. Quoted in Goen, "Introduction," *The Great Awakening*, p. 68.

32. Dwight, "Memoirs," pp. lxxxii–lxxxviii.

33. Jonathan Edwards, "An Account of His Conversion, Experiences, and Religious Exercises, Given by Himself" (orig. pub. 1765), in Samuel Hopkins, "The Life and Character of the Late Reverend Mr. Jonathan Edwards," *Jonathan Edwards: A Profile*, ed. David Levin (New York, 1969), pp. 26–30.

34. J. A. Albro, *The Lives of the Chief Fathers of New England: The Life of Thomas Shepard* (Boston, 1870) pp. 318–319, quoted in John E. Smith, "Introduction" to Edwards, *Religious Affections*, pp. 53–57.

In his short comparison of Shepard and Edwards, Smith argues that Shepard conceived of the affections and understanding as discontinuous faculties and taught that the former should be harnessed by the latter. Shepard's notion of the opposition of these faculties is perhaps not as sharp as Smith argues. Shepard's stress on the saint's apprehension of God's beauty suggests an experience in which sensibility is united with understanding.

35. Jonathan Edwards, *Religious Affections,* pp. 253–257. In his "Free-dom of the Will" (1754) (*The Works of Jonathan Edwards,* Vol. I, ed. Paul Ramsey [New Haven, 1957]), Edwards offered close proof that every act of will is compelled by the greater apparent beauty of its object. Once the reader grants Edwards' first statement that to will, to choose, and to prefer are synonyms, the logic of the treatise is invincible. If to will is to prefer, and we prefer what appears most agreeable, then "the will always is, as the greatest apparent good is." In proportion to his or her own sensitivity to beauty the viewer will perceive the beauty of the objects of perception. The saint, who perceives what is truly beautiful, wills the will of God.

In "A Divine and Supernatural Light," the truly "enlightened" person "does not merely rationally believe that God is glorious, but he has a sense of the gloriousness of God in his heart." The "actual and lively discovery of this beauty and excellency . . . is a kind of intuitive and immediate evidence." Seeing the beauties of divine things "does not leave room to doubt of their being of God" (pp. 128–130).

36. Jonathan Edwards, *The Nature of True Virtue,* ed. William Frankena (Ann Arbor, 1960), pp. 10, 61.

37. *Ibid.,* pp. 94–96. I am indebted to William A. Clebsch for calling this passage to my attention.

38. Quoted in Hopkins, "Life and Character of Edwards," p. 80.

39. Edwards defined the affections as "the more vigorous and sensi-ble exercises of the inclination and will of the soul" (*Religious Affections,* p. 96).

40. Jonathan Edwards, *Some Thoughts,* pp. 334–341.

41. *Ibid.,* pp. 335–336.

42. Dwight, "Memoirs," p. civ.

43. *Ibid.*

44. Quoted in Elisabeth D. Dodds, *Marriage to a Difficult Man: The "Uncommon Union" of Jonathan and Sarah Edwards* (Philadelphia, 1971), p. 99.

45. Dwight, "Memoirs," p. civ.

46. *Ibid.,* pp. cvii–cviii.

47. *Ibid.,* p. cviii.

48. *Ibid.,* p. cix.

49. The mystical union accomplished by divine love also gave Chris-tian unity to mankind. In their vision of Christian unity, New England Puritans sensed their community as the body of Christ. For compelling

analysis of this point see Sacvan Bercovitch, *The Puritan Origins of the American Self* (New Haven, 1975).

Chapter Three

1. Barbara J. Berg, *The Remembered Gate: Origins of American Feminism: The Woman and the City, 1800–1860* (New York, 1978), *passim*.

2. Cotton Mather, *Magnalia Christi Americana, or the Ecclesiastical History of New England*, ed. Raymond J. Cunningham (New York, 1970; orig. pub. 1702), pp. 3, 15–16. John Winthrop, "A Model of Christian Charity," in *The American Puritans: Their Prose and Poetry*, ed. Perry Miller (Garden City, N.Y., 1956), p. 3.

3. Sacvan Bercovitch, *The Puritan Origins of the American Self* (New Haven, 1975), *passim*.

4. Perry Miller, "Errand into the Wilderness," *Errand into the Wilderness* (New York, 1956), p. 15.

5. Thomas Prince, *The Christian History, Containing Accounts of the Revival and Propagation of Religion in Great Britain and America* (Boston, 1744–1745), pp. 56–64 and 66.

Timothy Dwight, in his epistolary *Travels*, described how the ambition to accumulate wealth increased during the latter half of the eighteenth century. For Dwight, the history of New England avarice waxed and waned in indirect proportion to religiousness. When French infidelity tainted the piety of New England youth during the wars of 1755 and 1776, the idolatry of wealth flourished. The purpose of French atheism was twofold: "to extend the reign, multiply the means, facilitate the progress, and establish the quiet of sin; the other, to place the world beneath the feet of philosophical pride, ambition, and avarice" (Timothy Dwight, *Travels in New England and New York*, ed. Barbara Miller Solomon [4 vols.; Cambridge, Mass., 1969], IV, 265; see also "Religion of New England," Letters I and II, *ibid.*, pp. 258–269).

6. Mary P. Ryan, *Womanhood in America: From Colonial Times to the Present* (New York, 1975), pp. 29–38. John Demos, *A Little Commonwealth: Family Life in Plymouth Colony* (Oxford, 1970), pp. 183–186, and Ryan, *Womanhood in America*, p. 39. Elisabeth Anthony Dexter, *Colonial Women of Affairs: A Study of Women in Business and the Professions in America before 1776* (Boston and New York, 1924), *passim*. Richard B. Morris, "Women's Rights in

Early American Law," *Studies in the History of American Law, with Special Reference to the Seventeenth and Eighteenth Centuries* (New York, 1930), pp. 126–200. Thomas Woody, *The History of Women's Education in the United States* (2 vols.; New York, 1929), I, 25–28, 147. Berg, *Remembered Gate,* pp.ii–29.

7. Arthur W. Calhoun, *A Social History of the American Family from Colonial Times to the Present* (3 vols.; New York, 1945), Vol. I: *The Colonial Period,* p. 116, and Woody, *History of Women's Education,* I, 137–147. As Cotton Mather put it in his *Ornaments for the Daughters of Zion* (1692), "sloth and idleness in husband or wife are sinful and shameful" (quoted in Ryan, *Womanhood in America,* p. 36).

8. "In Honour of that High and Mighty Princess Queen Elizabeth of happy memory," *Poems of Anne Bradstreet,* ed. Robert Hutchinson (New York, 1969), p. 108.

9. George Savile, Marquis of Halifax, "The Lady's New Year's Gift, or, Advice to a Daughter," in *Root of Bitterness: Documents of the Social History of American Women,* ed. Nancy F. Cott (New York, 1972), p. 78. Benson, *Women in Eighteenth-Century America,* p. 18.

The *Library* did include an anonymous selection from Mary Astell's *Serious Proposal to the Ladies* (1694), which suggested a "religious retirement" for learned women. Though she accepted the superiority of husbands to wives, Astell argued that women were not innately inferior. Astell's contribution notwithstanding, the *Library* assumed the separation of religious and social life and, in contrast to early New England life, represented the diminished social participation of women (see Benson, *Women in Eighteenth-Century America,* pp. 22, 29–32).

10. See the discussion of liberal theologians Jonathan Mayhew, Jediah Mills, and Charles Chauncy, in Joseph Haroutunian, *Piety versus Moralism: The Passing of the New England Theology* (New York, 1932), pp. 58, 135–139.

11. On more than one occasion these "Consistent" Calvinists defended Edwards' notion of religiousness from the perspective of "natural," or self-centered, virtue. Hopkins, for example, affirmed the necessity of regeneration on the grounds of man's innate sinfulness, but his definition of sin focused more on the individual will than on the unified corruption of the human race. He defended the doctrine of original sin by arguing that "God will answer some good end by all the sin and misery in the world." He upheld the goodness of God, but by defining sin as willful action against God, he assumed man's independence from

God's sovereignty. See Haroutunian, *Piety versus Moralism*, pp. 53–61, 140, 41.

12. Susanna Rowson, *Charlotte Temple: A Tale of Truth*, ed. Clara M. and Rudolf Kirk (New Haven, 1964). The earliest extant edition of *Charlotte Temple* was published in London in 1791. Quotations are taken from that edition, as republished in 1964.

Charlotte Temple was published in over two hundred American editions and was superseded as a best seller only by *Uncle Tom's Cabin*. Variously subtitled *A True Tale, Founded on Fact*, or *Founded on True Fact*, the novel was probably a fictionalized elaboration of the short life of Charlotte Stanley, who in 1774 eloped to America with John Montressor, a British Army officer (see Kirk, "Introduction," *Charlotte Temple*, pp. 15–30).

13. *Charlotte Temple*, pp. 60, 163.

14. *Ibid.*, pp. 26, 27, 60–63.

15. *Ibid.*, p. 161.

16. *Ibid.*, see pp. 155 and 134.

17. Charles Brockden Brown, *Alcuin: A Dialogue* (part of which was published in 1789, in magazine and pamphlet form), ed. Lee R. Edwards (New York, 1971). Mary Sumner Benson, *Women in Eighteenth-Century America: A Study of Opinion and Social Usage* (New York, 1935), pp. 172–175.

18. *Alcuin*, pp. 4, 29–30.

19. *Ibid.*, pp. 26, 41, 84–86.

20. *Ibid.*, pp. 29–30.

21. Charles Chauncy, "Enthusiasm Described and Caution'd Against: A Sermon Preach'd . . . the Lord's Day after the Commencement . . ." (Boston, 1742), reprinted in *The Great Awakening: Documents Illustrating the Crisis and Its Consequences*, ed. Alan Heimert and Perry Miller (Indianapolis and New York, 1967), p. 243.

In Chauncy's view efforts to make "assurance essential" to faith and "Knowledge of the Time and Manner of Conversion necessary to the Thing itself" were doctrinal errors and threats to social stability. Chauncy argued that revivalist ministers who "have gone about venting their own wild Imagination for divine Truths were misleading the people about the nature of Christianity." He advocated sober preaching that rationally justified Christian doctrine. "There is no Doctrine of Faith, but it perfectly accords with the Principles of true Reason" [Charles Chauncy, "Ministers Exhorted and Encouraged to Take Heed to Themselves, and to Their Doctrine" (Boston, 1744), in *American Christianity: An Historical Interpretation with Representative Documents*, ed. H.

Shelton Smith, Robert T. Handy, and Lefferts A. Loetscher (2 vols.; New York, 1960), I, 400–403.]

22. Alexander Garden, "Regeneration, and the Testimony of the Spirit; Being the Substance of Two Sermons . . . Occasioned by Some Erroneous Notions of Certain Men Who Call Themselves Methodists" (Charleston, 1740), in *The Great Awakening*, ed. Heimert and Miller, pp. 60–61.

23. See Ernest F. Stoeffler, *The Rise of Evangelical Pietism* (Leiden, 1965).

24. Jonathan Edwards, *Some Thoughts Concerning the Present Revival of Religion in New England*, reprinted in *Great Awakening*, ed. Goen, pp. 387, 490–495.

25. *The Bethlehem Diary*, Vol. I: *1742–1744*, trans. and ed. Kenneth G. Hamilton (Bethlehem, Pa., 1971), p. 145, entries for April 13 and 15, 1743.

26. *Ibid.*, p. 176 and p. 192 (entry for May, 1744).

27. Clifford W. Towlson, *Moravian and Methodist: Relationships and Influences in the Eighteenth Century* (London, 1957). C. F. Richter, *Hymnal of the Methodist Episcopal Church*, trans. John Wesley, arr. Lowell Mason (New York, 1878), p. 239, no. 394.

The Moravians who accompanied Wesley on his voyage to America in 1736 impressed him by their "meekness" and "humility" during a storm at sea (John Wesley, *The Journal of the Reverend John Wesley*, ed. John Emory [2 vols.; New York, 1855], I, 17, entry for Jan., 1736).

From 1736 through 1738, when John and his brother Charles experienced religious crises that shaped their future ministries, both sought guidance from Moravians in America and Germany. Though John Wesley and the Moravian leader Ludwig von Zinzendorf came to disagreements, the style of Moravian piety exercised a lasting influence on the Wesleys and on Methodism (see Towlson, *Moravian and Methodist*).

28. Francis Asbury, *The Journal and Letters of Francis Asbury*, ed. J. Manning Potts (3 vols.; London and Nashville, 1958), aboard ship on his way to America, I, 6, entry for Sept. 29, 1771; I, 45, entry for Sept. 30, 1772; II, 5, "An Address to the Annual Subscribers for the Support of Cokesbury College," May 18, 1787.

29. See Charles A. Johnson, *The Frontier Camp Meeting: Religion's Harvest Time* (Dallas, 1955), pp. 54, 57, 65, 97.

30. See Timothy Lawrence Smith, *Revivalism and Social Reform in Mid-Nineteenth-Century America* (New York, 1957), pp. 124–126.

31. Timothy Dwight, *Travels*, IV, 335.

32. Horace Bushnell, *Women's Suffrage: The Reform against Nature* (New

York, 1868), pp. 50-57, 86, 65-66. In Bushnell's romantic epistemology, beauty was apprehended by intuition, through poetic sensitivity rather than through rational understanding. For his discussion of the close relation between feminine and religious intuition see Horace Bushnell, *Nature and the Supernatural; as Together Constituting the One System of God* (New York, 1904; orig. pub. 1858), esp. p. 302.

33. Bushnell, *Women's Suffrage,* p. 171. Just as a mother can compel the love of those who realize how much she loves them, Christian wives can also enforce love in their husbands. In a letter of 1838, Bushnell described to his wife Mary "the great power you have over me," which though "silent" exerted a "hold deeper than consciousness itself." Because her existence was consumed in the steady nurture of his needs, she compelled him to "be her man" (*Life and Letters of Horace Bushnell,* ed. Mary Bushnell Cheney [New York, 1880], p. 111). Just as a believer surrenders to Christ's power when he experiences himself as the object of Christ's sacrifice, so a husband is possessed by the power of his wife when he finds himself the object of her martyrdom.

34. Edna Dean Proctor, *Life Thoughts, Gathered from the Extemporaneous Discourses of Henry Ward Beecher* (Boston, 1859), pp. 5, 31, 79. Beecher took the gentleness of motherhood as a symbol not only for God, but for the beauty of nature herself. In the *Star Papers; or, Experiences of Art and Nature* (New York, 1855), Beecher described the natural beauty of social cohesion: "Society grows, as trees do, by rings. There are innumerable circles formed, with mutual attraction" (p. 194). Organic metaphors for society served Beecher well in his argument that stability and hierarchy are sanctioned because they imitate nature.

35. Dwight Lyman Moody, *"The Gospel Awakening," Comprising the Sermons and Addresses, Prayer-Meeting Talks and Bible Readings of the Great Revival Meetings Conducted by Moody and Sankey . . . ,* ed. L. T. Remlap (Chicago, 1883), pp. 207, 289, 52, 164.

36. Mary Patricia Ryan, "American Society and the Cult of Domesticity, 1830-1860," Ph.D. diss., University of California at Santa Barbara, 1971. For an intellectual history of the novel see Ian Watt, *The Rise of the Novel: Studies in Defoe, Richardson, and Fielding* (Berkeley, 1967). For discussion of the American sentimental novel see Herbert Ross Brown, *The Sentimental Novel in America, 1789-1860* (New York, 1959), and Helen Papashvily, *All the Happy Endings* (New York, 1956).

37. Harriet Beecher Stowe, *Oldtown Folks,* ed. Henry F. May (Cambridge, Mass., 1966), pp. 152, 533, 483.

38. *Ibid.,* pp. 481-482.

39. Horace Bushnell, *Christian Nurture* (New Haven, 1967; reprint of 1861 ed.), pp. 4, 39–40; originally published as *An Argument for "Discourses on Christian Nurture"* (Hartford, Conn., 1847). Quotations here are taken from the elaborated version that appeared in book form in 1861, but cross-references to the 1847 *Argument* will also be included in the notes. For this note, see *Argument*, pp. 23, 30.

Bushnell did not argue for innate goodness but rather for an early and consistent education into goodness. Religious growth "involves a struggle with evil, a fall and a rescue" and the Christian essentials—"repentance, love, duty, dependence, faith"—could be inculcated through parental example: "If you inspire a child with right *feelings*, they will govern his actions."

Child-rearing manuals popular in America in the 1830's and 1840's offered practical advice similar to Bushnell's and implied religious values similar to those he developed fully. Lydia Maria Child's *Mother's Book* (1831) prescribed a program for instilling obedience and goodness in a child through the early education of his emotions. For Child, the affections were the source of "all our thoughts and actions." She warned against establishing *"rules* instead of inspiring *sentiments"* (Lydia Maria Child, *The Mother's Book* (New York, 1972; orig. pub. Boston, 1831), pp. 22, 67–68, 81, 76.

In Child's manual, as in Bushnell's theology, the subtle control of emotions guaranteed the peace of domestic bliss. Defining a good child as cheerful as well as pious and obedient, Child emphasized the happiness of being religious: a mother must teach that everything her child enjoys comes from God; above all, death should be treated with "cheerful associations," as a "privilege" and not a calamity to be feared. In the piety of domesticity home and heaven had almost everything in common.

40. *Christian Nurture*, pp. 14–15, 80, 193, 197 (*Argument*, pp. 19–20, 31–32).

41. Harriet Beecher Stowe, *Uncle Tom's Cabin* (New York, 1966; orig. pub. 1851–1852), pp. 161–162, 304.

42. *Ibid.*, pp. 199, 328, 343.

43. *Ibid.*, pp. 243–244.

44. Helen Sootin Smith, "Introduction" to Elizabeth Stuart Phelps, *The Gates Ajar* (Cambridge, Mass., 1964), p. vi. Both Stowe and Phelps are important figures in Ann Douglas' *The Feminization of American Culture* (New York, 1977). For a brilliant analysis of the related sociologies of

home and heaven see Douglas' chapter "The Domestication of Death,"
pp. 200–226.

45. Phelps, *Gates Ajar,* pp. 7–9, 89, 161.

46. *Ibid.,* pp. 92, 124, 95.

47. *Ibid.,* pp. 75, 84. For analysis of the consumer ethic of domestic
theology see Douglas, *Feminization of Culture,* pp. 5, 64–68. Henry Ward
Beecher's novel *Norwood; or, Village Life in New England* (New York, 1892),
applies religious consumerism to nature. In *Norwood* God tests the piety
of the heroine, Rose Wentworth, by allowing her to learn simultaneously that Barton has been killed and that he loves her. Rose reasons
that "since God has taken him into heaven, he will send over all things
that the heavens cover, something of his nobleness and honor," and her
delight mounts at the prospect of God's recompense for Barton's death:
"The sun shall be brighter to me for his sake; the earth, and all that
grows upon it, shall have new meaning now; and every sound that the
ear loves to hear shall be to me a part of his voice, saying, 'Rose, I love
thee!'" (pp. 498–499). Rose has made the correct response and soon
learns that Barton is alive. Her response is proof that she trusts in the
goodness of God and the serviceability of his natural products.
Beecher's God is neither transcendent nor critical—he is docilely available in nature and family ties. Beecher's novel, like his sermons, instructed Christians how to control passion, avoid discontinuity, and
domesticate nature.

48. Quoted in Smith, "Introduction" to Phelps, *Gates Ajar,* p. xxii.

49. America's Christian evangelicals worked to unify this division
between politics and religion. Those of the early nineteenth century,
like Lyman Beecher, used political metaphors to defend Christian theology. Later, more romantic evangelicals applied the domestic metaphors of their religiosity to the world outside the home.

Chapter Four

1. Henry Ward Beecher, *Lectures to Young Men, on Various Important
Subjects* (New York, 1853), pp. 123, 299, 208.

2. John Greenleaf Whittier, "The Witch of Wenham" *The Works of John
Greenleaf Whittier,* orig. pub. 1877; 7 vols. (Cambridge, Mass., 1892),
"Narrative and Legendary Poems," I, 360–369.

3. So worthy did Neal deem the endeavor to create a uniquely American literature that he had the Scotchman's taunt engraved on his tomb-

stone (John Neal, "Unpublished Preface," *Rachel Dyer*, ed. John D. Seelye [Gainsville, Fla., 1964], pp. ix–x).

4. Thomas Hutchinson reported that the eldest girl was thirteen, or at most fourteen. The girls who began the accusations—Elizabeth Parris and Abigail Williams—were eleven and twelve (Thomas Hutchinson, *The History of the Colony and Province of Massachusetts-Bay* [1768], ed. Lawrence Shaw Mayo [2 vols.; Cambridge, Mass., 1936], II, 15).

5. George Lyman Kittredge, *Witchcraft in Old and New England* (Cambridge, Mass., 1929), 368. In sum, thirty-four New Englanders died as a result of being accused of witchcraft. For documents of American witchcraft, see David Levin, *What Happened in Salem?* (New York, 1960). Original documents there are reprinted mostly from *Records of Salem Witchcraft, Copied from the Original Documents*, ed. William E. Woodward (2 vols.; Roxbury, Mass., 1864).

6. See Barbara Yoshioka, "Imaginal Worlds: Woman as Witch and Preacher in Seventeenth-Century England" (unpub. Ph.D. diss., Syracuse University, 1977), for discussion of the theology and practice of witchcraft and its relation to femininity.

7. Cotton Mather, "A Discourse on Witchcraft," *Memorable Providences, Relating to Witchcrafts and Possessions* (Boston, 1689), in Levin, *What Happened in Salem?* p. 99.

8. William Henry Herbert ("Frank Forester"), *The Fair Puritan: An Historical Romance of the Days of Witchcraft* (Philadelphia, 1875), pp. 14, 159, 23, 27.

9. *Ibid.*, p. 131.

10. *Ibid.*, pp. 171–173.

11. *Ibid.*, pp. 220–221.

12. James Kirke Paulding, *The Puritan and His Daughter* (2 vols.; New York, 1849), I, 199.

13. *Ibid.*, pp. 195, 203, 262, 269.

14. John W. DeForest, *Witching Times*, ed. Alfred Appel (New Haven, 1967), pp. 128, 82.

15. *Ibid.*, pp. 167–168.

16. Nathaniel Hawthorne, "Young Goodman Brown," reprinted in Levin, *What Happened in Salem?* p. 154.

17. Nathaniel Hawthorne, "Rappuccini's Daughter," *Nathaniel Hawthorne: Selected Tales and Sketches*, ed. Hyatt H. Waggoner (San Francisco, 1950), pp. 340, 359.

18. Nathaniel Hawthorne, "The Gentle Boy," *Selected Tales*, pp. 79–80, 83–84.

19. Nathaniel Hawthorne, *The Scarlet Letter* (New York, 1955), pp. 48, 256–258. Zenobia, of *The Blithedale Romance* (1852), has "preternatural" powers that inspire awe. She is an "enchantress" who always wears a "hot-house flower,—an outlandish flower,—a flower of the tropics, such as appeared to have sprung passionately out of a soil the very weeds of which would be fervid and spicy." When Zenobia's love for the cold-hearted Hollingworth is not returned she drowns herself in an effort to become a tragic heroine. By rendering Zenobia's death as pitiful, Hawthorne makes her fail in her efforts to symbolize the grand integrity of her passion (Nathaniel Hawthorne, *The Blithedale Romance* [New York, 1962], pp. 68–69, 276).

20. Herman Melville, *Pierre; or the Ambiguities* (New York, 1929), pp. 296, 62, 212–213.

21. *Ibid.,* p. 505.

Chapter Five

1. William Randall Waterman, *Frances Wright* (New York, 1924), p. 205; Johanna Johnston, *Mrs. Satan: The Incredible Saga of Victoria Woodhull* (New York, 1967), p. 126.

2. Frances Wright, *Views of Society and Manners,* ed. Paul R. Baker (Cambridge, Mass., 1963; orig. pub. 1821), pp. 217–222; and Baker, "Introduction" to Wright, *Views of Society,* xi.

3. Waterman, *Frances Wright,* p. 137.

4. *Ibid.,* pp. 179, 185–186, 169.

5. Orestes A. Brownson, *The Convert; or, Leaves from My Experience* (New York, 1857), p. 127, quoted in Baker, "Introduction" to Wright, *Views of Society,* p. xxi.

6. Theodore Tilton, "A Biographical Sketch of Victoria C. Woodhull," *The Lives and Writings of Notorious Victoria Woodhull and Her Sister Tennessee Claflin,* ed. Arlene Kisner (Washington, N.J., 1972), pp. 3–11. Johnston, *Mrs. Satan,* p. 15.

7. See Johnston, *Mrs. Satan,* pp. 48, 104.

8. *Ibid.,* pp. 18–19.

9. Victoria Woodhull, "Woman's Position," *Woodhull and Claflin's Weekly,* May 14, 1870, reprinted in *Lives and Writings,* p. 11; see Johnston, *Mrs. Satan,* p. 109. Johnston, *Mrs. Satan,* p. 63.

10. Stanton felt that "when the men who make laws for us in Washington can stand forth and declare themselves pure and unspotted

from all the sins mentioned in the Decalogue, then we will demand that every woman who makes a Constitutional argument on our platform shall be as chaste as Diana" (quoted in Johnston, *Mrs. Satan*, p. 82).

11. Harriet Beecher Stowe, *My Wife and I* (New York, 1967; orig. pub. 1871), pp. 250, 278.

12. Johnston, *Mrs. Satan*, pp. 86–90.

13. *Ibid.*, pp. 163, 172, 213–220.

Chapter 6

1. Joseph I. Dirvin, *Mrs. Seton: Foundress of the American Sisters of Charity* (New York, 1975), pp. 3–4, 11–13, 23, 28, 41, 49, 62, 65–66.

2. *Ibid.*, pp. 122–123.

3. *Ibid.*, pp. 131–132.

4. *Ibid.*, pp. 134, 137.

5. *Ibid.*, p. 138.

6. *Ibid.*, p. 136.

7. *Ibid.*, p. 133.

8. Annabelle M. Melville, *Elizabeth Bayley Seton, 1777–1831* (New York, 1951), p. 95; and Dirvin, *Mrs. Seton*, pp. 164, 169.

9. Melville, *Elizabeth Bayley Seton*, p. 98.

10. Dirvin, *Mrs. Seton*, pp. 423, 447, 450–451.

11. *Ibid.*, p. 454.

12. Melville, *Elizabeth Bayley Seton*, p. 98.

13. Dirvin, *Mrs. Seton*, p. 317.

14. Melville, *Elizabeth Bayley Seton*, p. 189.

15. Dirvin, *Mrs. Seton*, pp. 380, 378.

16. Elizabeth Stuart Phelps, *The Gates Ajar* (Cambridge, Mass., 1964).

17. Harriet Beecher Stowe, *Uncle Tom's Cabin* (New York, 1966; orig. pub. 1851–1852), pp. 243–244.

18. Dirvin, *Mrs. Seton*, p. 235.

19. *Ibid.*, pp. 276–277, 349–355, 398.

20. Quoted in Kathryn Kish Sklar, *Catharine Beecher: A Study in American Domesticity* (New Haven, 1973), pp. 176, 171–172.

21. Catharine E. Beecher, "An Essay on Cause and Effect in Connection with the Doctrines of Fatalism and Free Agency," *The American Biblical Repository*, Oct. 1839, quoted in Sklar, *Catharine Beecher*, pp. 142–143; and Catharine Beecher, *Common Sense Applied to Religion, or the*

Bible and the People (New York, 1857), quoted in Sklar, *Catharine Beecher*, p. 251.

22. Timothy L. Smith, *Revivalism and Social Reform in Mid-Nineteenth-Century America* (New York, 1957), *passim*.

23. Lyman Beecher's evangelical militarism was justified by his evangelical psychology: the unconverted, who were in mortal need of salvation, were capable of helping themselves to Christianity if given the opportunity. Like other contemporary evangelicals, Beecher qualified the Puritan doctrine that men were dependent on God for their virtue by preaching that men moved themselves toward God by their own moral improvement. In Beecher's theology, God led men toward salvation in ways amenable to human reason: "God governs mind by motive and not by force" (*The Autobiography of Lyman Beecher*, ed. Barbara M. Cross [2 vols.; Cambridge, Mass., 1961], II, 117). Beecher followed Nathaniel William Taylor's view that man "sins freely, voluntarily." Taylor's theology stressed individual moral responsibility rather than humanity's dependence on God or ontological statements about God's nature: "No man knows" whether "God could have . . . prevented all sin" (Taylor, *Concio ad clerum* [1828], quoted in Sidney Earl Mead, *Nathaniel William Taylor, 1786-1858: A Connecticut Liberal* [Chicago, 1942], p. 226).

24. With religion a voluntary affair, evangelical Protestants hoped America would voluntarily become a Protestant nation: "A *de facto* establishment grew where the old legal one had fallen" (Martin E. Marty, *Righteous Empire: The Protestant Experience in America* [New York, 1970], p. 44). For a discussion that disputes the religious basis of nineteenth-century social reformism and, in particular, the religious motivations of women reformers see Barbara J. Berg, *The Remembered Gate: Origins of American Feminism: The Woman and the City, 1800-1860* (New York, 1978), pp. 145-175.

25. Carroll Smith Rosenberg, *Religion and the Rise of the American City: The New York Mission Movement, 1812-1870* (Ithaca, N.Y., 1971), *passim*.

26. Catharine E. Beecher, *Treatise on Domestic Economy* (rev. ed.; New York, 1847), pp. 25-36. Catharine E. Beecher, *The Duty of American Women to Their Country* (New York, 1845), quoted in Sklar, *Catharine Beecher*, p. 174. Also see Sklar, *Catharine Beecher*, pp. xi-xv. In her first published work Beecher isolated two tests of Christian morality: "longing after purity" and ostensible, consistent moral behavior. In the rarified air of the home moral purity was a practical possibility for women while men

were drawn to immorality as they ventured outside the home. Beecher predicted "the most confirmed habits of cold, and revolting selfishness" for any "man that has been drawn from the social ties of home, and has spent his life in the collisions of the world" (Catharine Beecher, *The Elements of Mental and Moral Philosophy, Founded upon Experience, and the Bible* [Hartford, Conn., 1831], quoted in Sklar, *Catharine Beecher,* pp. 86–87).

27. Lyman Beecher to Catharine Beecher, July 8, 1830, in Beecher, *Autobiography,* II, 167.

28. Sklar, *Catharine Beecher,* pp. 113–117. Less than a year after Lyman delivered his *Plea* in Boston, and as some thought a result of it, the Ursiline Convent was burned in nearby Charlestown (Ray Allen Billington, *The Protestant Crusade, 1800–1860* [New York, 1938], pp. 70–76).

29. Billington, *Protestant Crusade,* esp. pp. 99–100.

30. Quoted in Sklar, *Catharine Beecher,* p. 172.

31. Beecher, *Autobiography,* I, 368–375, and Sklar, *Catharine Beecher,* p. 79.

32. Elizabeth Peabody, *Guide to Kindergarten and Intermediate Class* (New York, 1877), p. 38. Gladys Brooks, *Three Wise Virgins* (New York, 1957), pp. 70–76. Brooks' three wise virgins are Dix, Peabody, and Catharine Sedgwick.

Elizabeth Peabody was an active supporter of the educational experiments of her brother-in-law Horace Mann. Peabody's contributions to the theory and practice of American education were centered in a high valuation of woman's maternal virtues and a commitment to institutionalizing those virtues within systems of public education. Peabody was also the owner of Boston's West Street Bookstore, gathering place for romantic philosophers.

Like other heroines of reform, Dorothea Dix expressed an almost boundless capacity for serving others. Her life, like Beecher's and Seton's, was characterized by a pattern of excessive work, collapse, and recovery for work. Her "queer and arbitrary" righteousness increased with her age, and at sixty-one she was fired for abrasiveness as the Union Army's Superintendent of Nurses. But by her aggressive sacrifice of self for "poor, sick, insane people" she won a place in the heart of her country: "My eyes fill with tears at the hourly heart-warm welcome, the confidence, the cordial good will, and the succession of incidents, proving that I do in very truth dwell in the hearts of my countrymen. . . . A Gentleman in the State Service said to me, 'You are a moral autocrat; you speak and your word is law.' People say, 'O you are no stranger, We have known you years and years'" (Brooks, *Three Wise Virgins,* pp. 70–76).

33. (John Angell James, "The Influence of Christianity on the Condition of Woman," *Young Lady's Guide* [New York, 1870], pp. 441–468).

34. Louise Porter Thomas, *Seminary Militant* (Portland, Me., 1937), p. 25. Catharine Beecher's vision of a national system of moral education spearheaded by women is a competing example of domestic mission. There were differences between the religious and pedagogical theories of Lyon and Beecher.

First, Lyon's religious fervor contrasts with Beecher's moralism. While Beecher disparaged the fatalism of Jonathan Edwards' theology, Lyon campaigned for the republication of his work and was righteously critical of the public demand for "lighter trash" (*Mary Lyon through Her Letters,* ed. Marion Lansing [Boston, 1937], p. 141).

Second, the curricula of Beecher's schools stressed training in the science of domestic economy. By contrast, the Mount Holyoke curriculum was modeled on those of Yale and Harvard. Further, Mary Lyon was herself a chemist and her school the first to offer women a systematic study of the sciences. Though Lyon insisted that education was always and only a means to Christian service, her biographers attest to the tension in her own life between intellectual ardor and religious obligation. There was a "fire burning" in Lyon's "bones" to provide women the training to lead useful and intellectual lives.

Third, Lyon and Beecher differed over endowment and tuition policy. Beecher's Hartford Seminary was funded by several wealthy individuals; Mount Holyoke by numerous small contributions. Green velvet bag in hand, Lyon canvassed New England, soliciting funds from middle-class wives. A class-conscious principle stood behind Holyoke's form of endowment—Holyoke educated daughters of families of moderate means. "The middle class," wrote Lyon, "contains the main springs and main wheels, which are to move the world." And thus at Holyoke tuition was lower than at Hartford, which attracted daughters of the upper-middle class. Lyon promised "the bringing of a liberal education within the means of the daughters of the common people" (Lyon, *Letters,* pp. 35–36, 61, 106, 176, 152).

35. Lyon, *Letters,* p. 277.

36. Thomas, *Seminary Militant,* pp. 65, 85–107, 31–32, 44.

Chapter Seven

1. *The Years and Hours of Emily Dickinson,* ed. Jay Leyda (2 vols.; New Haven, 1960), "Mount Holyoke Journal, October 2, 1847," I, 123; "Emily Norcross to Mrs. Porter," I, 134–135; "Mary C. Whitman to Mrs. Porter," I, 136. For the most thorough biographical account of Emily Dickinson's life see Richard B. Sewall, *The Life of Emily Dickinson* (2 vols.; New York, 1974).

2. "Mount Holyoke Journal, February 6," Dickinson, *Years and Hours,* I, 136. "To Jane Humphrey, 23 January, 1850," *The Letters of Emily Dickinson,* ed. Thomas H. Johnson (2 vols.; Cambridge, Mass., 1958), I, 83. "Emily Dickinson to Abiah Root, 7 & 17 May, 1850," Dickinson, *Letters,* I, 97. "To Abiah Root, 29 January, 1850," Dickinson, *Letters,* I, 89. "To Austin Dickinson, 16 November, 1851," Dickinson, *Letters,* I, 158.

3. "To Abiah Root, late 1850," Dickinson, *Letters,* I, 104, 99. "September 13, 1852," Dickinson, *Years and Hours,* I, 255.

4. *The Complete Poems of Emily Dickinson,* ed. Thomas H. Johnson (Boston, 1957). Page references to Dickinson's poems included in the text are to this edition.

5. Dickinson's religious identity seems to have crystalized sometime during the late 1850's. John Cody's hypothesis that during this period she suffered psychotic breakdown, successfully concealed by her family, may be accurate (*After Great Pain: The Inner Life of Emily Dickinson* [Cambridge, Mass., 1971], pp. 344–349). Certainly she emerged from a period of nearly total seclusion with a new sense of herself as a poet and with an almost boundless energy for writing. She had experienced religious sanctification. The experience seems to have entailed both an acceptance of her finitude and a new commitment to poetry.

6. See Wallace Stevens, "Notes toward a Supreme Fiction," *The Collected Poems of Wallace Stevens,* ed. Stevens (New York, 1954), pp. 380–408. For philosophical discussion of the psychological and literary significance of domestic space see Gaston Bachelard, *The Poetics of Space,* trans. Maria Jolas (New York, 1964).

7. For definition and discussion of "liminal" experiences within the context of the anthropological study of religious rituals, see Victor Turner, *The Ritual Process: Structure and Anti-Structure* (Chicago, 1969).

8. For philosophic discussion and literary criticism of the relation between color and consciousness see William Gass, *On Being Blue: A Philosophical Inquiry* (Boston, 1976).

Chapter Eight

1. Mary Baker Eddy, *Science and Health with Key to the Scriptures* (Boston, 1934; orig. pub. 1875), *passim*.

2. *Ibid.*, pp. 249, 331, 335, 516, 517, 592, 58.

3. *Ibid.*, pp. 29, 332.

4. For historical discussion of Mary's holiness in relation to her virginity see Marina Warner, *Alone of All Her Sex: The Myth and the Cult of the Virgin Mary* (New York, 1976). For discussion of Mother Ann Lee and her disciples see Edward D. Andrews, *The People Called Shakers* (New York, 1953).

5. Eddy, *Science and Health*, pp. 558-560.

6. Stephen Gottschalk, *The Emergence of Christian Science in American Religious Life* (Berkeley, 1973), p. 166; Edwin Franden Dakin, *Mrs. Eddy: The Biography of a Virginal Mind* (New York, 1929), pp. 337-338: and Eddy, *Science and Health*, pp. 562-565.

7. Robert Peel, *Mary Baker Eddy: The Years of Discovery* (New York, 1966), pp. 195-199.

8. Gottschalk, *Emergence of Christian Science*, p. 244. See also Robert Peel, *Mary Baker Eddy: The Years of Trial* (New York, 1971), pp. 223-225. Dakin, *Mrs. Eddy*, pp. 413-414. Peel, *The Years of Trial*, pp. 133, 141-244, and Dakin, *Mrs. Eddy*, pp. 351-357.

9. The theology that denied disease, death, and matter implicitly affirmed health and wealth. Just as a diseased body indicated erroneous thinking, so a healthy body indicated a right-thinking mind. A similar logic may apply to success as well as health. The increasing appeal of Christian Science to business men after 1890 and the upwardly mobile, middle-class status of Christian Science membership since 1900 suggest that prosperity could become an indirect sign of religious virtue (see Gottschalk, *Emergence of Christian Science*, pp. 249-259). For discussion of Christian Science administration see Gottschalk, *Emergence of Christian Science*, pp. 181-193, and Dakin, *Mrs. Eddy*, pp. 259-272.

10. Quoted in *The American Woman: Who Was She?* ed. Anne Firor Scott (Englewood Cliffs, N.J., 1971), p. 67. A college experience redirected Addams' life, as it did the lives of many other women who worked to reform Victorian conventions about women and Christianity.

11. Jane Addams, "The Subjective Necessity for Social Settlements" (orig. pub. 1893), *The Social Thought of Jane Addams*, ed. Christopher Lasch (New York, 1965), pp. 42-43, and Allen F. Davis, *American Heroine: The Life*

and Legend of Jane Addams (New York, 1973), p. 52. Davis' book is an exemplary biography. I am particularly indebted to his thorough and provoking discussion of the relation between Addams' own life and public perceptions about her.

12. Jane Addams, "The Objective Value of a Social Settlement" (orig. pub. 1893), in Lasch, *Social Thought*, pp. 44–61, 36–38.

13. Jane Addams, *Twenty Years at Hull-House* (New York, 1910), p. 48.

14. See Davis, *American Heroine*, pp. 67–134.

15. Addams, "Subjective Necessity," pp. 40–42. Italics mine.

16. For formal presentation of the philosophy of pragmatism in its most idealist form see Charles Sanders Peirce, "Evolutionary Love," *The Monist* (1893).

17. Davis, *American Heroine*, pp. 194, 60–62, 200–201.

18. *Ibid.*, pp. 229, 240–241. I follow Davis for this story.

19. *Ibid.*, pp. 252, 263–265.

20. *Ibid.*, pp. 110–134. Florence Kelley's name usually accompanied Jane Addams' on the spider charts and Bolshevist lists of the 1920's. Unlike Addams, Kelley described herself as a socialist throughout her career. Kelley's socialism had religious dimensions. Her sensitivity to social injustice had its source in the religious commitment to justice and pacifism that defined her Quaker heritage. Throughout her life Kelley assumed herself to be a Christian, at moments of stress compared her life with Christ's, and at the end of her life returned to the Quaker fold. During her public years, Kelley's language was secular—philosophically socialist and practically centered on the legal, medical, and moral problems of the working class. Like Addams, Kelley translated Christian idealism into a language of social concern and largely dispensed with the rituals and formulas of ostensible spirituality (Josephine Goldmark, *Impatient Crusader: Florence Kelley's Life Story* [Urbana, Ill. 1953], pp. 106–107, and William L. O'Neill, *Everyone Was Brave: A History of Feminism in America* [Chicago, 1969], 138). O'Neill's title comes from Newton Baker's remark about Kelley: "Everyone was brave from the moment she came into the room."

As general secretary of the National Consumer's League, Kelley became the nation's most effective reformer. The small and tightly organized NCL worked effectively for protective labor legislation during the progressive era. With the help of NCL research, Louis Brandeis and Felix Frankfurter defended a number of important minimum-wage and maximum-hour court cases. As William O'Neill remarked of the vitality and efficiency of the NCL's legal work: "Dollar for dollar and woman for woman, it was the best buy in the history of social feminism" (*Everyone Was Brave*, p. 153). The Shepard-Towner Maternity and Infancy Protection Act passed in 1921 as a direct outgrowth of NCL work. In one historian's estimate, the Shepard-Towner Act links progressivism with the reform measures of the New Deal, and the social feminists who supported the Act assume a unique historical role in an era otherwise characterized by "normalcy," red-baiting, picture palaces, and bootlegging (see Stanley Lemons, *The Woman Citizen: Social Feminism in the 1920's* [Chicago, 1973]).

Despite her knowledge of Marxism and her reputation for noncompromise, Kelley operated from what finally must be called mixed idealisms. She so tenaciously pursued protective legislation for women and children that the means supplanted the end of social transformation. Her first project at the NCL made it possible for department store consumers to purchase only those garments produced in factories and shops with acceptable labor practices. Approved employers comprised a "white list," and in the case of underwear manufacture, garments made under fair conditions received white labels (Goldmark, *Impatient Crusader*, pp. 54–57). A strategy that focussed on the moral sentiments of middle-class consumers may have been effective, but fell within Kelley's own category of "bourgeois Philanthrophy." Middle- and upper-class guilt motivated a "patch and darn" philanthrophy that functioned not to transform but to ameliorate and stabilize the class structure of capitalism (O'Neill, *Everyone Was Brave*, p. 134; Goldmark, *Impatient Crusader*, p. 77).

Kelley's compromise with radical socialism stemmed from her conviction that conventionally structured families make the building blocks of any just society. In her book, *Modern Industry in Relation to the Family, Health, Education, and Morality* (New York, 1914), she related the cultural transformations wrought by industrialism to "the American ideal of the home." For Kelley, "the paradox of Modern Industry" was that while industrialism improved "the material basis of family life," it simultaneously destroyed the ideal roles formerly experienced in agricultural society—"the father the breadwinner, the mother the homemaker, . . . the boys helping their fathers with the chores, and the girls learning under their mothers' eyes the arts of the housewife" (*Modern Industry*, pp. 3–4).

21. Lemons, *Woman Citizen*, pp. 209–235. O'Neill, *Everyone Was Brave*,

pp. 181–204, 227–232 (I follow O'Neill for the useful distinction between social feminism and hard-core feminism). Davis, *American Heroine,* pp. 187–189. *The Woman's Protest* (1912–1918) and *The Woman Patriot* (1918–1930), journals representing the conservative woman's point of view, defined radicalism as a threat to single-family stability and woman's place in the home. Social feminists expanded their maternal idealism to apply to the social community and hoped to establish social justice through legislation encouraging traditional family patterns among the working classes. More radical feminists, who fought sexual inequality and opposed any association between gender and profession, chose the home as the object of scientific analysis and reform. Home-consciousness retained its centrality for women engaged in transforming—as well as for those engaged in perpetuating—Victorian culture.

22. Jane Addams, "A Function of the Social Settlement" (orig. pub. 1899), in Lasch, *Social Thought,* pp. 184–189.

23. Roy Lubove, *The Professional Altruist: The Emergence of Social Work as a Career, 1880–1930* (Cambridge, Mass., 1965), pp. 49–51. Judith Ann Trolander, in her *Settlement Houses and the Great Depression* (Detroit, 1975), uses the feminine pronoun in all her references to the social worker.

24. Lubove, *Professional Altruist,* pp. 55–84, 118 ff.

25. June Sochen, *Movers and Shakers: American Women Thinkers and Activists, 1900–1970* (New York, 1973), p. 31.

26. See Betty Friedan, *The Feminine Mystique* (New York, 1963), for a feminist critique of conventions about femininity. Although Friedan's book addresses the emergence of the feminine mystique after World War II, there are many points of resemblance between the feminine mystique and the earlier theology of domestic pietism.

27. Though an architect was commissioned, the plan was abandoned in 1915, ostensibly because of high mortgage rates (Sochen, *Movers and Shakers,* pp. 37–39).

28. Other contemporary women espoused even more radical philosophies. Marxists like Rose Stokes, Elizabeth Flynn, and Kate O'Hare spoke for the industrial proletariat and looked toward communism. Anarchist Emma Goldman found the revolution of society the prerequisite for individual freedom. These women understood the exploitation of women as a corollary of capitalism and advocated sexual equality as part of a new order of things. They were feminists because they were political radicals. In distinction, Rodman and Eastman were feminists who were radical at those points where their demands for equality

threatened the social order. The difference between the two groups was essentially one of class. Goldman, Stokes, Flynn, and O'Hare spoke for the economically disinherited. The Feminist Alliance spoke for the economically secure but dependent women who demanded individual integrity and direct political and economic power (Sochen, *Movers and Shakers,* pp. 53–65).

29. Quoted in Sochen, *Movers and Shakers,* p. 39.

30. Charlotte Perkins Gilman, *The Home* (New York, 1903), pp. 64–65, 78–80.

31. *Ibid.,* pp. 49, 55.

32. *Ibid.,* pp. 60, 11, 49.

33. Eddy, *Science and Health,* pp. 592, 58, 595.

34. Addams, *Twenty Years,* 82–83.

Chapter Nine

1. Charlotte Perkins Gilman, "The Yellow Wall Paper," in *The Oven Birds: American Women on Womanhood, 1820–1920,* ed. Gail Parker (Garden City, N.Y., 1972), pp. 317–318.

2. *Ibid.,* pp. 334, 329, 318.

3. *Ibid.,* p. 319.

4. *Ibid.,* pp. 321–323, 329–331.

5. *Ibid.,* pp. 334–335.

6. Richard Warrington Baldwin Lewis, *Edith Wharton: A Biography* (New York, 1975), p. 121.

7. *Ibid.,* pp. 76–79. Also see Cynthia Griffin Wolff, *A Feast of Words: The Triumph of Edith Wharton* (New York, 1977), pp. 77–91. Wharton, Gilman, and Jane Addams were all treated for depression by Weir Mitchell, the renowned physician of wealthy women suffering nervous disorders.

8. Edith Wharton, *The House of Mirth* (New York, 1962), pp. 144, 114. Mrs. Peniston's "purple drawing room" bore the likeness of "a well-kept family vault, in which the last corpse had just been decently deposited" (p. 250).

9. Quoted in Stanley Lemons, "Introduction," *The Woman Citizen: Social Feminism in the 1920's* (Chicago, 1973).

10. *House of Mirth,* pp. 15, 6, 116.

11. *Ibid.,* p. 64.

12. *Ibid.,* pp. 75, 191, 201.

13. *Ibid.,* p. 359.

14. This argument recurs throughout Wolff's book. For its first full statement see *Feast of Words*, pp. 86–91.

15. *Ibid.*, p. 413. Also see pp. 192, 206, 211, 223, and 155 for examples of Wharton's statements about herself that involve the metaphor of house.

16. Lewis, *Edith Wharton*, pp. 259–260.

17. One evening, Henry James read aloud to Edith Wharton from Walt Whitman's *Leaves of Grass*, whom they agreed was America's best poet. They stayed up late talking about him and reciting favorite passages. One need only think of the freedom that enchanted both James and Wharton to imagine with what sweetness Whitman's free style must have been shared by two of the most crafted writers of American psychological fiction. When James closed the conversation that evening, he remarked, "Oh, yes, a great genius; undoubtedly a great genius! Only one cannot help deploring his too-extensive acquaintance with the foreign languages" (Lewis, *Edith Wharton*, pp. 120–121).

18. See Mircae Eliade, "The Symbolism of the Center", *Cosmos and History: The Myth of the Eternal Return* (New York, 1959), pp. 12–17. Mircea Eliade, *The Sacred and the Profane: The Nature of Religion* (New York, 1959), especially "Sacred Space and Making The World Sacred," pp. 20–67. I am indebted to Catherine L. Albanese, *Sons of the Fathers: The Civil Religion of the American Revolution* (Philadelphia, 1976), for her pathfinding use of such categories of comparative religion as sacred space to understand civil religion in America.

Chapter Ten

1. Martha Graham, press interview, 1935, in Merle Armitage, *Martha Graham* (New York, 1966; orig. pub. 1937), pp. 106–107.

2. Armitage, *Martha Graham*, p. 97.

3. *Ibid.*, p. 96.

4. Martha Graham, "Dancers' World," video film, 1957.

5. For a general history of modern dance see Margaret Lloyd, *The Borzoi Book of Modern Dance* (New York, 1949). For a history of Humphrey's life and philosophy see *Doris Humphrey: An Artist First* (Middletown, Conn., 1972), which was begun as an autobiography and edited and completed after Humphrey's death by Selma Jeanne Cohen. For Humphrey's own analysis of the craft of modern choreography, see Doris Humphrey, *The Art of Making Dances* (New York, 1959).

6. Doris Humphrey, "What Shall We Dance About?" *Trend: A Quarterly of the Seven Arts* (June-July-Aug., 1932), quoted in the Appendix to *An Artist First*, pp. 252–254.

7. Don McDonagh, *Martha Graham* (New York, 1973), pp. 101–103.

8. *Ibid.*, pp. 6, 65, 134.

9. *Ibid.*, p. 55, and Lloyd, *Borzoi Book*, p. 52.

10. McDonagh, *Martha Graham*, pp. 131–133.

11. *Ibid.*, p. 147.

12. *Ibid.*, p. 190.

13. *Ibid.*, p. 186.

14. *Ibid.*, pp. 296, 298. Graham performed centrally in all her dances and continued to dance and deny her roles to others until 1969, when she retired from performing at the age of sixty-seven. She saw herself as God's greatest acrobat, the human soul who comprised the whole circus (see McDonagh, *Martha Graham*, p. 234).

Index

Activism, 96, 123–24, 126, 162, 165–66
Addams, Jane, 162–69, 170, 171, 174–75, 224, 227
Albanese, Catherine, 228
Alcuin: A Dialogue (Charles Brockden Brown), 61–63, 170
American Tract Society, 125–26
Analogy, 48–50, 77
Anarchy, 94, 167–68, 226
Antinomianism, 37, 96, 110
Asbury, Francis, 7, 66
Astell, Mary, 61, 210
Authority, 5, 9–10, 37, 39, 56–57, 72–73, 78, 110, 120–21, 152, 155–56, 161, 166. *See also* Power
Awful Disclosures of the Hotel Dieu Nunnery of Montreal (Maria Monk), 122
Axis mundi, 188

Bachelard, Gaston, 222
Bayley, Richard, 111
Beauty, 78–79, 153, 198, 200; domestic, 3–4; and freedom, 182; God's, 20, 27–29, 42, 48, 78; and grace, 20–23, 27–29, 34, 39–43, 48–51, 193–94; natural, 3–4, 89; and sexuality, 84–86, 88–90, 92–94; woman's, 57, 60–61, 183
Beauty of Holiness (Phoebe Palmer), 67
Beecher, Catharine, 5–6, 11, 105, 110, 119–26, 162, 173–74, 219–20, 221
Beecher, Harriet. *See* Stowe, Harriet Beecher
Beecher, Henry Ward, 7, 15, 52, 68–69, 84, 105, 119, 213, 215
Beecher, Isabella. *See* Hooker, Isabella Beecher
Beecher, Lyman, 119–24, 204, 215, 219

"Belle-ideal" of womanhood, 52
Bercovitch, Sacvan, 8–9
Bethlehem Diary, 64–65. *See also* Moravians
Bible, 54, 91, 129, 155, 158–59; literary criticism of, 70
Biography, as genre, 10–14
Blood, Colonel James Harvey, 102–3
Body, 37, 48, 89, 106–8, 115, 134, 157, 169, 178, 186–87, 190–93, 200, 207; of Christ, 114, 138
Boyce, Neith, 180
Bradstreet, Anne, 34–37, 39, 56, 115, 187
Bradstreet, Simon, 35–36
Bride-consciousness, 8, 19, 27, 50, 123–24, 136, 194
Brown, Charles Brockden, 58, 63, 170
Brownson, Orestes, 102
Bruté, Gabriel, 114
Buell, Samuel, 46
Bushnell, Horace, 15, 52, 67–68, 70, 72–73, 213, 214
Bushnell, Mary, 213

Calvin, John, 200
Calvinism, 58, 71, 196
Cartwright, Peter, 204
Catharine Beecher: A Study in American Domesticity (Kathryn Kish Sklar), 11. *See also* Beecher, Catharine
Catholicism, 64, 75, 112–19, 121–23, 125, 168, 195
Charlotte Temple (Susanna Rowson), 59–61, 182, 211
Chauncy, Charles, 63–64, 210, 211
Child, Lydia Maria, 214
Chopin, Kate, 180

Christ, 9, 31, 35, 53, 90, 126, 128; as
    Bridegroom, Lover, and Spouse, 23–
    30, 65–66, 115; as Child, 74–76;
    Emily Dickinson's, 135–36, 138; as
    Idea, 157; as Light, 21–22, 87; sacra-
    mental presence of, 113–15; as Son,
    115–16; suffering of, 65, 75, 113–16;
    woman as, 67–69. *See also* God
Christian Nurture (Horace Bushnell),
    72–73
Christian Science, 78, 115–62, 174,
    223. *See also* Eddy, Mary Baker
Church, 79, 91; as Bride of Christ, 23;
    Catholic, 112, 113–14, 138; as home,
    72, 150–51, 161, 174; Puritan under-
    standing of, 23–25
Church of Christ Science. *See* Christian
    Science
Claflin, Roxana, 106
Claflin, Tennessee Celeste ("Tennie
    C."), 103
Clebsch, William A., v, ix, 203
Codman, Ogden, 181
Cody, John, 222
Colman, Benjamin, 25–27, 28
Communion. *See* Sacrament
Communitas, 121
Congregationalism. *See* Church; Puri-
    tans
Consumerism, 77. *See also* Materialism
Conversion, 16, 111, 123–24, 126, 146,
    151. *See also* Transformation
Cooper, James Fenimore, 96
Copland, Aaron, 200
Cotton, John, 206
Covenant of grace. *See* Grace

Dance, 17, 114, 144–45, 189–201
D'Arusmont, William Phiquepal, 101
Davenport, John, 33
Davis, Allen F., 203, 223–26
Death: as best part of life, 76–77; Emily
    Dickinson's relation to, 132–33, 141–
    43, 198; Elizabeth Seton's, 114–16;
    and sexuality, 36–37, 84, 156, 187,
    194, 196
Decoration of Houses (Edith Wharton and
    Ogden Codman), 181

DeForest, John W., 86, 91–92, 93
Devil, 54, 87. *See also* Evil; Satan
Dewey, John, 169
Dickinson, Emily, 3–4, 16–17, 19, 129–
    54, 167, 175, 182, 196, 200, 203, 222
Dillard, Annie, 203
Dix, Dorothea, 124–25, 220–21
Domestic consciousness, 5, 10, 177–88.
    See also Home; Pietism, domestic
Domesticity, 70–78, 104; beauty and
    pleasures of, 3–5; confinements of,
    106, 191, 172–73; conventional, 117;
    Emily Dickinson's, 135, 138, 144,
    150–51; as politics, 119–20; as sci-
    ence, 124
Douglas, Ann, 14–15, 77
Duncan, Isadora, 192
Dwight, Timothy, 39–40, 209

Eastman, Crystal, 170, 171, 226–27
Ecstasy, 16, 20–21, 36, 44, 48, 52, 75,
    110–11, 114; Emily Dickinson's, 135,
    137, 141, 144–45; Martha Graham's,
    195–96; Edith Wharton's, 186–88
Eddy, Mary Baker, 155–62, 174
Education, 56, 73, 101, 105, 118–27,
    162–64, 174, 221
Edwards, Jonathan, 4, 8, 15, 40, 60, 63–
    64, 195, 200, 203; as interpreter of
    his wife's religious experiences, 20–
    21, 39, 44–45, 110–11; theology of,
    22, 29, 193–94, 206; marriage, 40–43;
    psychology of, 58, 119, 207, 208
Edwards, Jonathan, Jr., 58
Edwards, Sarah Pierrepont: ecstatic
    experiences of, 20–23, 43–48, 52, 60,
    110–11, 114, 134, 198; as interpreter
    of her husband, 45–47; life and repu-
    tation, 39–41, 199–200
Effeminacy, 66
Elizabeth, Queen of England, 56
Ely, Ezra Stiles, 101
Emerson, Ralph Waldo, 4, 203
Emmons, Nathaniel, 58
Emotion, 46, 56–58, 63–67, 168, 192–
    93. *See also* Passion
Enthusiasm, 43, 63, 64–67, 100
Episcopalians, 91, 111

Evil, 83–99, 156, 158, 162, 183. *See also* Devil; Satan

Fair Puritan (William Henry Herbert), 88–90
Family, 70, 73–78, 108, 121, 168, 173, 225; claim, 163, 167; pietism, 110
Fanaticism, 89–92, 95
Fantasy, 77–78, 179
Feast of Words: The Triumph of Edith Wharton (Cynthia Wolff), 185
Feminine mystique, 14, 170, 226
Feminism, 62, 168, 170–71, 180, 224–26
Feminist Alliance, 170, 227
Feminization of American Culture (Ann Douglas), 14–15, 77
Fertility rites, 70. *See also* Ritual
Few Days in Athens (Frances Wright), 100
Fiction, 117–18, 176, 180; Emily Dickinson's religion of, 15–16, 137, 139, 143–44; in relation to theology, 11–16, 58–59, 70–73, 158, 181, 185; about witchcraft, 84–98
Finney, Charles Grandison, 204
Fiske, Fidelia, 127–28
Flynn, Elizabeth, 226–27
Freedom, 47, 60, 90, 95, 102, 125–26, 143–45, 179–80, 182–86, 191, 193, 197
Free love, 100–1, 103–6, 109
Friedan, Betty, 14, 226
Fuller, Margaret, 15
Fullerton, Morton, 187

Garden, Alexander, 64
Gass, William, 222
Gates Ajar (Elizabeth Stuart Phelps), 76–77, 117
Gender, 38, 61, 157–58
"Gentle Boy" (Nathaniel Hawthorne), 94–95
Gilman, Charlotte Perkins, 171–80, 191, 227
Glaspell, Susan, 180
God, 12, 27, 33, 38, 55, 76, 155, 200; as babe, 113; beauty of, 20, 27–29,

42, 48, 78; dark side of, 92; Emily Dickinson's, 129–36, 138–40, 150–52; Mary Baker Eddy's, 157–61; Sarah Edwards', 39–41, 43–48, 60; feminine characteristics of, 4, 15, 30–37, 52–53, 83; as mother, 68–69; of pietists, 64–65; Puritan understanding of, 20–27, 48–50, 54, 87, 200; in sacraments, 112–15; transformation of, 51, 58, 61
Goddess, 69, 199
Godey's Ladies Book, 70
Godwin, William, 61
Goldman, Emma, 226–27
Grace, 16–17; covenant of, 50, 205; through dance, 17, 189–201; Sarah Edwards' experience of, 21–22, 44–45; as an esthetic, 176; love as, 71; as religious experience, 26, 31, 37–39, 155; Elizabeth Seton's cultivation of, 111–15; and virtue, 110–11, 125–28
Graham, Martha, 17, 189–201, 229
Great Awakening, 21, 43–44, 46, 63–64; second, 120

Halifax, Lord, 56–57
Hawkins, Eric, 195, 196–97
Hawthorne, Nathaniel, 80, 92–96, 217
Heaven, 37, 69–77, 87, 89, 111, 158–59, 172, 188, 200; Emily Dickinson's, 139–41, 145, 151; Queen of, 195
Hell, 84, 105, 201
Hellion, 95, 100
Hemingway, Ernest, 96
Herbert, William Henry, 86, 88–90, 92, 93
Holiness, 39, 53, 93, 105, 109, 134, 138; movement, 66–67
Home, 54, 61, 84, 90, 105, 106, 108, 121, 196, 199, 220; and church, 161; Emily Dickinson's understanding of, 138–41, 144, 150–51; as economic center, 55; feminist, 170–76; as heaven, 4, 69, 71, 73–77; nature as, 92, 150–51; as religious kingdom, 72–73; Universal, 104; universe as, 4–6, 125, 150–51, 193

Home (Charlotte Perkins Gilman), 172–74

Hooker, Isabella Beecher, 104

Hooker, Thomas, 15

Hopkins, Samuel, 39–40, 58, 210–11

House of Mirth (Edith Wharton), 181–85

Housecleaning, 3–4, 114, 130, 164, 182–83

Hull House, 164–65, 166–69, 174–75

Humility, 33–34, 44, 48, 54, 134

Humphrey, Doris, 192, 228

Hutchinson, Anne, 31, 34, 37–38, 95, 96, 155, 167

Hysteria, 177–79

Immortality, 76, 80, 136–37, 198–99

Incest, 96–97

Independence, 47, 100, 161, 210–11

Innocence, 60, 91, 138–39

Interiors, 177–88, 197–200

James, Henry, 228

James, William, 4, 6, 8, 166, 169, 203

Jesus. *See* Christ; God

Jones, Lucretia, 181

Kelley, Florence, 224–25

Kemble, Frances, 104

Ladies Library, 56

Lady's New Year Gift (Lord Halifax), 56–57

Lafayette, Marquis de, 100, 101

Lectures to Young Men (Henry Ward Beecher), 84

Lee, Mother Ann, 158

Lewis, R. W. B., 180–81

Liberty, 100. *See also* Freedom

Lindsay, Vachel, 195

Literalism, 61, 88

Lyon, Mary, 126–27, 129–30, 221

MacDonagh, Don, 197

Madness, 94, 96–97, 142–43, 146, 176–80, 197

Madonna. *See* Virgin Mary

Magnalia Christi Americana (Cotton Mather), 53–54

Mann, Horace, 220

Marriage, 61, 90, 101–2, 106, 122, 164; as analogy for grace, 25–28, 49; Emily Dickinson's view of, 130–31, 136; Jonathan and Sarah Edwards' as exemplary, 43; Charlotte Perkins Gilman's, 179–80; and incest, 96; and prostitution, 103; Puritan view of, 23–24, 38–39, 49; Victorian, 84. *See also* Union

Martyrdom, 70, 127

Mary. *See* Virgin Mary

Materialism, 55, 77, 90, 117, 156

Mather, Cotton, 53–54, 87

Melville, Herman, 96–98

Methodism, 66

Miller, David, 203

Miller, Perry, 54

Missionaries, 120–22, 125–27

Mitchell, Weir, 227

Modern art, 188–93, 200, 201

Monk, Maria, 122

Moody, Dwight Lyman, 15, 52, 68–69, 204

Moral energy, 110, 183. *See also* Virtue, moral

Moralism, 99, 110, 165

Morality, 60, 97, 103, 168, 219–20

Moral superiority of women, 5–6, 120–21

Moravians, 64–65, 212

Morgan, Edmund, 206

Mother: spiritual authority of, 68–69, 71, 73, 78, 119–20, 153, 172, 195; as representative Christian, 119; God as, 152, 157; -love, 83, 124, 157–58, 174; Virgin Mary as, 112–13, 115–17

Motherhood, 75, 95, 105, 135, 159, 164; feminist view of, 170–71

Mount Holyoke Female Seminary, 126–27, 129–30, 162, 163–64, 221

Mysticism, 111, 134, 155–56, 186–88

Mythology, 96–97, 125, 171–73, 175–76, 180, 194–97

Nashoba, 100–1

Nature, 90, 192; beauty of, 3–5; as home, 92, 150–51; and witchcraft,

85, 88, 93–94, 145–51; woman's, 52, 97

Nature of True Virtue (Jonathan Edwards), 42

Neal, John, 86

Norcross, Emily, 129

Novels, 11–13, 59–63, 70–77, 79–83, 86–92, 95–98, 104–5, 181–84. *See also* Fiction

Nuns, 118–19, 122, 137–38

Occult, 106–8. *See also* Witchcraft

O'Hare, Kate, 226–27

Old Town Folks (Harriet Beecher Stowe), 71–73

O'Neill, William, 224–25

Organizationalism, 121, 127, 161–62, 165, 169. *See also* Pragmatism; Professionalism

Owen, Robert, 100, 101

Paganism, 125–26, 148. *See also* Witchcraft

Palmer, Phoebe, 66–67

Parable of the Ten Virgins (Thomas Shepard), 24–25, 31

Park, Edwards Amasa, 70

Passion, 30, 43, 70, 83–98, 116, 177, 196, 197, 200–1; Anne Bradstreet's, 34–35; Emily Dickinson's, 134–35, 149, 196; Edith Wharton's, 186–88

Paulding, James Kirke, 86, 90–91, 92, 93

Peabody, Elizabeth, 124–25, 220

Personality, 71, 80–81, 180, 190, 191, 199, 201; Emily Dickinson's, 133–34, 137, 148, 150, 151–53; Mary Baker Eddy's, 159; Virgin Mary's, 112

Phelps, Austin, 70, 76

Phelps, Elizabeth Stuart, 76–77, 117–18

Pierre (Herman Melville), 96–98

Pietistical enthusiasm. *See* Enthusiasm

Pietism, domestic, 71, 108, 116, 168, 174 (*see also* Domestic consciousness; Domesticity; Home); Emily Dickinson's transvaluation of, 135, 138, 151, 180, 226; Mary Baker Eddy's

transvaluation of, 156–57; family, 110; occult form of, 106

Plea for the West (Lyman Beecher), 122

Poe, Edgar Allan, 140–41

Politics, 79, 119–20, 165–67, 226–27; as masculine sphere, 61–62, 109–10. *See also* Reform

Power, 9–10, 31, 38, 48, 55, 57, 59, 61–62, 67, 78, 110, 118, 120–21, 176, 186, 187, 189, 193–95, 198, 200; Jane Addams' relation to, 164, 168; Emily Dickinson's relation to, 131, 133–37, 146, 148–50, 152; Mary Baker Eddy's relation to, 155, 157, 160–61; God's diminished, 61, 69; Virgin Mary's, 112. *See also* Authority

Pragmatism, 79, 161–62, 164–66, 169, 180. *See also* Organizationalism; Professionalism; Progressivism

Primitivism, 173, 190–92, 195. *See also* Modern art; Paganism

Prince, Thomas, 55

Professionalism, 124–25, 162, 164, 169–71, 201. *See also* Addams, Jane; Beecher, Catharine; Organizationalism; Pragmatism

Progressivism, 165–66, 170

Prostitution, 103, 152

Protestantism, 101, 103, 118–23, 219

Puritan and His Daughter (James Kirke Paulding), 90–91

Puritan Origins of the American Self (Sacvan Bercovitch), 8–9

Puritans: influence of, 19–20; influence on Martha Graham, 193–96, 199–201; romantic perceptions about, 84–96; social life of, 23–24, 55–56; spirituality of, 6, 8, 23–24, 27, 30, 39, 53–54, 65, 193; theology of, 48–50, 87

Quakers, 95, 105, 224

Quimby, Phineas T., 159–60

Rachel Dyer (John Neal), 86

"Rappuccini's Daughter" (Nathaniel Hawthorne), 94

Rationalism, 57–58, 62–63, 92, 100, 102, 170

Reason, 56–58, 84, 100–1, 142, 146, 219

Reform, 103, 105–6, 109–10, 118, 120, 124, 125, 162–63, 168–69, 171, 219. *See also* Virtue, moral

Religious enthusiasm. *See* Enthusiasm

Revivalism, 13, 66, 101, 102, 106, 120, 126, 127, 168

Ritual, 87, 112, 114, 180, 183, 192–93, 195

Rodman, Henrietta, 170–71, 174, 175–76, 181, 191, 226–27

Romanticism, 70, 79, 83–98, 117, 128, 150, 171. *See also* Imagination

Rome, 121–22; as wicked mother, 64. *See also* Catholicism

Rowson, Susanna, 58–61, 63. See also *Charlotte Temple*

Sacrament: God embodied in, 112, 114–15; Puritan understanding of, 23–24; romantic love as, 71

Sacred space, 76, 78, 108–9, 141, 174–76, 186–88, 189. *See also* Church; Home; Space

Sacrifice, 67–68, 78, 105; Catharine Beecher's understanding of, 110, 119–20; Emily Dickinson's, 130–31, 135; Elizabeth Seton's, 116, 118. *See also* Christ; Mother; Motherhood

Saint, 49, 52, 54, 84, 110, 115, 127–28; Jane Addams as, 116; as bride, 8, 23–26, 52; as virgin, 24, 52; as wife, 23, 26, 37, 52. *See also* Bride-consciousness; Mother; Sainthood

Sainthood, associated with femininity, 8–10, 27, 34, 166

Salvation, 104–5, 127. *See also* Heaven; Saint; Sainthood; Sanctification

Sanctification, 26, 28, 37, 39, 77, 134, 137. *See also* Marriage; Sacrifice; Salvation; Union

Sand, George, 104

Satan, 43; Mrs., 100. *See also* Devil; Evil

Scarlet Letter (Nathaniel Hawthorne), 95–96

Science, 78–79, 169–70, 221; domestic, 124, 126. *See also* Christian Science

Science and Health (Mary Baker Eddy), 156–59, 161

Scripture. *See* Bible

Secularism. *See* Professionalism

Self, 15, 22, 38, 42, 54, 105, 119, 123, 151–53, 177–88, 190–91. *See also* Personality

Self-sacrifice. *See* Sacrifice

Seton, Annina, 116

Seton, Cecilia, 118

Seton, Elizabeth, 110–19, 137–38, 155

Seton, Rebecca, 116–17

Seton, William, 111–12

Sexuality: demonic, 83–107, 122–23; in relation to spiritual passion, 29–30, 37, 42–43, 66, 109, 122–23, 134–37, 157–58, 195–99. *See also* Free love; Marriage; Passion; Witchcraft

Shakers, 158

Shepard, Joanna, 31–34, 41

Shepard, Thomas, 15, 24–28, 31–33, 41–42, 60, 65, 207

Sin, 40, 41, 72, 92, 93, 178, 194, 210. *See also* Evil

Sisterhood, 119, 201

Sisters, 96–97, 126. *See also* Nuns

Sisters of Charity, 116, 118–19, 121. *See also* Seton, Elizabeth

Sklar, Kathryn Kish, 11, 203

Slavery, 73–75, 106

Smith, John E., 207

Some Thoughts Concerning the Recent Revival (Jonathan Edwards), 21, 43

Space, 96, 177–201; domestic, 5, 138–47, 150–51, 170–76; environmental, 5, 10, 150–51. See also *Axis mundi*; Sacred Space

Spiritualism, 102–4, 106–7, 159–60

Standish, Miles, 194

Stanton, Elizabeth Cady, 104, 217–18

St. Denis, Ruth, 192

Stokes, Rose, 226–27

Stowe, Harriet Beecher, 12, 71–76, 77, 104–5, 117–18, 158

Stuart, Moses, 76

Suffering: Jane Addams' view of, 163; of Christ, 65, 75, 113–16; Mary Baker

Eddy's view of, 156, 159–60, 161; transvaluation of, 111–12

Suffrage, 67, 101, 104, 168

Surrender, 55, 102, 107, 135. *See also* Passion; Sacrifice

Taylor, Edward, 7, 27–31, 38, 65

Taylor, Elizabeth Fitch, 31

Taylor, Nathaniel William, 219

"Terminus" (Edith Wharton), 186–88

Theology: of the body, 107; decline of, 15, 51–53, 58, 63, 68–70, 79–81; Mary Baker Eddy's, 156–59; in relation to fiction, 12–15, 58–59, 70–73, 88; Martha Graham's, 191–94; of happiness, 77; Puritan, 49–50; of witchcraft, 84

Tilton, Elizabeth, 105

Transformation: environmental, 146–48, 169; of God, 51, 58; spiritual, 16–17, 117, 151, 177–88, 190–201

Treatise on Domestic Economy (Catharine Beecher), 124

Treatise on the Religious Affections (Jonathan Edwards), 8, 42

Turner, Victor, 222

Twain, Mark, 77, 96

Uncle Tom's Cabin (Harriet Beecher Stowe), 12, 73–76, 117, 158

Union, 26, 28, 30, 35, 38, 39, 42–43, 49–50, 208–9; of church and state, 101. *See also* Marriage; Mysticism; Sexuality

Unitarianism, 92, 125

Vanderbilt, Cornelius, 103

Varieties of Religious Experience (William James), 8

Vere, Lady Mary, 33

Virgin Mary, 17, 95, 157–58, 195, 196, 201, 223; Emily Dickinson's, 137–38, 152; Elizabeth Seton's, 110, 112–13, 115–17

Virgin, 136, 195

Virginity, 98

Virtue, 67, 91, 174, 200; beauty of, 22, 39; Sarah Edwards', 40–41, 47; fixed,

93; and gender, 59–61, 84; and grace, 110–11; maternal, 85, 119–20; moral, 58, 110, 119–26, 161–69, 190; true, 42–43

Volunteers, 120, 169

Way of Holiness (Phoebe Palmer), 67

Wesley, Charles, 212

Wesley, John, 212

Wharton, Edith, 180–88, 191, 227, 228

Whitman, Walt, 187, 228

Whittier, John Greenleaf, 81–85

Whore, 98, 106. *See also* Imagination; Prostitution

Wickes, Frances, 197

Wife, 19, 55, 83, 97, 127, 205–6; poems of Emily Dickinson, 136–37; exemplary, 32–34, 37, 47, 50

Willard, Frances, 183

Winthrop, John, 30–31, 49, 54

Winthrop, Margaret, 30–31, 49

Witchcraft, 83–98, 146–50, 199, 216. *See also* Imagination; Paganism; Romanticism; Witches

Witches, 83, 87, 95, 99–100, 146, 149, 152–53, 197, 199. *See also* Emily Dickinson; Martha Graham; Victoria Woodhull; Frances Wright

Witching Times (John W. DeForest), 91–92

"Witch of Wenham" (John Greenleaf Whittier), 84–85

Wolff, Cynthia, 185

Wollstonecraft, Mary, 61, 104

Woman, 101; Jane Addams' definition of, 164; as Christ-like, 67–68; purified, 106

Woman and Economics (Charlotte Perkins Gilman), 172

Womanhood, 164, 167; and Christianity, 108, 170; idealization of, 52, 56–57; perversions of 122–23

Women: in Christian Science, 160–61; organization of, 118–21; perceptions about, 11–15, 55, 61, 63, 83, 87; status of, 52, 55–56, 100–2, 125–26

Women's Christian Temperance Union, 183

Women's Suffrage: The Reform Against Nature (Horace Bushnell), 67
Woodhull, Canning, 102
Woodhull, Victoria, 99–100, 102–9, 155, 167
Woodhull and Claflin's Weekly, 103–5
Wright, Frances, 99–102, 104, 106–7

"Yellow Wall Paper" (Charlotte Perkins Gilman), 177–80
"Young Goodman Brown" (Nathaniel Hawthorne), 93–94
Young Lady's Guide (American Tract Society), 125–26

Zinzendorf, Ludwig von, 212